Realized
RELIGION

Research on the
Relationship
between Religion
and Health

Realized
RELIGION

Theodore J. Chamberlain
and Christopher A. Hall

Templeton Foundation Press
Philadelphia & London

Templeton Foundation Press
Five Radnor Corporate Center, Suite 120
100 Matsonford Road
Radnor, Pennsylvania 19087

Library of Congress Cataloging-in-Publication Data
Chamberlain, Theodore J.
    Realized religion : research on the relationship between religion and health / Theodore J. Chamberlain and Christopher A. Hall.
        p.   cm.
    Includes bibliographical references.
    ISBN 1-890151-45-9 (cloth : alk. paper)
    1. Health—Religious aspects.   2. Health—Religious aspects—Bibliography.
I. Hall, Christopher A. (Christopher Alan), 1950—   II. Title.
BL65.M4 C48   2000
291.1′75—dc21

                                                            00-064935

Designed by Martha Farlow
Typeset by G & S Typesetters, Inc.
Printed in the United States of America

00 01 02 03 04 05 06   10 9 8 7 6 5 4 3 2 1

Contents

PART THREE

The Relationship of Realized Religion
to Future Research

Acknowledgments

WE WOULD LIKE to acknowledge the assistance of Christine Weigel, who was our research assistant, and Jaynette Arrington, who also assisted with research and attended to the manuscript as it developed. We are grateful to the John Templeton Foundation, which provided funding support for this project.

Realized
RELIGION

Introduction

Realized Religion Defined

TO BE RELIGIOUS, in the ordinary sense of the word, is to engage in a never-ending quest for spiritual fulfillment, to seek purpose and meaning in the face of the confusion, complexity, and occasional chaos that life presents to each of us. To be religious is to journey toward peace and comfort sometimes found in and through the structure of doctrine, religious ritual, and the spiritual disciplines. To be religious is to place trust in a higher authority by yielding one's own independence and self-serving will to the presumed omniscience of an all-wise and knowledgeable God. To be religious is to act "morally" with a sense of justice and with care for the well-being of others. To be religious, at least for Christians, is to hope for life after death, to be finally reconciled with the God of the universe; it is to engage life in the here and now with an expectation for spiritual reunion in the hereafter.

But what of health, happiness, well-being, psychological integration, and even prosperity? Are these the fruits of religion? Few religions teach that believers should expect health or wealth as a primary reward for being religious (although some "name it, claim it" forms of charismatic Christianity actually might). In the end religious people suffer—witness the ancient travails of Job and the modern-day afflictions of the Palestinians, Bosnians, Irish, Jews, and Kosovars—and religious people die (perhaps having lived slightly longer).

Religion and Health

The question for us in this bibliographic essay is whether being religious enhances health, even if being healthier is not the primary motivation for being religious. Dale Matthews, a medical professor and practicing physician, testifies to the power that faith and religious commitment exert on the health, well-being, and even the healing of persons. While his observations are largely anecdotal, they are the observations of a man of faith who truly believes in the efficacy of medicine as well as the power of belief. He is part of an emerging and increasingly significant effort to study the relationship between religion and health, an effort that has led to what some have called a new era of medicine, a potentially "revolutionary convergence of medicine and faith which is transforming the way that people seek healing" (Matthews, 1998, p. 2).

Studying the relationship between medicine and belief is a complex enterprise requiring a rigorous empirical research methodology. Studying something as subjective and elusive as faith and belief is extremely challenging; some would assert that it is an impossible task, and others might say that it is possible, but not especially desirable. That might be because faith is by definition mysterious, spiritual, subjective, and idiosyncratic (witness the continuous multiplication of Protestant denominations). These matters are not easily examined by science, which has justly earned the reputation for establishing reliable, objective "facts" or knowledge based on rationality, reason, and an underlying attitude of skepticism.

Realized Religion

What do we mean by realized religion? Religion is defined as a system of religious attitudes, beliefs, and practices held with ardor and faith (Merriam-Webster, 1997). Faith is defined as a firm belief in something for which there is no proof (p. 418). St. Paul describes faith as "the substance of things hoped for, the evidence of things not seen" (Heb. 11:1). How can science measure trust and hope in matters believed with ardor but nevertheless unseen? How does science account for religious fervor based on evidence that is nevertheless lacking in proof? This conundrum creates a complicated challenge for those who attempt to study religion and faith from a scientific perspective.

We have chosen to focus on the term "realized" and apply it to the term "religion" in order to approach the conundrum of studying the mystery of faith from the perspective of objective scientific methodology. The word realized is defined as "to bring into concrete existence" (p. 973). Thus, religion is realized when the essential elements of religion (faith and trust) are made operational by being brought into "concrete existence." Better health, a higher degree of well-being, more marital satisfaction, less addiction, less suicide, and a better likelihood of healing have been found in a series of empirical studies presented in the following chapters to be the byproduct of religion realized. These crucial elements of life are the manifestation of religion being made real, of religion being brought into concrete existence.

Religion versus Science

Some researchers maintain that efforts to study the existence of a relationship between faith and medicine have been hindered by a long-standing antipathy toward religion from the scientific community. Evidence for such antipathy is garnered from polls, which point to a disparity in religiosity between scientists and the general population of the United States.

The religion versus science equation describes a tension between trust and doubt that has historically created hostile camps, each tending to demonize the other. What is now emerging is the application of objective scientific methodology to subjective religious experience. The context is religion and health, a place where the debate has often focused on the presumed adverse effects of religion on health and where now the evidence increasingly suggests otherwise.

Levin (1994) contends that very few of the four hundred or so empirical studies dating back to the nineteenth century, which deal with the health effects of religiosity, ever set out explicitly to study religion as a variable. Furthermore, he maintains that "salient ideological and institutional barriers within academic medicine [have] discouraged the dissemination of positive findings" (p. 1475). He describes these barriers as attitudes typified by such statements as "religion is unimportant," "this is bad science," and finally "religion is not real" (p. 1475).

Defining Religion

We believe that religion is indeed real and furthermore that religion realized can often have a profound influence on one's psychological, emotional, spiritual, and physical health and well-being. The reality of religion is essentially a matter of faith. Matters of faith by definition create serious problems for science. Anthropologist Clifford Geertz (1973) provides a helpful definition of religion, a definition that is largely based on the ethereal qualities of religion including symbols, moods, and conceptions of existence that seem uniquely real or realistic; the operative word being "seem." According to Geertz, religion is

(1) a system of symbols which acts to (2) establish powerful, persuasive, and long-lasting moods and motivation in and by (3) formulating conceptions of a general order of existence and (4) clothing these conceptions with such an aura of factuality that (5) the moods and motivations seem uniquely realistic (p. 90).

It is at this junction that faith intrudes on objective reality and science becomes increasingly nervous, if not skeptical. The intellectual gap that exists between the domain of faith and the domain of science no doubt accounts for why Levin (1994) believes that "mainstream scientists and scholars seem positively oblivious to the presence of the expanding literature base of empirical data supportive of a salutary role for religion" (p. xi). However, many observers have perceived a radical change in this historic nonrelationship, so much so that religion has now become a subject of serious interest to researchers in medicine, epidemiology, gerontology, and other sociomedical disciplines. According to Levin, "the growth in this nascent field is exemplified by an explosion of publications, organizations, and funded research" (p. xv).

Larson is one of the heroes in the emerging field of the epidemiology of religion. Larson, who founded the National Institute for Healthcare Research, has had an important influence on the generation and quantification of empirical research on spirituality and health. He has also done significant work in the clinical and educational applications of religion and spirituality to psychiatric residency programs. His *Faith Factor Bibliography Series* is a comprehensive overview of decades of research summarizing scientific evidence that deals with the link between religious commitment and health. *Volume 1: An Annotated Bibliography of Clinical Research on Spiritual Subjects* summarizes the findings of 158 studies on spirituality and various outcomes (Matthews, Larson, and Barry, 1993). *Volume 2: An Annotated Bibliography of Systematic Reviews and Clinical Research on Spiritual Subjects* contains the detailed abstracts of 35 research reviews on various aspects of spirituality and health (Larson, 1993). *Volume 3: Enhancing Life Satisfaction* contains abstracts of 79 newer general research studies published after 1993 that confirm the observations reported in volumes 1 and 2 (Matthews and Larson, 1995). *Volume 4: Prevention and Treatment of Illness, Addictions, and Delinquency* contains detailed abstracts of 92 original research studies on the relationship of spirituality to the prevention and treatment of illness, addictions, and delinquency (Matthews and Saunders, 1997).

According to Sherrill and Larson (1994), some researchers have asserted that religion plays an important role in the promotion of health and well-being, while, at the same time, most have avoided doing the research necessary to validate these claims. Larson calls this phenomenon the "forgotten factor." Sherrill and Larson assert that less than 5 percent of the nearly 1,100 quantitative articles published in the two leading psychiatry journals contain a quantified religious variable, and, even then, the only religious variable used was that of denominational affiliation. Larson contends that among the reasons for such an impoverished representation of religious variables in the leading clinical journals is what he calls the anti-tenure factor (ATF), an anti-religious bias found among academic researchers, which has worked against persons interested in exploring religious issues and religious variables scientifically and which, furthermore, has augured against promotion and tenure decisions within leading colleges and universities. While there are some encouraging signs of change, Larson believes that researchers continue to fear that the study of religion and health is a dead-end street on which to build an academic career; research in this field has been hindered accordingly.

This book is an attempt to chronicle the relative value of religion (realized religion) in terms of its effect on the various dimensions of living, including mental health, psychopathology, alcohol use and abuse, marital stability, and other forms of psychological and physical well-being and healing. We believe that when all of the evidence is examined, it will become clear that religion indeed has a positive effect on health, particularly mental health. We believe that the explosive burst of new research, which has appeared over the last twenty years, clearly demonstrates the various health benefits that accrue to believers because of their faith and their religious commitment. The scientific evidence convincingly demonstrates that the natural by-product of religion realized is longer life, less illness, better physical and mental health, more marital stability, less divorce, less suicide, and less abuse of alcohol and other substances.

Dale Matthews is professor of medicine at Georgetown University and, with David Larson, the author of three volumes of the aforementioned four-volume annotated bibliography of clinical research on spiritual subjects. In his most recent book, *The Faith Factor*, Matthews (1998) details the ways in which faith and religious commitment have contributed to health benefits, as well as healing benefits. He believes that a fair reading of the growing scientific evidence establishes that faith is good for your physical, emotional, and spiritual health, which leads to the inevitable conclusion that faith is indeed "good medicine." As Matthews contends, "the soundness of

the faith-factor data is confirmed by the replicability of these findings: in one review, over 75 percent of the 325 studies of different
types, undertaken by hundreds of different researchers, have produced findings indicating the benefits of religious involvement to
health and well-being" (p. 37).

In a particularly provocative article entitled *Religion and Health: Is
There an Association, Is It Valid, and Is It Causal?* Levin (1994) answers his first question affirmatively, claiming that there is indeed a
clear association between religion and health. According to Levin,
data from multiple studies show a definite trend toward better
health where there are higher levels of faith and religiosity.

In answering his second question, Is the relationship between
religion and health valid? Levin cites as evidence that more than
75 percent of the published studies in this field demonstrate ways in
which being religious affects health positively. And finally, in answering the question, Is it causal? Levin says, "Perhaps." Matthews
(1998) also addresses the causality question and does so by caution-
ing patience and urging further study. "But as we await new findings,
the data we have today are strong enough from a scientific point of
view to warrant the attention of scientists, physicians, and even
skeptics" (p. 40). He concludes that there is a great need for many
more well-designed, scientifically rigorous studies before causation
can be answered with a "yes" or "no."

Religion as Illusion

Of course the epitome of those who disavow the reality of religion
is Sigmund Freud, the father of psychology. In *Totem and Taboo*
(1950), Freud saw an evolutionary progression from magic to religion and believed that science would eventually expose religion as
an illusion, a childish, wishful desire to explain God, the origins of
life, and the mystery of death. Freud believed that religion was "the
universal obsessional neurosis of humanity . . . a system of wishful
illusions together with a disavowal of reality" (p. 71). According to
Freud, religion provides an illusion of an all-powerful God who is
conjured up to symbolically reduce the unconscious anxiety that is

the core of psychopathology and that exists as a result of primitive fears of annihilation, as well as threats to the ego that come from distorted memories and the real dangers of living. According to Jones and Butman (1991), the Freudian perspective is "that religion is seen as a kind of universal neurosis that civilization substitutes for a more authentic personal reality based on scientific knowledge" (p. 77). Some religions have at times distorted reality and created oppressive environments in such a way as to give credence to Freud's theory of neurosis.

Religion is realized in the macro sense when the essential elements of religion become operational and are made real in the service of economic, political, cultural, and religious progress. We believe that most major world religions work to enhance social cohesion while also promoting social, cultural, and religious values and norms, which generally lead to more fully functioning societies. This is one aspect of realized religion.

However, the primary aspect of religion realized is not macro but micro. Religion is made operational and made real on a personal basis when it provides a sense of meaning and purpose for living life, coupled with a hope for the future. Religion realized in a micro context provides beliefs and traditions that hold people together, that tend to promote humanistic values, and that lead to the practice of forgiveness, reconciliation, and social justice.

In his book, *Stages of Faith*, Fowler (1991) explores the difference between religion, faith, and belief. He defines religion as the cumulative traditions of the various expressions of faith of people in the past, dependent on ongoing remembering and reenactment of belief (as in the sense of holding certain ideas to be true). He defines faith as the element of trust and loyalty to the transcendent; "the most fundamental category is the human quest for relation to transcendence" (p. 17). Fowler has coined the term "faith development," which refers to the developmental process of finding and making meaning as a human activity. Fowler's approach to faith development is influenced by the interdisciplinary approach of Erikson (1950, 1958, and 1969). Erikson is a psychoanalytically oriented theorist who is known as a nondogmatic, emancipated Freudian.

Erikson's model of the life cycle, his eight stages of man, is a kind of mosaic of human development in which mind, body, and social milieu merge in a dynamic process of identity formation. For Erikson, development is a product of the interaction of heredity and the environment. In that regard, Erikson is known as a psychosocial theorist rather than a psychosexual (Freudian) theorist.

In *Identity: Youth in Crisis* (1968), Erikson put forth his stage theory of development. According to Erikson, in each stage there is an encounter or conflict with the individual and the environment, which fosters a "psychosocial crisis." The psychosocial crisis is not a cataclysmic, end-of-the-world type of crisis. Rather, a psychosocial crisis is a normative, age-appropriate crisis in which the individual is pressured by internal needs and external demands to solve the crisis in favor of psychosocial growth. A crisis according to Erikson is a period of active decision making and a time of heightened vulnerability to the opportunity for growth. Erikson speaks of "the epigenetic principle," in which, as the life cycle unfolds, there is a proper or appropriate time for each psychosocial crisis. Erikson's stages are sequential with the first four stages roughly parallel to Freud's oral, anal, phallic, and latency stages. Erikson's stages are:

1. trust versus mistrust
2. autonomy versus shame
3. initiative versus guilt
4. industry versus inferiority
5. identity versus identity diffusion
6. intimacy versus isolation
7. generativity versus stagnation
8. integrity versus despair

According to Erikson, development proceeds by critical steps, at age-appropriate times. The decision the individual makes consciously and unconsciously is to adapt or not to adapt to the challenge of growth and maturation. Each stage of the life cycle is based on a psychosocial crisis, with the resolution of each crisis leading to personality integration and inadequate resolution hindering subsequent development.

For Erikson, the development of a religious sense is related to the first stage of his eight-stage schema. According to Erikson, during the first year of life the psychosocial crisis is trust versus mistrust. Acquisition of trust is not simply that the infant comes to trust that the world is safe as much as the infant comes to understand that the world is orderly and predictable. This is often associated with the reliability of the primary caregivers. Erikson suggests that this first stage is where religion is born, where the capacity for hope is fostered, and where trust in God is established.

For Erikson, the term identity crisis is used to signify the universal quest to answer the question, Who am I? Erikson sees identity as the need to define one's self clearly and consistently and in such a way as to have the emerging self-definition be in essential harmony with the perceptions of others. Identity involves a progressive continuity with the past and a promise of continuation in the future. The identity crisis is resolved, as all psychosocial crises are resolved, through a process of conflict with the environment, leading to a psychosocial crisis that is then resolved when the person emerges as identity achieved. Identity achievement means that the adolescent has actively struggled with issues pertaining to worldview, belief system, philosophy of life, and career choice. These issues will present the individual with a certain amount of internal crisis or "active decision making" where the individual examines the expectations of parents, church, and culture and begins to make choices and commitments that become internalized into the ego as identity formation.

Kohlberg defines cognition or thinking as the active process of putting things together or relating events. According to Kohlberg, the cognitive connecting process is accomplished through cognitive stages and thus is developmental. Kohlberg acknowledges his debt to Piaget, the great Swiss psychologist, and claims that these stages are sequential, invariant, and hierarchical. Fowler's six stages of faith development closely follow Kohlberg's six stages of moral development, which are built on Piaget's stage theory. Fowler's stages of faith are as follows.

Primal Faith (infancy): Fowler (1991) suggests that this stage deals with the development of trust formed through the mutuality of relationships with parents, the environment, and others, which then creates the context for the development of a concept of God.

Intuitive-Projective Faith (early childhood): This stage focuses on imagination, which is stimulated by stories and symbols and not yet limited by logic. Faith in this stage is characterized by magical thinking and fantasy.

Mythic-Literal Faith (childhood and beyond): According to Fowler, children in this stage begin to develop the ability to think logically and begin to order the world with "categories of causality, space, and time; to enter into the perspective of others; and to capture life meanings and stories" (p. 25). This stage leads to the acquisition of faith that is literalistic and primarily based on the faith of one's parents.

Synthetic-Conventional Faith (adolescence and beyond): Children in this stage are characterized by increasing cognitive ability which, according to Fowler, provides the opportunity to take on the perspective of others and to integrate new and diverse self-images into a coherent identity. The substance of faith continues to be primarily conventional and conforming to that of parents, peers, and other authority figures.

Individuative-Reflective Faith (young adulthood and beyond): This is the stage in which individuals begin to reflect critically upon their beliefs and values and come to see themselves as part of a larger social system. As they begin to "own their own faith," they internalize authority on the one hand and assume responsibility for their choices of commitments, beliefs, ideology, and lifestyle on the other. This process includes doubting, questioning, and sometimes rejecting traditional beliefs. According to Fowler, this reflection opens the way for "critically self-aware commitments in relationships and vocation" (p. 25).

Conjunctive Faith (mid-life and beyond): This stage is characterized by paradox, which entails the embracing of the polarities of one's life, including the need for taking "multiple interpretations of reality" (p. 25), involving "symbol and story, metaphor and myth" (p. 25).

Universalizing Faith (mid-life and beyond): This stage, which most persons never obtain, is characterized by being "grounded in a one-

ness in the power of being." Persons who do reach this stage see
their visions and commitments freeing themselves for investment
in love, "devoted to overcoming division, oppression, and violence,
and in effective anticipatory response to an inbreaking common-
wealth of love and justice" (p. 25). Mother Teresa, Dietrich Bonhoeffer, and Martin Luther King might be examples of the universalizing faith stage.

Fowler's stages provide a developmental framework or structure
to conceptualize how people make meaning and how they explain
the ordinary and extraordinary events of life. They are also a helpful
way to demonstrate the developmental process of religion realized,
of faith being brought into concrete existence.

Consequences of Religion Realized

Most religions teach, and most adherents of religion believe, that
there are consequences of religious commitment. The implications
of religion, the religious effects of realized religion, are also called
the consequential dimensions of religiosity. According to Stark and
Glock (1968), the consequences of religion have to do both with what
the individual receives as a result of being religious as well as what
the individual is expected to give. The consequences of religion realized may be either immediate or long-term, and they deal with the
behavior and the attitudes individuals might hold as a consequence
of being religious. "In the language of Christian belief, the consequential dimension deals with man's relation to man rather than
man's relation to God" (Glock, 1962, S-99). This aspect of religiosity is related to the theological notion of "works." The consequential
dimension is the fifth and last dimension of Glock's core dimensions
of religiosity, which he maintains are applicable to all the world's
religions. The core dimensions are 1) the experiential, 2) the ritualistic, 3) the ideological, 4) the intellectual, and 5) the consequential.

According to Glock, experiential dimensions are subjective
experiences based on the sense that a religious person will gain
knowledge of "ultimate reality" and experience "religious emotions" such as exultation, humility, joy, peace, and a passionate

sense of union with the divine. The ritualistic dimension provides for religious practices such as worshipping, praying, and so on. The ideological dimension recognizes that religious people hold to certain beliefs and doctrines that constitute both a world view and a belief system. The intellectual dimension, like the ideological dimension, deals with people's knowledge of the religious teachings and doctrines to which they subscribe. The consequential dimension then is the implementation of the attitudes and behaviors that are based on religious belief, practice, experience, and knowledge.

Faith versus Placebo

In his book, *Timeless Healing: The Power and Biology of Belief*, Herbert Benson (1996) explains how belief and faith are not only emotionally and spiritually beneficial but "vitally important to physical health" (p. 11). Benson, a practicing physician and professor of medicine at Harvard Medical School, has done considerable research on the biology of belief in an attempt to show how the power of belief affects our well-being and physical health.

Benson defines what he calls the relaxation response as a bodily calm that leads to a lowering of blood pressure, heart rate, breathing rate, and metabolic rate. He suggests that the relaxation response is the opposite of the well-known flight or fight response to threat and danger.

Benson believes that there is scientific evidence to support the notion that "remembered wellness" (the ability to "remember" the calm and confidence associated with health and happiness) is not limited to emotional and psychological memory but includes physical memory as well. The term "remembered wellness," which he uses as a synonym for the placebo effect, is based on the contention that it is belief in the treatment that contributes to superior outcomes. In fact, Benson contends that "depending on the condition, sometimes affirmative beliefs are all we really need to heal us" (p. 21). Benson asserts that his review of the literature indicates that remembered wellness is 70 percent to 90 percent effective, a success rate double or triple that which has always been attributed to the placebo effect. According to Benson, remembered wellness includes the beliefs and expectations of both the patient and the caregiver.

Benson asserts that there has always been the placebo; "early medicine and its cross-cultural cast of characters—priests, healers, sorcerers, medicine men, witch doctors, witches, shamans, midwives, herbalists, physicians, and surgeons—relied exclusively on scientifically unproved potions and procedures, the vast majority of which had no physical value in and of themselves, some of which did more harm than good" (p. 107). He points out that many patients did get better and that their improved health was due primarily to the natural course of their disease or illness, as well as to the power of their belief that they would get better, rather than to any inherent value of medicine.

The placebo effect is one of the most powerful forces in medicine. It is established in scientific research that when a pharmacologically inert substance, in some cases a "sugar pill," a placebo, is given as a drug to patients in research studies, they often experience a change in their condition as a result of their expectations for change. Often individuals taking a placebo experience as much improvement as individuals taking an actual medication. The placebo effect then seems to be related to patients' expectations of positive results, their belief in the effectiveness of the placebo, and the reputations and expectations of the physicians involved.

Certainly the placebo effect occurs when a person expects benefit from a procedure or drug that is in reality neutral in its effect. The central aspect of a placebo is that the individual believes that the treatment will help, and it is that expectation that results in therapeutic gain. Many studies have documented the effects of the placebo on the reduction of physical symptoms. Most researchers believe that the placebo effect is related to suggestion and suggestibility. To statistically control for this variable, researchers use a common experimental approach, "double-blind" method, in which neither the researcher nor the subject is aware of whether the medication is real or a placebo.

To reiterate, the underlying psychological principles of the placebo are belief and expectation, and clearly belief and expectation are also the essential elements of faith, which is an essential element of religion. The placebo phenomenon points out just one of the many complexities inherent in any attempt to ascertain just how faith relates to health. Faith is generally construed to be built on a foundation of transcendence; that is, there is an expectation that religion realized (made concrete) is based on more than an illusion (placebo), that God is at work on behalf of the believer, that it is the transcendent intersecting of the human with the divine that accounts for the positive effect of religion on health and not simply the placebo phenomenon.

Jerome D. Frank (1973), in his classic book *Persuasion and Healing*, points out how sick people interact with both family and culture. When people are physically ill they have difficulty managing their emotions, which can lead to interpersonal conflict, a diminishment of self-esteem, and a growing sense of hopelessness. According to Frank, hopelessness can impede recovery from illness and perhaps even hasten death. Alternatively, hope and expectation often play a crucial role in recovery and healing and Frank observes that "favorable expectations generate feelings of optimism, energy, and well-being and may actually promote healing especially of those illnesses with a large psychological or emotional component" (p. 136). Even Freud (1953) agrees that "expectation colored by hope and faith is an effective force with which we have to reckon . . . in all our attempts at treatment and cure" (p. 289).

Why Religion Is Good Medicine

We might ponder the essential question, Why is religion good for human health? The answer is multifaceted and includes social and psychological aspects as well as spiritual and theological ones.

It is clear that all religions are characterized by certain moral teachings that prescribe acceptable behavior and proscribe unacceptable behavior. For example, many religious systems oppose "worldliness" or what some religions call sin, and their teachings serve to keep their people from the "contaminating" influence of perceived sinful behavior. For example, both Christian and Muslim conservatives instruct their members to avoid alcohol and drugs, and to abstain from sexual intimacy apart from marriage between a man and a woman. These teachings often result in behavior that promotes health—physically, socially, interpersonally, and, as expected, spiritually. We actually do know that nonsmokers are at a reduced risk for cancer, heart disease, emphysema, and a host of other physical maladies. Those who abstain from alcohol enjoy significant health benefits, not the least of which is the avoidance of alcohol addiction. Persons who practice sexual fidelity within a traditional marriage avoid sexually transmitted diseases and are at a lower risk for HIV and AIDS. It seems increasingly clear that a byproduct of being religious is engaging in behavior that leads to better health.

Religiosity also has important social benefits, not the least of which is a social support system provided by church membership and church attendance, both of which have the additional benefit of establishing important and sometimes vital social networking, leading to beneficial effects on psychological and physical health. Social involvement also provides a necessary element of "community," which promotes altruistic behavior, ethical conduct, and sometimes social change, witness the abolitionist movement and the advent of various faith-based nongovernmental agencies such as the Mennonite Central Committee, the Catholic Relief Agency, and World Vision.

Religion provides people with a sense of purpose and meaning, and an interpretative framework for confronting the ethical dilemmas of human existence. Religion also provides answers to the essential religious questions such as Why is there evil? Why is there sickness? What happens to us when we die? and What about human suffering? Religious answers to these questions provide solace to existential anxiety and effectively serve to ameliorate the stresses of human existence by enabling people to better cope with the afflictions inherent in being human and being alive.

Most religions validate human life and provide an explanation for the inevitability of death. Belief in an afterlife as a reward or pun-

ishment for moral choices can promote moral behavior while enriching the meaning of living a "good" life.

We conclude that religion, with the possible exception of extreme
fundamentalisms, is generally good for human health because it
promotes a healthy lifestyle, opposes self-indulgent and self-destructive behavior, encourages moral behavior, provides vital social
support and an ethical value system, establishes an interpretative
framework to understand the complexities of life and human existence, and promotes spiritual growth, which generally assists believers in overcoming the stresses and vicissitudes of living. Furthermore, religion provides access to a divine force (God) who has
the perceived power (sovereignty) to influence human events (transcendence) and who hears requests (prayers) that are health promoting if not healing.

Theologians have long grappled with the illness/sin and health/
salvation equation. In the Christian biblical narrative, Jesus is asked
by his disciples, who with Jesus had noticed a blind man passing by,
"Rabbi, who sinned, this blind man or his parents, that he should be
born blind?" (John 9:2).

Jesus takes this teachable moment to address the prevailing view
that sin might be responsible for causing physical afflictions, that
sickness is actually caused by sin. Jesus answers his disciples by
telling them that neither the blind man nor his parents had sinned.
Jesus seems to be clear that there is no direct link between sin and
sickness.

Jesus teaches his disciples that the blind man, and presumably
his parents, might be an instrument of a larger, more complex divine plan, and that his blindness provided an opportunity to demonstrate that "the works of God might be displayed in his life" (v. 3).
Then Jesus heals the man of his blindness.

This biblical teaching underscores the truth that there have always been saints who are sickly and sinners who are robust and that
the Christian doctrine of the sovereignty of God allows for a divine
purpose to be achieved in oblique, nondirect, nonintrusive, and
highly paradoxical ways.

Harold Koenig is professor of psychiatry and medicine as well as director of the Program on Religion, Aging, and Health at Duke University. His recent book, *Is Religion Good for Your Health?* (1997), provides a careful review of the effects of religion on the health and well-being of people. He concludes that the data demonstrate a link between religion and health "although they do not prove beyond all doubt that mature religion causes better health" (p. 119). Nonetheless Koenig is prepared to say that "a strong religious faith and active involvement in the religious community helps prevent or reduce depression, anxiety, high blood pressure, stroke, heart attack, cancer, and may add years to life" (p. 119).

Why Religion Is Accused of Causing Harm

Koenig is confident that religion, particularly Judeo-Christian religion, has positive effects on health, and that whatever adverse and negative effects do exist have been overemphasized. That is not to say that religion has not been misused or caused serious harm. There have always been neurotic and deeply pathological uses of religion that have caused hurt and even disaster for individuals, families, and societies. The tragedies of Jonestown and Waco are examples of how deviance can cause immense damage in the name of religious beliefs and conviction.

It was William James (1902) who first addressed the question of healthy and unhealthy religion in his classic book, *Varieties of Religious Experience.* James was a pragmatist and an empiricist who provided psychological insight into the process of religious conversion. James used a phenomenological approach to the psychology of religion in which he drew upon dramatic and intense biographical "case studies" to illustrate some of the more extreme forms of religious experience. For example, James cited John Bunyon and St. Augustine as reportedly having suffered from some form of serious melancholia and depression.

Freud (1953) has had perhaps the most significant effect on the development of psychiatry and psychology. As a physician, Freud was deeply connected with neuropsychiatry and committed to a medical view that mental processes were a function of biological mechanisms. Freud's view of psychoanalysis was that with the help of an analyst, and through free association and the interpretation of dreams, patients could discover the unconscious psychodynamic mechanisms that determine and explain behavior.

In his recent book, *Freud versus God* (1998), Blazer compares Christianity and psychoanalysis by suggesting that both share 1) the necessity of integrating one's personal story, 2) an emphasis on being delivered from guilt, and 3) a determination to expose one's deepest thoughts through a confessional process. "For the Christian the context was biblical narratives, for psychoanalysis it was the dominant myth of society" (p. 16). According to Blazer, both Christianity and psychoanalysis saw guilt as the central problem facing humanity and "release from guilt as the key to healing. Confession to a sympathetic and confidential confessor was central to healing on the couch and in the church" (p. 66).

Freud regarded Christianity as a collective neurosis based on the suppression of natural instinctive impulses (sex and aggression). Freud viewed religion as an illusion that cannot be proved and he believed that as scientific knowledge increased, "the need of humankind for religious dogma will diminish. Religion will ultimately be replaced by science, as there will no longer be a need for religion" (p. 69).

Koenig discusses Pruyser's explication of specific ways that religion can be used negatively thereby causing harm and damage. It is Pruyser's theory that religious people who are neurotic and disturbed often sacrifice their intellect and their reason and assume a "blind faith" orientation to life rather than adopting a proper balance of faith and reason. He points out that low self-esteem and psychological wounds sometimes cause pathological bitterness, hatred, and a desire for revenge, which Koenig suggests are sometimes channeled into religious fervor. "Such persons use religion as a way to release their hatred and aggressive impulses onto others, cleverly cloaking them in theological terms that are expressed with pious, better-than-thou attitudes" (p. 106).

According to Pruyser, religion can also be used for controlling the thoughts (brainwashing) and behaviors of religious adherents, especially those who might be excessively needy, psychologically weak, or dependent personalities. It is this context from which cults with charismatic but authoritarian leaders emerge. Pruyser also contends that excessive suffering that leads to a seeking after martyrdom "bespeaks a wish for self-destruction either by masochistic urges or as a necessary atonement for some real or imagined wrongdoing which an implacable conscience demands" (p. 341).

Persons who suffer from obsessional thinking, defined as recurrent thoughts and beliefs that dominate thinking and which might include incessant prayers, compulsive confessionals, and church attendance, may experience pathological guilt or anxiety. According to Koenig (1997), instead of being an authentically religious person, the obsessional person "may be driven by deep anxieties and insecurities rather than by a love for God or for holiness" (p. 108).

Finally, Pruyser contends that religion can be used to reinforce negative or undesirable character traits, leading to highly self-righteous persons who manipulate others or perhaps deceive others with dishonest or fraudulent schemes. In the early 1990s John Bennett, a Philadelphia businessman, developed a Ponzi scheme called New Era Philanthropy in which he used Christian notions of "giving" to dupe countless religious schools, churches, colleges and universities, social agencies, and relief organizations into "investing" in his organization, which he claimed would double their money, thereby providing even more resources for advancing God's kingdom. His fraudulent scheme eventually collapsed from the weight of the financial deception as well as from the underlying pathology of Bennett himself, who was apparently a narcissist who viewed himself as special and anointed by God. He "sold" his fraudulent scheme using the language of religious service and mission. When his scheme collapsed, the scandal led to significant harm for numerous not-for-profit religious and cultural organizations, colleges, and universities all of whom depend on fundraising to support their missions. Bennett lost his home and possessions and, following his conviction for fraud, was imprisoned (Cohen, 1995).

Koenig (1997) points out that in all of these neurotic uses of religion it is "the person's insecurity or mental disturbance—not the religious doctrine—that drives behavior" (p. 110); religion thus becomes a tool to justify or implement pathological tendencies.

We conclude that scientific evidence supports the contention that religion is good for human health, and when individuals misunderstand religion or misuse religion in the service of their own emotional, psychological, or spiritual pathologies, it is not religion per se that is pathological, but rather the abuse of religion that is sick, harmful, and sometimes evil.

We have approached this study with a Christian faith commitment that embraces the notion that religion is beneficial for living a meaningful life. Nonetheless, we found the information presented here to be compelling in its own right, and we believe that our faith bias does not unduly influence the findings presented in this work.

References

Baldwin, J. M. (1906). *Social and Ethical Interpretation in Mental Development*. New York: Macmillan.

Benson, H. (1975). *The Relaxation Response*. New York: William Morrow.

Benson, H. (with Marg Stark). (1996). *Timeless Healing: The Power and Biology of Belief*. New York: Fireside.

Cohen, M. (August 1995). "The 'Gun' Nuzzles Against His Temple." *The Philadelphia Magazine*, 100–203.

Dewey, J. (1930). "Experience and Conduct." In C. Murchison (Ed.), *Psychologies of 1930*. Worchester: Clark University Press.

Erikson, E. (1950). *Childhood and Society*. New York: Norton.

Erikson, E. (1958). *Young Man Luther: A Study in Psychoanalysis and History*. (Austen Riggs Center, Monograph No. 4). New York: Norton.

Erikson, E. (1968). *Identity: Youth and Crisis*. New York: W. W. Norton.

Erikson, E. (1969). *Ghandi's Truth*. New York: Norton.

Fowler, J. W. (1991). *Stages of Faith: The Psychology of Human Development and the Quest of Meaning*. San Francisco: Harper & Row.

Fowler, J. W., Nipkow, K. E., and Schweitzer, F. (1991). *Stages of Faith and Religious Development: Implications for Church, Education, and Society*. New York: Crossroads Publishing Company.

Frank, J. D. (1973). *Persuasion and Healing*. Baltimore: Johns Hopkins University Press.

Freud, S. (1927). *Future of an Illusion*, standard edition. London: Hogarth Press.

Freud, S. (1950). *In Totem and Taboo*. Translated by James Strachey. New York: Norton.

Freud, S. (1953). *The Complete Psychological Works of Sigmund Freud*, vol. 7. Edited and translated by J. Strachey. London: Hogarth Press.

Geertz, C. (1973). *The Interpretation of Cultures: Selected Essays*. New York: Basic Books.

Glock, C. Y. (July/August 1962). "On the Study of Religious Commitment." *Religious Education*, S-98–110.

Harper Study Bible (Revised Standard Version). (1952). New York: Harper & Row.

James, W. (1902). *The Varieties of Religious Experience*. New York: Longman, Green, and Company.

Jones, S. L., and Butman, R. E. (1991). *Modern Psychotherapies: A Comprehensive Christian Appraisal*. Downers Grove, IL: Intervarsity Press.

Koenig, H. G. (1997). *Is Religion Good for Your Health? The Effects of Religion on Physical and Mental Health*. New York: Haworth Pastoral Press.

Kohlberg, L. (1966). "A Cognitive Developmental Analysis of Children's Sex-Role Concepts and Attitudes." In E. Maccoby (Ed.), *The Development of Sex Differences*. Stanford, CA: Stanford University Press.

Kohlberg, L. (1968). "Preschool Education: A Cognitive-Developmental Approach." *Child Development* (in press).

Kohlberg, L. (1969). "Stage and Sequence: The Cognitive-Developmental Approach to Socialization." In D. A. Goslin (Ed.), *Handbook of Socialization Theory and Research* (pp. 347–480). Chicago: Rand McNally.

Kohlberg, L. (1969). *Stages in the Development of Moral Thought and Action*. New York: Holt, Rinehart and Winston.

Kohlberg, L. (1976). "Moral Stages and Moralization: The Cognitive-Developmental Approach." In T. Lickona (Ed.), *Moral Development and Behavior: Theory, Research, and Social Issues* (pp. 62–64, 338). New York: Holt, Rinehart and Winston.

Larson, D. B. (December 1993). *The Faith Factor: Vol. 2. An Annotated Bibliography of Systemic Reviews and Clinical Research on Spiritual Subjects*. Washington, DC: National Institute for Healthcare Research.

Levin, J. S. (1994). "Religion and Health: Is There an Association, Is It Valid, and Is It Causal?" *Social Science and Medicine, 38*(11), 1475–1482.

Loevinger, J. (1966). "The Meaning and Measurement of Ego Development." *American Psychologist, 21*, 195–217.

Matthews, D. A. (with Connie Clark). (1998). *The Faith Factor: Proof of the Healing Power of Prayer*. New York: Penguin Group.

Matthews, D. A., Larson, D. B., and Barry, C. P. (July 1993). *The Faith Factor: Vol. 1. An Annotated Bibliography of Clinical Research on Spiritual Subjects*. Washington, DC: National Institute for Healthcare Research.

Matthews, D. A., and Larson, D. B. (April 1995). *The Faith Factor: An Annotated Bibliography of Clinical Research on Spiritual Subjects: Vol. 3. Enhancing Life Satisfaction.* Washington, DC: National Institute for Healthcare Research.

Matthews, D. A., and Saunders, D. M. (July 1997). *The Faith Factor: An Annotated Bibliography of Clinical Research on Spiritual Subjects: Vol. 4. Prevention and Treatment of Illness, Addictions, and Delinquency.* Washington, DC: National Institute for Healthcare Research.

Mead, G. H. (1934). *Mind, Self, and Society.* Chicago: University of Chicago Press.

Merriam-Webster's Collegiate Dictionary, 10th ed. (1977). Springfield, MA: Merriam-Webster.

Piaget, J. (1962). *The Moral Judgment of the Child.* New York: Collier.

Pruyser, P. (1977). "The Scary Side of Current Religious Beliefs." *Bulletin of the Menninger Clinic, 41,* 329–348.

Sherrill, K. A., and Larson, D. B. (1994). "The Anti-Tenure Factor in Religious Research in Clinical Epidemiology and Aging." In. J. S. Levin (Ed.), *Religion in Aging and Health: Theoretical Foundations and Methodological Frontiers* (pp. 149–177). Thousand Oaks, CA: Sage.

Spilka, B. (1989). "Functional and Dysfunctional Roles of Religion: An Attributional Approach." *Journal of Psychology and Christianity, 8,* 5–15.

Stark, R., and Glock, C. Y. (1968). *American Piety.* Berkeley: University of California Press.

PART ONE

The Relationship of Realized Religion to Prayer and Healing

1

The Role of Prayer
in Health and Healing

WILLIAM JAMES (1963) defined prayer broadly but in elegantly simple terms as "every kind of law and communion or conversation with the power recognized as divine. . . . It is the very soul of religion" (p. 464).

Researchers interested in investigating the literature dealing with the nature and efficacy of prayer will soon discover that this is a subject that has historically been largely unexplored from an empirical approach. According to Finney and Malony (1985b), "Nowhere is the longstanding breach between psychology and religion more evident than in the lack of research on prayer. Only a few studies exist in spite of the fact that prayer is of central religious importance" (p. 104).

Petitionary Prayer

Francis Galton (1883) conducted the first empirical study of petitionary prayer in 1872, which led him to conclude that "there is no statistical evidence for the objective value of petitionary prayer and intercessory prayer" (Finney and Malony, 1985b, p. 107). Later Galton (1883) was to write:

> It is asserted by some, that men possess the faculty of obtaining results over which they have little or no direct personal control, by means of devout and earnest prayer, while others doubt the truth of this assertion. The question regards a matter of fact, that

has to be determined by observation and not by authority; and it is one that appears to be a very suitable topic for statistical inquiry. . . . Are prayers answered or are they not. . . . Do sick persons who pray or are prayed for, recover on the average more rapidly than others? (p. 277).

Galton drew his conclusions regarding prayer after testing the hypothesis that prayer would enhance the well-being of those who prayed, as well as the well-being of those who were prayed for, particularly when contrasted with those for whom prayer was not a factor at all. Galton examined Guy's table of the average life span of the English aristocracy and noted that the British royal family enjoyed a relatively modest life expectancy despite the long-standing practice of the English people of praying for their sovereigns. Galton also noted that the clergy of the day experienced a shorter life expectancy than lawyers or physicians and seemed to have a pattern of poor health in general. He further observed that the mortality rate of missionaries was no better than for the general population and might actually be worse. He commented on the high rate of insanity among the nobility and the common incidence of religious madness among them. On the basis of these observations, Galton concluded that there was little statistical evidence for the efficacy of petitionary prayer, reasoning that if the English people prayed so often and so hard for the well-being of the royal family, the nobility, the clergy, and their missionaries then surely they should live longer and presumably better than the average citizen.

Galton's (1883) study came under strong attack from the church, which led to the omission of his study from subsequent editions of his book, *Inquiries into Human Faculty*. The general attitude adopted by the Church of England was that religion was not an acceptable area for scientific inquiry, research, or study. The church asserted that evidence about the efficacy of prayer should come only from divine revelation and not from science. This schism between the ecclesiastical community and the scientific community, while not at all new, nonetheless laid the foundation for the continuing adversarial relationship between faith and reason that is still evident today and which contributes to the paucity of empirical research in the area of prayer.

Galton's study raised a number of very interesting questions about the nature of petitionary prayer and the possibility of studying it empirically. For example, can or should prayerful people expect a positive response to all petitions? Indeed, what constitutes a positive response? Healing, health, wealth, inner peace, deeper spirituality? If people do not receive what is construed to be an immediate positive response to a petition, should they immediately deduce that the prayer was ineffective or unanswered? For example, if God does not answer a petition or answers "no" or perhaps "later" does that petition or the "answer" still qualify as efficacious? Is the intensity of a prayer or its repetition or duration related to its efficacy? What theological considerations enter into the question of efficacy? Is the righteousness of the intercessor related to the efficacy of the request? What criteria are to be employed in determining efficaciousness? Can the intricacies and complexities of God's responses to prayer be adequately and accurately observed and measured? And finally, what kind of experiment would effectively control for all the variables involved? Meadow and Kahoe (1984), authors of a textbook on the psychology of religion, caution:

> If a deity can meaningfully answer a believer's prayer, and if prayer is to remain a spiritual rather than a magical exercise, then surely that same deity would make sure that all empirical studies of the efficacy of prayer will turn out inconclusive! The evidence of the effectiveness of prayers, as they touch events in the material world, remains outside the domain of science. The faithful who want to believe can believe, and the skeptic who chooses not to believe could not be convinced (p. 120).

Perhaps a closer look at attempts to study petitionary prayer will prove helpful, or at least demonstrate the inherent difficulties entailed in this type of research.

Finney and Malony (1985b) cite William Parker's 1957 research, published as *Prayer Can Change Your Life*, as the next major study of the effects of verbal prayer after Galton's 1872 study. The subjects for Parker's study were forty-five volunteers ranging in age from twenty-two to sixty. All were suffering from either psychosomatic complaints or subjective emotional distress.

Parker's nine-month-long experiment included pre-testing and post-testing using a battery of psychological tests. Parker's volunteers were placed into one of three groups. Group 1 received weekly sessions of individual psychotherapy. This group reported gains of 65 percent in the psychological conditions of its members. Group 2 consisted of practicing Christians who agreed to pray daily for God to help them overcome their problems. Group 2 reportedly experienced no measurable improvement. Group 3 was a prayer therapy group that followed a program developed to enhance spiritual growth through self-analysis, spiritual guidance, and group therapy. Group 3 reportedly improved by 72 percent (Finney and Malony, 1985b, p. 108).

Unfortunately, there are design problems associated with this study, including the fact that there was no random assignment to the treatment groups. However, the positive outcome of the prayer therapy group does suggest that prayer in this format may have an ameliorating effect on psychological well-being. Regrettably, it is not possible to parse out the effect of the "prayer" from the self-reflective and group functions of the group 3 program.

Joyce and Welldon (1965) conducted research on petitionary prayer in 1965, investigating the efficacy of prayer in thirty-eight patients suffering from various forms of rheumatic disease and receiving treatment in two outpatient clinics in a London hospital. Patients were matched in pairs by day of visit, sex, age, and primary clinical diagnosis; half were also matched by marital status and religious faith. One of each pair was assigned to a prayer treatment group by means of a coin toss. Neither patient nor physician was aware of who was receiving prayer. Information about each patient receiving treatment was relayed to the leader of a prayer group, without identifying the patient. The prayer group was made up of one to five members who prayed for these patients on a bi-weekly basis for up to an hour. At the end of six months all of the patients were examined by their treating physicians to determine if there had been any changes in their conditions. Of the thirty-eight patients in the study, twenty-six remained unchanged. Six showed improvement, of whom five had been prayed for on a regular basis. As Koenig, Smiley, and Gonzales (1988) summarized in their review of this study, the result, though suggestive, "was not statistically significant" (p. 90).

P. J. Collipp (1969) was prompted by the findings of Joyce and Welldon in England to do a similar study in the United States. The focus of his research was children with terminal cancer and their families. Koenig, Smiley, and Gonzales (1988) described Collipp's study as "one of the few objective studies of the consequences of prayer" (p. 90). The names of ten patients from a group of eighteen children with leukemia were selected randomly and sent to ten Protestant families who organized a prayer group that prayed for them on a daily basis. Those praying were not told that this was a study on the efficacy on prayer, nor were the patients' physicians informed that a prayer group was praying for their patients. After fifteen months of regular prayer, seven of the ten children were still alive. Of the eight children in the control group, only two were still alive. Collipp concluded that "the small number of patients in this study precludes definitive conclusions about the efficacy of prayer. Our data does support the concept, however, that prayers for the sick are efficacious" (p. 202). Collipp went on to state, "among the plethora of modern drugs, it seems inappropriate that our medical literature contains so few studies on our oldest and, who knows, perhaps most successful form of therapy. Every physician has prescribed this remedy and nearly every physician has seen it succeed" (p. 204). Matthews, Larson, and Barry (1993) reviewed Collipp's research and found that the overall design of Collipp's study was appropriate and believed that his conclusions may have been acceptable had a much larger number of children been tested and the same differences in the two groups maintained (70 percent in prayer group versus 25 percent in control, p. 57).

Rosner (1975) also reviewed Collipp's work and concluded that design flaws invalidated Collipp's finding that prayers for the sick are efficacious. He further asserted that a precise scientific, statistically sound study of prayer has yet to be reported. While Rosner does not discount the reality or efficaciousness of prayer itself, he doubts that prayer can ever be effectively subjected to empirical analysis.

Carson and Huss (1979) examined the use of prayer and Bible reading by a nursing staff as part of the treatment plan for chronic undifferentiated schizophrenics who had not responded to psychotherapy. An experimental group of ten Christian schizophrenics met individually with nursing students for a period of ten weeks. These sessions began and closed with a written prayer and included the reading of Scriptures that focused on the love of God and the worth of each individual to God. Patients in the control group were treated with normal psychotherapeutic techniques. Carson and Huss reported that patients in the treatment group who received prayer and Bible study developed further in their abilities to express anger and aggression, became more hopeful about changing their conditions, displayed more appropriate affect, and decreased their somatic complaints. However, Finney and Malony (1985b) critiqued this study for having "serious design deficiencies which make the results only suggestive" (p. 109).

In 1979 Elkins, Anchor, and Sandler set out to compare the effect of prayer in reducing anxiety with the effects of certain muscle relaxing exercises. They discovered that prayer, whether of a petitionary or reflective variety, failed to significantly reduce anxiety as measured by either electromyogram readings or Speilberger's State-Trait Anxiety Inventory (STAI). The group that received the muscle relaxation exercise experienced significant reductions in both the objective and subjective measures of anxiety. Those members of the prayer group who rated prayer as having high significance in their lives did show greater tension reduction than those in the group who considered prayer to be of less significance. The researchers concluded that the muscle relaxation exercises caused significant reductions in objective and subjective measures of anxiety, whereas prayer did not.

Matthews, Larson, and Barry (1993) commented that the study by Elkins, Anchor, and Sandler was "noteworthy for the clarity of its presentation and design," while its small sample size limited its validity: ". . . no sample size or power calculations were performed to set up an appropriate size with adequate power to say with a reasonable degree of certainty that no effect of prayer took place. . . . Larger studies are necessary to answer the question more definitively" (p. 90).

Intercessory Prayer

In ground breaking research that has received much notice, R. C. Byrd (1988) investigated the therapeutic effect of intercessory prayer on coronary care patients, producing results that Koenig, Smiley, and Gonzales (1988) described as "nothing short of remarkable" (p. 91). Byrd conducted a double blind randomized test of prayer efficacy on a sample of 393 coronary care patients at San Francisco General Hospital. One hundred ninety-two of these patients were randomly assigned to be prayed for daily by volunteer "intercessors" who were "born again" Christians with an active Christian life "as manifested by daily devotional prayer and active Christian fellowship with a local church" (pp. 826–827). A broad range of denominations was represented among the intercessors, including both Protestants and Roman Catholics. Byrd studied these groups for a period of ten months and found that:

> Only three of the "treated" (those patients who were actively "prayed for") compared with eighteen of the "control" patients required antibiotics, while only six of the treated and eighteen of the control suffered from pulmonary edema. None of the treated and twelve of the control group had to be intubated (a breathing tube placed into the lungs to provide artificial respiration) (Koenig, Smiley, and Gonzales, 1988, p. 91).

Later Byrd (1995) further concluded that in twenty-one of the twenty-six categories monitored by the study, patients fared better when they received prayer.

Matthews, Larson, and Barry (1993) reviewed Byrd's (1988) study and found it to be well designed and well executed, utilizing a classic methodology for intervention evaluation. They described it as the only study asserting that "patients in a coronary care unit benefit from prayer to the Judeo-Christian God" (p. 50).

Trier and Shupe (1991) examined the relationship between prayer and healing and have hypothesized that prayer would typically be used in conjunction with orthodox medical treatment rather than as a substitute for it, and that people who were suffering from chronic medical problems, that is, those problems medical professionals were unable to heal, would pray more often than those persons suffering from acute or severe illnesses.

Trier and Shupe (1991) used a random sample of 352 midwesterners; respondents were asked about their utilization of a variety of health services, the incidence of chronic and acute illnesses, and their satisfaction with the therapies that had been employed. Prayer was listed as one of the possible therapies to choose from during the interview. Those subjects who did mention praying were asked if they did so for the following concerns: health, personal relationships, and financial-material needs. The subjects were given a measurement of religiosity, which focused on church attendance, reading the Bible, praying, and watching television evangelists. The subjects were also given a religious orthodoxy measure that from a theological perspective seems to be somewhat simplistic.

Nonetheless, Trier and Shupe (1991) reported that close to 30 percent of the respondents reported using prayer for "healing and health maintenance" (p. 354). They found no evidence that prayer was used in lieu of standard medical practices; rather, they suggested that prayer works in harmony with biomedicine and as a supplement to it. Interestingly enough, they also found that people reported praying as frequently for acute illnesses as they did for chronic health problems. Trier and Shupe, therefore, concluded that medical professionals would be wise to recognize that their patients see no contradiction between prayer and standard medical practices. In fact, empirical evidence seems to demonstrate "that prayer is attitudinally and holistically interwoven with many persons' views of their own health and healing—and therefore it is a socially 'real' aspect of treatment and recovery" (p. 356).

King and Bushwick (1994) interviewed 203 family practice adult

in-patients at two hospitals regarding their views on the relationship between religion and health. According to the authors, religion
is rarely mentioned in medical school classes, and medical students
are generally taught that a discussion of a patient's religious and
spiritual beliefs is inappropriate. This practice is in direct contrast
to the findings of this study, which revealed that many patients express positive feelings toward physicians' involvement in spiritual
issues. King and Bushwick found that 77 percent of the patients said
physicians should consider patients' spiritual needs, 37 percent
wanted their physicians to discuss religious beliefs with them more
frequently, and 48 percent wanted their physicians to pray with
them. However, 68 percent said that their physician had never discussed religious belief with them. King and Bushwick concluded
that although many patients desire more frequent and more in-
depth discussion about religious issues with their physicians, physicians in general do not discuss these issues with their patients.

However, this reality might be changing. A 1997 report indicated
that at least thirty of the top medical schools in the United States
now offer teaching programs on the subject of faith and the role of
prayer in the healing process compared to only three medical
schools in 1993 (Holmes, 1998, p. 16).

Saudia and colleagues (1991) conducted a recent investigation
into the relationship between the helpfulness of prayer as a direct
action coping mechanism and health locus of control for patients
about to undergo cardiac surgery. Ninety-six out of one hundred patients reported using prayer as a coping mechanism in dealing with
the stress of surgery, which suggests that prayer can be regarded as a
valuable asset in coping with impending life-threatening surgery.
These results confirmed the studies by Sodestrom and Martinson
(1987) on cancer patients, and by Fordyce (1982) on hospitalized
adults. Benson's (1996) observation that prayer is effective in providing physiologic responses such as decreased heart rate, decreased blood pressure, and decreased incidence of angina in cardiac patients is also consistent with the findings of Saudia and
colleagues (1991), who concluded that prayer was perceived as a
helpful coping mechanism for such cardiac patients.

Bearon and Koenig (1990) examined religious cognitions and the use of prayer in dealing with both health and illness. Forty adults aged sixty-five to seventy-four were interviewed about their perceptions of God's role in health and illness. They were asked how they utilized prayer in response to their physical symptoms. Bearon and Koenig discovered that most "held a belief in a benevolent God but were not clear about God's role in health and illness" (p. 249). Over half of those people interviewed had prayed in response to a symptom the last time they had experienced it. Those symptoms that were discussed with a physician or those symptoms for which drugs had been prescribed were the most likely to be prayed over. The least-educated respondents and the Baptists in Bearon and Koenig's sample were the most apt to pray.

Developmental Aspects of Prayer

In 1991, Scarlett and Perriello conducted a fascinating study on the development of prayer in adolescence. They defined mature prayer by pointing to the famous story of Abraham Lincoln, who when one of his generals is reported to have said prior to an important battle, "I pray God is on our side," was said to have responded, "No, General, let us pray we are on God's side" (p. 65). Their view is that mature prayer functions as a way to change a person's attitude so as to determine what should be an individual's desires, wants, and wishes. Thus in Lincoln's case, he appears to have been concerned not only with winning the battle and the war, but in being justified in the winning.

Immature prayer seems to begin as simple wish fulfillment and addresses a God out there, or up there, a God whom we try to command to intervene directly to do our will "if we have been good and perhaps even if we have not been good" (p. 65). Mature prayer seems to become increasingly dialogical and interactive. In the process of praying, we receive something in return: "a thought, a feeling, a newly apprehended truth, insight, or directive rather than a direct divine action" (p. 65).

According to Scarlett and Perriello (1991), "prayer begins as an effort to bend God to our will" (p. 66). Developmentally, it functions first and foremost as an attempt to change the reality outside of ourselves. It begins as talking at rather than with God. It is primarily petitionary. We are asking God to give us something: health, money, freedom, peace, and such. But with age and maturity, prayer becomes increasingly a way to discover and mold ourselves to what is felt to be God's will, to feel connected to God in order to cope with or change troublesome feelings, and to experience closeness or even union with God for its own sake.

The design of this study focused on solicited prayers and answers to questions about prayer among eighty-nine middle-class adolescents and young adults from Catholic schools. The authors asked the subjects to write prayers for six hypothetical situations. The responses were divided into the following general types: 1) requests, 2) confessions, 3) thanksgivings, and 4) expressions of thoughts, feelings, and questioning.

The results indicated that seventh graders were more direct in their requests, making very little effort to search for the right wish, or wrestle with feelings, or try to overcome any perceived distance between themselves and God. The ninth graders also focused on requests; however, their prayers included an increase in the responses that dealt with changes in feelings.

The prayers of undergraduate college students showed definite signs of searching, struggling, and doubting. "In examining their prayers, one can sense their considerable effort to understand and communicate feelings as well to question old ways of wishing and thinking about God. The result is a more intimate praying, or at least a praying that seems more intent on revealing the self as one might do in dialogue with a friend" (p. 71).

Scarlett and Perriello (1991) concluded that the results of their statistical analysis on solicited prayers indicate a shift during adolescence away from the use of prayer to request changes in objective reality and toward the use of prayer to change or cope with feelings and to increase intimacy with God.

Tamminen's (1991) research of Finnish third graders who were asked to complete the sentence "I think prayer is . . ." found that

these children responded most often that prayer is "asking something from God" (p. 221). He concluded that there is a difference in
the nature of prayers according to the age of the person praying. Like
Scarlett and Perriello, he concluded that younger children are likely
to ask for concrete things, while older children and adolescents are
more apt to pray for spiritual gain. This would be entirely consistent
with the cognitive developmental theory of Piaget as well as the faith
formation stage theory of Fowler.

It might be helpful to provide a brief explanation or definition of
various types of prayer. Petitionary prayers include those prayers for
which something is asked, presumably for the benefit of the petitioner. Intercessory prayers involve the asking of something for
someone else. Prayers of confession include the awareness of and
repentance for wrongdoing and generally include the asking of forgiveness. Worshipful prayer includes adoration or the giving of
honor and praise to God.

A number of studies have examined what people are thinking and
doing when they pray. In a project conducted twenty-four years ago,
Long, Elkind, and Spilka (1967) investigated children's conceptions
of prayer. They interviewed 160 elementary school children from
ages five to twelve and observed a three-stage development in their
conceptions of prayer. At the first stage (ages five to seven), the
global, or undifferentiated stage, notions of prayer tended to be
"vague and indistinct." The child has "a dim awareness that prayers
were somehow linked with the term 'God' and with certain learned
formulae. . . . There was little real comprehension of the meaning of
prayer" (p. 104).

At the second stage (ages seven to nine), the concrete differenti-
ated stage, prayer tends to be an impersonal and externalized activity. "At this stage children never rose above the actual behaviors associated with prayer to its mental and affective aspects which to the
older child and adult are its essence" (p. 105).

In the third stage, the abstract stage (ages nine to twelve), prayer
had become less impulsive and a more satisfying and deeper spiritual experience. Prayer had "emerged as a type of private conversation with God involving things not talked about with other people"

(p. 106). Prayer had become a sharing of intimate communication with God. Children at this stage appear to be able to distinguish between "what one thinks and what one says" and also seem to recognize that prayer "involves the nonmaterial mental activity such as thought and belief" (p. 106). Hence, children no longer consider dogs and cats capable of prayer. Conceptions of prayer were generally more "abstract and circumscribed." With increasing age, prayer also changed from a focus on "egocentric wish fulfillment (candy, toys, etc.) to altruistic moral and ethical desires (peace on earth, etc.)" (p. 101).

Several studies indicate a developmental pattern with respect to prayer that is consistent with Piaget's stages of moral and cognitive development (Godin and Van Runey, 1959; Goldman, 1964; Long, Elkind, and Spilka, 1967). According to Finney and Malony (1985b), a number of studies have indicated that as one develops and matures there is a concomitant decline in the belief that prayer will have direct material consequences. The authors concluded that research on the development of the concept of prayer in childhood and adolescence shows that "a child's concept of prayer develops from vague association with the term 'God' to private conversation with God in which very intimate things are shared" (p. 106).

A more recent study by Janssen, De Hart, and Den Draak (1990) focused on a content analysis of the praying practices of Dutch youth. Janssen, De Hart, and Den Draak stressed that their research did not start with a preliminary concept concerning the nature of prayer. "We simply asked our subjects to describe how *they* defined prayer. Consequently, the main data were spontaneous, written, self-formulated answers to questions about the definitions, motivations, and methods of prayer" (p. 100).

The authors were interested in the structure and content of prayer. They defined structure and content as including the need for prayer or why people pray, the method of prayer or how people pray, the direction of prayer or to whom people pray, and what might be the effects of prayer.

The authors drew a sample of 192 students from 5,000 Dutch high school pupils who had been surveyed previously about political and religious matters. The sample consisted of 60 Catholic, 71 Protestant (34 Dutch Reformed and 37 Calvinist), and 61 non-affiliated high school pupils. Each pupil was asked three open-ended questions: (1) What is prayer to you? (2) At what moments do you feel the need to pray? and (3) How do you pray? (p. 100)

The authors found that praying at all stages was generally motivated by personal problems such as sickness, death, war, disaster, examinations, problems of others, and sin. These "needs" comprise 85 percent of all prayer responses. While 60 percent of the needs pertained to "personal problems," only 20 percent of the "needs" related to issues pertaining to personal happiness. Thirty-three percent of the prayers consisted of asking or wishing for something. Sixty percent were directed to God, while 11 percent prayed to "someone," 13 percent prayed to "spirits/powers" and 2 percent directed their prayers to "Mary/Jesus." In terms of times and places, young people pray at night in bed. Only 11 percent mentioned that they pray in church and most preferred to pray in silence and alone.

Prayer was seen by most respondents as a coping strategy for dealing with the tragedies of life, and at times as a "motivational device" or "anticipatory action for changing things according to one's wishes" (p. 99). Janssen, De Hart, and Den Draak (1990) also noted that one's conception of God affects how prayer takes place. For those who conceive of God in personal terms, prayer will be practiced as a "dialogue," while for those who conceive of God as "an indefinable power," prayer will be viewed in terms of meditation (p. 106).

It is interesting to note that according to Janssen, De Hart, and Den Draak, most respondents prayed when they were in trouble. However, when they were ill, they did not pray for an immediate cure; they prayed instead for help, trust, and blessing. The authors concluded that "praying seems to be primarily a way of coping with inevitable, incurable unhappiness" (p. 105). The authors further deduced that there is ample evidence to regard the importance of petitionary prayer as "an involuntary cry for help, not mitigated by the availability of real help" (p. 105). Finally, the authors concluded that praying is very often stimulated by incurable and insoluble problems; therefore, it functions primarily as a coping mechanism for the person who prays.

Moberg and McEnery (1976) analyzed the prayer habits and attitudes of Catholic students from 1961–1971. They noted that the rank order of reasons for praying remained constant over four factors: (1) a desire to converse with God; (2) feelings of dependence; (3) a sense of obligation; and (4) intercession.

Thouless and Brown (1964) studied the beliefs of adolescent girls in terms of the efficacy and appropriateness of petitionary prayer. The primary finding of the study indicated that belief in the causal efficacy of prayer decreased with increasing age, while there was no corresponding decrease in the belief in the appropriateness of petitionary prayer.

The Nature of Religious Experience in Prayer

Empirical research has also been conducted on a somewhat different form of prayer, namely *contemplative prayer*, a form of prayer defined by Finney and Malony (1985a) as:

> a particular form of Christian prayer in which one gives one's full attention to relating to God in a passive, nondefensive, nondemanding, open way. It is a patient waiting on God to deepen one's confidence in God's power and love. Having been made more secure by increased confidence in God, one is freed to love others more unconditionally. The essence of CP is a particular type of interpersonal stance toward God (p. 173).

Finney and Malony (1985a) examined the possibility of using contemplative prayer as an adjunct to psychotherapy. They hypothesized that when contemplative prayer is used in association with standard psychotherapeutic techniques, psychotherapy would improve and spirituality would be enhanced. Nine subjects were involved in the experiment, three males and six females ranging in age from twenty-one to fifty-eight. All were currently in individual insight-oriented psychotherapy. The dependent measures employed were (a) patients' ratings of distress on target complaints (those complaints that the patients wanted to see changed by therapy); (b) the trait anxiety scale of the Speilberger State-Trait Anxiety Inventory, composed of 22-item scales measuring state or trait anxiety; (c) the Stein and Chu adaptation of Barron's ego-strength scale; (d) Batson's inventory of religiosity, a 6-scale, 70-item inventory on intrinsic and extrinsic religiosity; (e) Hood's mysticism scale, a 32-item measure of reported mystical experience; and (f) the Pauline Comparison Scale, a 5-item scale designed by Finney and Malony to measure "the degree to which one views religion as providing an emotional independence from one's circumstances" (p. 286).

Finney and Malony (1985c) attained only "modest" support for the hypotheses that when contemplative prayer is used as an adjunct to psychotherapy, both psychotherapy and spirituality would gain. They did find psychotherapeutic improvement as indicated by a "marked decrease in distress on target complaints" (p. 288). Two subjects who did not show this pattern of distress decrease also averaged a significantly less period of time in contemplative prayer. However, because similar trends were not observed for trait anxiety or ego strength, Malony and Finney were not sure if the decline in distress was due to therapy alone. A significant correlation was observed for all subjects between the practice of contemplative prayer and lower trait anxiety, but this might have been because they practiced contemplative prayer when they were less anxious. The most that can be said is that "the data provide modest circumstantial evidence for the association of CP with psychotherapeutic improvement" (p. 288).

Finney and Malony (1985c) concluded that more research was needed that recognizes the complex nature of contemplative prayer and they specifically suggested two areas for further exploration: (1) the psychotherapeutic effect of contemplative prayer, and (2) the effect of contemplative prayer on individual perceptions and experiences of reality.

Hood, Morris, and Watson (1989) observed that those empirical studies that had been done on prayer largely centered on petitionary prayer, leaving contemplative or mystical prayer overlooked or ignored.

Mystical prayer, or what might be termed silent contemplation, has been ignored by psychologists despite its obvious relationship to meditation and mysticism, topics that are of continued research interest in the empirical psychology of religion. Furthermore, it is quite likely that mystical prayer rather than petitionary prayer characterizes mature religiosity (Allport, 1950). If so, measures of mysticism ought to be relevant to assessing prayer experience (p. 39).

The intrinsic/extrinsic distinction, first put forth by Allport (1950), has proved to be a helpful, if also controversial, means of measuring religiosity. According to Allport, people with an extrinsic orientation to religious life tend to view their religion instrumentally, as a means to an end. Alternatively, people with an intrinsic orientation, whom Allport and others would describe as possessing a more mature religious outlook, see their religious lives as an end in themselves. These researchers set out to investigate whether intrinsic/extrinsic orientation was correlated with prayer experiences and found that intrinsic persons were more likely to interpret their prayer experiences in meaningful religious terms than extrinsic persons. Hood, Morris, and Watson (1989) concluded that intrinsic individuals tend to engage in contemplative or what the authors called mystical prayer. Furthermore, intrinsic individuals are more likely to report imagery during prayer or meditation. In contrast, extrinsic people do not tend to identify prayer or meditative experiences as mystical at all. It is interesting to note that extrinsic people apparently do not reach a state of contentlessness (an emptying of the mind from concrete distractions) during prayer, perhaps because their prayers are more likely to be petitionary rather than mystical in nature. According to Hood, Morris, and Watson, extrinsic persons are not at all comfortable with contemplative or mystical prayer.

A number of studies that are somewhat peripheral to a bibliography on prayer have explored the nature of mystical experience and noted its relationship to contemplative/mystical prayer. Hay and Morisy (1978) observed that people who claimed mystical experiences were also more likely to report a high level of psychological well-being than people not in this category.

Ralph Hood, Jr., frequently in collaboration with Paul Watson and Ronald Morris, has extensively studied the nature of mystical experience; personality correlates of mystical experience; the measurement of mystical experience; mystical experience as related to church attendance; stress and the elicitation of mystical experience; and religious orientation and the experience of transcendence, mystical experience, and intense religious experiences. Hood (1989) has also explored the relationship between theology and religious experience. It should be noted that "religious experience" or "mystical experience" is a broader category than prayer itself, but insights gained in examining these broader categories might well enlighten our understanding of prayer. Others who have investigated mystical experience include Thomas and Cooper (1978), Margolis and Elifson (1979), and Spanos and Moretti (1988).

The number of studies focusing on prayer and human well-being remain small in number, though there are signs that at least some researchers are currently working to alleviate this deficit. The dearth of studies on prayer and well-being is surprising, especially when one notes that members of the Christian Association for Psychological Studies (CAPS) apparently employ prayer on a frequent basis in psychotherapy. Christian psychotherapists surveyed in 1982 demonstrated a strong belief in the importance of prayer. Most felt free to use prayer in psychotherapy sessions, whether it be silent prayer, audible prayer, or asking clients to pray for themselves outside of therapy. Therapists prayed for their clients and expected prayer to affect therapy outcome. The CAPS survey appeared to demonstrate clearly that "most of this population is very supportive of the use of prayer in the process of counseling, and tend to use prayer where it is appropriate and feasible. There are very few who remain skeptical as to the usefulness of prayer" (Lange, 1983, p. 49).

Clearly, if prayer is perceived to be a therapeutic value by Christian professionals in the health field, more empirical work is in order.

Carlson, Bacaseta, and Simanton (1988) studied the effects of devotional meditation (DM) on physiological and psychological variables related to stress. They defined devotional meditation as a period of prayer and meditative reading of biblical material. They reported partial confirmation for their hypothesis that religious persons engaging in DM would experience physiological and psychological changes similar to those reported for persons using progressive relaxation exercises. They went on to speculate that the results of their study might be explained in terms of the unique spiritual resources inherent among a Christian population, which might foster such physiological and psychological relaxation.

Poloma and Pendleton (1989) have conducted one of the few research investigations that has studied the relationship between prayer and quality of life. Drawing from the annual Akron Area Survey, which includes a number of "quality of life" domains, the authors randomly selected and then obtained 560 completed telephone interviews. The authors began by dividing prayer into four categories: ritual prayer, petitionary prayer, colloquial prayer, and meditative prayer. Ritual prayer defines those prayers that include recitation of prepared prayers available through reading or from memory. Petitionary prayer includes those requests to meet the specific material needs of one's self or one's friends. Colloquial prayer incorporates within a conversational style various petitionary elements such as asking for God's guidance, blessing, forgiveness, and lessening of the world's suffering. It also includes conversational prayers of thanksgiving and love. Meditative prayer includes components of intimacy, a perceived personal relationship with the divine, such as "being in the presence of God," "thinking about God," and "adoring, reflecting, and communicating with God" (p. 47). The authors found that meditative prayer seems to be moderately although significantly related to quality of life and religious satisfaction. Ritual prayer was found to have a positive relationship with negative affect, suggesting that those who use ritual prayer as their primary form of praying are more likely to be sad, lonely, depressed, and tense. Only colloquial prayer was found to be a predictor of happiness.

The authors went on to report that people with high general life satisfaction tend to have lower levels of education, relatively higher income, and pray more often. Persons with higher incomes who have prayer experiences and who engage in meditative prayer are more likely to score higher on the existential quality of life scale. "Prayer experiences" refers to what happens spiritually, psychologically, and physically when one engages in prayer.

> In other words, those with higher incomes and more frequent prayer experiences, who engage in meditative prayer, believe they have a meaning, purpose, and sense of direction in life. Those who said they were most happy with their lives, taking all things together, have high incomes, engage in the colloquial form of prayer, often have prayer experiences, but paradoxically pray less frequently (p. 50).

That leaves us to ponder the paradox: why do seemingly happier people apparently pray less? It is interesting to note that those with higher happiness scores are more likely to use a conversational, verbal prayer style than any other form. The authors concluded, therefore, that it may be that unhappy people tend to use ritualistic prayers. However, saying prayers ritualistically without corresponding prayer experiences seems unlikely to alleviate the unhappy feelings. Finally, those who pray often and who do have prayer experiences are more likely to use meditative prayer forms rather than verbal ones and are more likely to score higher on the religious satisfaction scale.

According to Poloma and Pendleton (1989), the type of prayer—meditative, ritual, petitionary, or colloquial—may be more important than the frequency of prayer. They concluded with confidence that religiosity and prayer contribute to quality of life and perceptions of quality of life.

While empirical research investigating the relationship between prayer and health does seem to be increasing somewhat of late, the overall paucity of studies existent continues to limit whatever conclusions can be drawn. There seems to be no certainty to be derived from the empirical research that even begins to address a causal relationship between prayer and outcomes. Therefore, Galton's (1883) conclusion that if a large number of people pray for the health of the king, then the king certainly should be healthy, is necessarily unwarranted when there are clearly many other intervening variables that need to be taken into account. Nor can we judge either the efficacy of the prayer or the relative righteousness of the person offering the prayer in terms of specific outcomes. History is replete with examples of religious persons on both sides of war who prayed fervently for victory for their side. Neither the righteousness of the person praying nor the righteousness of the cause will necessarily affect the immediate outcome. Furthermore, we should not necessarily conclude that such prayers go "unanswered." The closest empirical research comes to addressing this issue is Byrd's (1988) well-designed study, which suggests how intercessory prayer might work to promote healing. However, it does seem possible to conclude that prayer that is mature and that is characterized by meditative, mystical, and fuller religious experience appears to be related to at least some aspects of adjustment, happiness, general life satisfaction, and perhaps healing.

Prayer has long been utilized as a resource for coping with the various stresses of life. McCullough (1995) reported in his very useful review of the theoretical and empirical literature on the relationship between prayer and health that studies support the notion that prayer can be an effective resource for coping with chronic pain and other medical problems. "Studies support these observations and suggest that prayer is a popular and effective way to cope with many life stressors, including muscular skeletal pain (Cronan, Kaplan, Posner, Bloomer, and Kosen, 1989), physical symptoms (Bearon and Koenig, 1990; Koenig, George and Siegler, 1988), the death of a spouse (Gass, 1987) and stress before heart surgery (Saudia, Kinney, Brown, and Young-Ward, 1991)" (p. 18).

Benson (1996) claimed in his book, *Timeless Healing*, that we are "wired to believe, that our bodies are nourished and healed by prayer and other exercises of belief" (p. 305). He asserted that there is a phenomena, which he calls "bodily calm," that is the opposite of the well-known fight or flight response. Benson called the "bodily calm" response the "relaxation response," a state in which blood pressure is lowered and heart rate, breathing rate, and metabolic rate are decreased. "The relaxation response yields many long-term benefits in both health and well-being and can be brought on with very simple mental focusing or meditation techniques" (pp. 16–17).

Theological Implications of Prayer

Sanders (1998) has written an enormously provocative book, which among other matters deals with the implications that prayer has for philosophical, systematic, and biblical theology. His book, *The God Who Risks: A Theology of Providence* (1988), suggests a working model of "relational theism," which holds that God has the freedom to interact openly with humanity (through prayer). Relational theism, also known as openness theology, refers to "any model of the divine-human relationship that includes genuine give-and-take relations between God and humans such that there is a receptivity and degree of contingency in God" (p. 12). Openness theology holds that God takes risks by engaging us in a reciprocal relationship that does not have preordained or guaranteed outcomes. According to this theology, God is open to changing the outcome of human events as a result of the prayers of a petitioner, hence God may actually change a divine decision when God believes such a change is warranted (perhaps in response to the fervent prayer of a righteous individual). Openness theology clashes with some interpretations of classical theism, which hold that God knows all (omniscience) and determines all events, personal or corporate solicitations (prayers) notwithstanding.

Presumably an individual who prays to God believes that God hears, cares, and is influenced by the prayer and by the relative righteousness of the person who offers the prayer. In theological terms, we are dealing with issues of providence and sovereignty.

"Providence refers to the way that God has chosen to relate to us and provide for our well-being" (p. 11). It is God's activity in our world and in human life. As Helm suggests in his recent book, *The Providence of God* (1994), providence, most simply put, refers to God's constant provision. Further, providence incorporates whom it is that God provides for, what God provides, and how God provides. The no-risk view of sovereignty contends that God is in absolute control of history, determining every event, every life, every death, and each individual success or failure. Sovereignty, providence, and prayer are clearly entangled in the perennial free will/determinism, free will/predestination debate. Part of the theological mystery with respect to providence and sovereignty is, if God controls every human event, how is it that God would or could respond to the petitions (prayers) of human beings? Sanders poses the possibility of a form of petitionary prayer that he calls "impetratory" prayer, defined as the receiving of something *because* an individual actually requests it through the act of a petitionary prayer.

We may wonder, Does God ever respond to us and do something that God would otherwise not do *only* because we ask for it? Does God ever not do something he would otherwise do because we ask for it? How shall we understand James's assertion that "you have not because you ask not (4:2)" (p. 268)? Could this last question be reframed as, You receive because you ask? Another perplexing question is, If God knows everything, why does he need to be prayed to anyway?

We see again the complexity inherent in attempts to measure prayer by rational, statistical, or even empirical means (such complexity begs the aforementioned theological questions). It is clear that social science has not yet made terribly helpful or significant contributions toward our understanding of just how the power and mystery of prayer, an essentially spiritual phenomenon, intersects with the divine/human equation.

It seems clear that ever since Galton published his findings and concluded that there is no statistical evidence for the objective value of petitionary and intercessory prayer that social science research examining the spiritual reality of prayer has met with great resistance from the religious community, which continues to be understandably reluctant to subject spiritual experience to empirical testing.

And yet, Finney and Maloney (1985b) point out there is an opportunity for much further empirical investigation of prayer, including studying the "motives for prayer, the differential effects of various kinds of prayer, the psychological processes active in prayer . . . the effects of prayer on religious and spiritual development . . . and finally the relationship of Christian prayer to other major religions" (p. 113).

References

Allport, G. W. (1950). *The Individual and His Religion*. New York: Macmillan.

Allport, G. W. (1954). *The Nature of Prejudice*. Cambridge, MA: Addison

Allport, G. W. (1959). "Religion and Prejudice." *Crane Review*, 2, 1–10.

Allport, G. W. (1966). "The Religious Context of Prejudice." *Journal for the Scientific Study of Religion*, 5, 447–457.

Allport, G. W., and Ross, J. M. (1967). "Personal Religious Orientation and Prejudice." *Journal of Personality and Social Psychology*, 5(4), 432–443.

Bearon, L. B., and Koenig, H. G. (1990). "Religious Cognitions and Use of Prayer in Health and Illness." *The Gerontologist*, 30(2), 249–253.

Benson, H. (with Marg Stark). (1996). *Timeless Healing: The Power and Biology of Belief*. New York: Fireside Press.

Byrd, R. C. (1988). "Positive Therapeutic Effects of Intercessory Prayer in a Coronary Care Unit Population." *Southern Medical Journal*, 81(7), 826–829.

Byrd, R. C. (1995). "The Therapeutic Effects of Intercessory Prayer." *Journal of Christian Nursing*, 12(1), 21–23.

Carlson, C. R., Bacaseta, P. E., and Simanton, D. A. (1988). "A Controlled Evaluation of Devotional Meditation and Progressive Relaxation." *Journal of Psychology and Theology*, 16(4), 362–368.

Carson, V., and Huss, K. (1979). "Prayer: An Effective Therapeutic and Teaching Tool." *Journal of Psychiatric Nursing*, 17(3), 34–37.

Collipp, P. J. (1969). "The Efficacy of Prayer: A Triple-Blind Study." *Medical Times*, 97(5), 201–204.

Cronan, T. A., Kaplan, R. M., Posner, L., Blumberg, E., and Kozin, F. (1989). "Prevalence of the Use of Unconventional Remedies for Arthritis in a Metropolitan Community." *Arthritis and Rheumatism*, 32, 1604–1607.

Elkins, D., Anchor, K. N., and Sandler, H. M. (1979). "Relaxation Training and Prayer Behavior as Tension Reduction Techniques." *Behavioral Engineering*, 5(3), 81–87.

Finney, J. R., and Malony, Jr., H. N. (1985a). "Contemplative Prayer and Its Use in Psychotherapy: A Theoretical Model." *Journal of Psychology and Theology,* *13*(3), 172–181.

Finney, J. R., and Malony, Jr., H. N. (1985b). "Empirical Studies of Christian Prayer: A Review of Literature." *Journal of Psychology and Theology, 13*(2), 104–115.

Finney, J. R., and Malony, Jr., H. N. (1985c). "An Empirical Study of Contemplative Prayer as an Adjunct to Psychotherapy." *Journal of Psychology and Theology, 13*(4), 284–290.

Fordyce, E. M. (1982). "An Investigation of Television's Potential for Meeting the Spiritual Needs of Hospitalized Adult Patients." Ph.D. diss., Catholic University of America. Washington, DC: *Dissertation Abstracts International.*

Freud, S. (1953). *The Complete Psychological Works of Sigmund Freud.* Edited and translated by J. Strachey. Volume 7. London: Hogarth Press.

Galton, F. (1883). *Inquiries into Human Faculty.* London: Macmillan.

Gass, K. A. (1987). "Coping Strategies of Widows." *Journal of Gerontological Nursing, 13,* 29–33.

Godin, A., and Van Rooey, B. (1959). "Immanent Justice and Divine Protection." *Lumen Vitae, 14,* 129–148.

Goldman, R. (1964). *Religious Thinking from Childhood to Adolescence.* London: Rutledge.

Hay, D., and Morisy, A. (1978). "Reports of Ecstatic, Paranormal, or Religious in Great Britain and the United States: A Comparison of Trends. *Journal for the Scientific Study of Religion, 17*(3), 255–268.

Helm, P. (1994). *The Providence of God.* Downers Grove, IL: Intervarsity Press.

Holmes, C. S. (July 13, 1998). "Winding Paths Meet: Healing and Faith Find a Connection." *Christianity Today,* 16.

Hood, Jr., R. W. (1970). "Religious Orientation and the Report of Religious Experience." *Journal for the Scientific Study of Religion, 9,* 285–291.

Hood, Jr., R. W. (1972). "Normative and Motivational Determinants of Reported Religious Experience in Two Baptist Samples." *Review of Religious Research, 13,* 192–196.

Hood, Jr., R. W. (1973). "Forms of Religious Commitment and Intense Religious Experience." *Review of Religious Research, 15,* 29–36.

Hood, Jr., R. W. (1973). "Religious Orientation and the Experience of Transcendence." *Journal for the Scientific Study of Religion, 12,* 441–448.

Hood, Jr., R. W. (1975). "The Construction and Preliminary Validation of a Measure of Reported Mystical Experience." *Journal for the Scientific Study of Religion, 14,* 29–41.

Hood, Jr., R. W. (1976). "Conceptual Criticisms of Regressive Explanations of Mysticism." *Review of Religious Research, 17,* 179–188.

Hood, Jr., R. W. (1976). "Mystical Experience as Related to Present and Antici-
pated Future Church Participation." *Psychological Reports, 39*, 1127–1136.

Hood, Jr., R. W. (1977). "Differing Triggering of Mystical Experience as a Function of Self Actualization." *Review of Religious Research, 18*, 264–270.

Hood, Jr., R. W. (1978). "Anticipatory Set and Setting: Stress Incongruities as
Elicitors of Mystical Experience in Solitary Nature Situations." *Journal for the
Scientific Study of Religion, 17*, 279–287.

Hood, Jr., R. W. (1980). "Psychological Strength and the Report of Intense Religious Experience." In John R. Tisdale (Ed.), *Growing Edges in the Psychology of
Religion* (pp. 291–297). Chicago: Nelson-Hall.

Hood, Jr., R. W. (1989). "The Relevance of Theologies for Religious Experiencing." *Journal of Psychology and Theology, 17*(4), 336–342.

Hood, Jr., R. W., and Hall, J. R. (1980). "Gender Differences in the Description
of Erotic and Mystical Experiences." *Review of Religious Research, 21*, 195–207.

Hood, Jr., R. W., Hall, J. R., Watson, P. J., and Biderman. M. (1979). "Personality
Correlates of the Report of Mystical Experience." *Psychological Reports, 44*,
804–806.

Hood, Jr., R. W., and Morris, R. J. (1981). "Knowledge and Experience Criteria in
the Report of Mystical Experience." *Review of Religious Research, 23*(1), 76–84.

Hood, Jr., R. W., Morris, R. J., and Watson, P. J. (1989). "Prayer Experience and
Religious Orientation." *Review of Religious Research, 31*(1), 39–45.

Hood, Jr., R. W., Morris, R. J., and Watson, P. J. (1990). "Quasi-Experimental
Elicitation of the Differential Report of Religious Experience among Intrinsic
and Indiscriminately Pro-Religious Types." *Journal for the Scientific Study of
Religion, 29*(2), 164–172. Cf. also Holm, N. G. (1982). "Mysticism and Intense
Experiences." *Journal for the Scientific Study of Religion, 21*(3), 268–276.

James, W. (1963). *The Variations of Religious Experience.* New York: University
Books.

Janssen, J., De Hart, J., and Den Draak, C. (1990). "A Content Analysis of the
Praying Practices of Dutch Youth." *Journal for the Scientific of Religion, 29*(1),
99–107.

Joyce, C. R. B., and Welldon, R. M. C. (1965). "The Objective Efficacy of Prayer."
Journal of Chronic Disease, 18, 367–377.

King, D. B., and Bushwick, B. (1994). "Beliefs and Attitudes of Hospital Inpatients About Faith Healing and Prayer." *The Journal of Family Practice, 39*(4),
349–352.

Koenig, H. G., George, L. K., and Siegler, I. C. (1988). "The Use of Religion and
Other Emotion-regulating Coping Strategies among Older Adults. *The Gerontologist, 28*, 303–310.

Koenig, H. G., Smiley, M., and Gonzales, J. P. (1988). *Religion, Health, and Aging:
A Review and Theoretical Integration.* New York: Greenwood Press.

Lange, M. A. (1983). "Prayer and Psychotherapy: Beliefs and Practice." *Journal of Psychology and Christianity*, 2(3), 36–49.

Long, D., Elkind, D., and Spilka, B. (1967). "The Child's Conception of Prayer." *Journal for the Scientific Study of Religion*, 6, 101–109.

Margolis, R. D., and Elifson, K. W. (1979). "A Typology of Religious Experience." *Journal for the Scientific Study of Religion*, 18(1), 61–67.

Matthews, D. A., Larson, D. B., and Barry, C. P. (1993). *The Faith Factor: An Annotated Bibliography of Clinical Research on Spiritual Subjects*. Washington, DC: National Institute for Healthcare Research.

McCullough, M. E. (1995). "Prayer and Health: Conceptual Issues, Research Review, and Research Agenda." *Journal of Psychology and Theology*, 23(1), 15–29.

Meadow, M. J., and Kahoe, R. D. (1984). *Psychology of Religion*. New York: Harper & Row, 120; quoted in Margaret M. Poloma and Brian F. Pendleton. (1991). "The Effects of Prayer and Prayer Experiences on Measures of General Well-Being." *Journal of Psychology and Theology*, 19, 172.

Moberg, D. O., and McEnery, J. N. (1976). "Prayer Habits and Attitudes of Catholic Students, 1961–1971." *Social Science*, 51(2), 76–85.

Parker, W. R., and St. Johns, E. (1957). *Prayer Can Change Your Life*. Carmel, NY: Guideposts.

Poloma, M. M., and Pendleton, B. F. (1989). "Exploring Types of Prayer and Quality of Life: A Research Note." *Review of Religious Research*, 31(1), 46–53.

Rosner, F. (1975). "The Efficacy of Prayer: Scientific vs. Religious Evidence." *Journal of Religion and Health*, 14, 294–298.

Sanders, J. (1998). *The God Who Risks: A Theology of Providence*. Downers Grove, IL: Intervarsity Press.

Saudia, T. L., Kinney, M. R., Brown, K. C., and Young-Ward, L. (1991). "Health Locus of Control and Helpfulness of Prayer." *Heart and Lung*, 20(1), 60–65.

Scarlett, W. G., and Perriello, L. (1991). "The Development of Prayer in Adolescence." *New Directions for Child Development*, 52, 63–76.

Sodestrom, K. E., and Martinson I. M. (1987). "Patients' Spiritual Coping Strategies: A Study of Nurse and Patient Perspectives." *Oncology Nursing Forum*, 14(2), 41–46.

Spanos, N. P., and Moretti, P. (1988). "Correlates of Mystical and Diabolical Experiences in a Sample of Female University Students." *Journal for the Scientific Study of Religion*, 27(1), 105–116.

Tamminen, K. (1991). *Religious Development in Childhood and Youth: An Empirical Study*. Helsinki: Suomalainen Tiedeakatemia (Finnish Academy of Science and Letters,).

Thomas, L. E., and Cooper, P. E. (1978). "Measurement and Incidence of Mystical Experiences: An Exploratory Study." *Journal for the Scientific Study of Religion*, 17(4), 433–437.

Thouless, R. H., and Brown, L. B. (1964). "Petitionary Prayer: Belief in Its Appropriateness and Causal Efficacy Among Adolescent Girls." In A. Godin (Ed.), *From Religious Experience to a Religious Attitude* (pp. 123–126). Brussels: Lumen Vitae Press.

Trier, K. K., and Shupe, A. (1991). "Prayer, Religiosity, and Healing in the Heartland, USA: A Research Note." *Review of Religious Research, 32*(4), 351–358.

Bibliography

Anthony, D., T. Robbins, M. Doucas, and T. E. Curtis. "Patients and Pilgrims." *American Behavioral Scientist* 20 (1977): 861–886.

Benson, Herbert. "The Relaxation Response and Norepinephrine: A New Study Illuminates Mechanisms."
Benson "reviews the historical usage of the relaxation response as well as more recent techniques, which include autogenic training, progressive relaxation, and hypnosis. All relaxation practices, both religious and secular, employ the basic steps of the repetition of a word, sound, prayer, or phrase and the adoption of a passive attitude toward other thoughts. The relaxation response appears to be an integrated hypothalamic response resulting in generalized decreased sympathetic nervous system activity, including decreased oxygen consumption, heart rate, arterial blood pressure, respiratory rate, and arterial blood lactate. Although the physiologic changes of the RR are consistent with decreased sympathetic nervous system activity, direct measurement of plasma norepinephrine (PN) during its elicitation has not revealed significant decreases in the hormone's concentration. In an experiment by J. W. Hoffman et al., after 30 days of regular elicitation of the RR in experimental subjects, the PN response to graded stress was augmented over and above change. It is concluded that the observations are consistent with reduced norepinephrine end-organ responsivity and may be a mechanism through which the physiologic changes persist longer than just during the elicitation of the response." (PsycLIT Database AN: 71-25276)

Benson, H. "The Faith Factor." *American Health* 5 (1984): 50–53.

Bolley, Alfons. "Recent Research into the Psychology of God-Consciousness in Meditation." *Lumen Vitae* 16 (June, 1961): 223–232.

Brown, L. B. "Ego-Centric Thought in Petitionary Prayer: A Cross-Cultural Study." *Journal of Social Psychology* 68 (1966): 197–210.

Byrd, R. C. "The Positive Therapeutic Effects of Intercessory Prayer in a Coronary Care Unit Population." *Southern Medical Journal* 57 (1988): 5–15.

Canesi, A. "Vorlaufige Untersuchungen uber die Psychologie des Gebets." *Archives Religionspsychology* 6 (1936): 13–72.

Committee on Psychiatry and Religion. "Mysticism: Spiritual Quest or Psychic Disorder?" *Group for the Advancement of Psychiatry* 9 (1976): 718–822.

Davidson, J. "Physiology of Meditation and Mystical States of Consciousness." *Perspectives in Biology and Medicine* 19 (1976): 345–380.

Davis, T. N. "Can Prayer Facilitate Healing and Growth? *Southern Medical Journal* 79, no. 6 (June 1986): 733–735.

DeBlassie, Paul A., III. "Christian Meditation: A Clinical Investigation." *Dissertation Abstracts International* 42 (1981): 1167B

Deikman, A. J. "Deautomatization and the Mystic Experience." *Psychiatry* 29 (1976): 324–338. Also in John R. Tisdale, *Growing Edges in the Psychology of Religion*, Chicago: Nelson-Hall, 1980, 201–217.
Deikman argues that mystic experience such as that attained in contemplative prayer is the result of deautomatization. In deautomatization "hierarchically ordered structures of perception and cognition, structures that ordinarily conserve attentional energy for maximum efficiency in achieving the basic goals of the individual," are set aside "in favor of alternate modes of consciousness whose stimulus processing may be less efficient from a biological point of view but whose very inefficiency may permit the experience of aspects of the real world formerly excluded"(215–16). The stimuli being processed through this mode are still difficult to determine and one's presuppositions about the nature of reality will largely determine one's interpretation.

Douglas-Smith, Basil. "An Empirical Study of Religious Mysticism." *British Journal of Psychiatry* 118 (1971): 549–554.

Driskill, Joseph D. "Meditation as a Therapeutic Technique." *Pastoral Psychology* 38, no. 2 (1989): 83–103.
Driskill argues that the use of Christian meditation as a therapeutic technique has been lost and needs to be reclaimed as an effective tool. Definitions of meditation found in religious literature and in the social sciences are clarified, and recent literature in the human sciences journals is reviewed. Suggestions for the integration of counseling and meditation in a unified theoretical model are included. (PsycLIT Database, AN: 77-20727)

Duke, James T., and Barry L. Johnson. "Spiritual Well-Being and the Consequential Dimension of Religiosity." *Review of Religious Research* 26, no. 1 (September 1984): 59–72.
This study explores the consequential aspect of religion. Seven religiosity factors are identified: public and private devotion, belief, integrity, loving service, spiritual well-being, and the Beatitudes. Interrelationships between factors are also explored. The relationship between prayer and other consequential factors was found to be weak in intrinsic spirituality. Spiritual well-being was more closely related to extrinsic rather than intrinsic factors. (Sociological Abstracts AN: 8403514)

Dunning, Laurie Elizabeth. "Beneficial Characteristics of Prayer Expressed by School Age Children Subsequent to Painful Procedures." *Dissertation Abstracts International* 25, no. 4 (1987), 358.

Earle, Jonathan B. "Cerebral Laterality and Meditation: A Review of the Literature." *Journal of Transpersonal Psychology* 13 (1981): 155–173.

Elkind, D. "The Development of Religious Understanding in Children and Adolescents." In *Research on Religious Development*, edited by M. P. Strommen, 655–685. New York: Hawthorn Books, 1971.

Ellens, J. H. "Communication Theory and Petitionary Prayer." *Journal of Psychology and Theology* 5 (1977): 48–54.

Finney, John R. "Contemplative Prayer as an Adjunct to Psychotherapy." Ph.D. diss., Fuller Seminary, 1984.

Galanter, Marc, and Peter Buckley. "Evangelical Religion and Meditation: Psychotherapeutic Effects." *Journal of Nervous and Mental Disease* 166 (October 1978): 685–691.

Galton, F. "Statistical Inquiries into the Efficacy of Prayer." *Fortnightly Review* 18 (Vol. 12, no. 68 New Series) (1872): 125–135.

Giardini, Fabio. "The Conscious and Unconscious Mind in Prayer." *Journal of Psychology and Christianity* 6, no. 1 (Spring 1987): 5–20. Giardini discusses "the different kinds of attention possible in acts of prayer and suggests that these types include active attention, receptive attention, and ecstatic attention. The difference between attentiveness and awareness called forth by active and receptive attention is compared with ecstasy and the effect of ecstatic attention in prayer. The role of unconscious awareness in prayer is discussed, and psychological literature referring to this form of awareness is reviewed. It is concluded that the attention of the mind in prayer takes different forms and can be entirely absorbed into God in ecstasy or expanded beyond explicit awareness through unconscious awareness of His presence." (PsycLIT Database AN: 75-19826)

Gibbons, D., and J. DeJarnette. "Hypnotic Susceptibility and Religious Experience." *Journal for the Scientific Study of Religion* 11 (1972): 152–156.

Gibson, Rose C. "Blacks at Middle and Late Life: Resources and Coping." *Annals of the American Academy of Political and Social Science* 464 (November 1982): 79–90.

Godin, A., ed. *From Religious Experience to a Religious Attitude.* Brussels: Lumen Vitae Press, 1964.

Godin, A., and B. Van Rooey. "Immanent Justice and Divine Protection." *Lumen Vitae* 14 (1959): 129–148.

Goleman, D. "The Faith Factor." *American Health* 3, no. 3 (1984): 48–53.

Griffith, E. E., T. English, and V. Mayfield. "Possession, Prayer, and Testimony: Therapeutic Aspects of the Wednesday Night Meeting in a Black Church." *Psychiatry* 43, no. 2 (May 1980): 120–128.

A study of the support mechanisms at work in a church service, with the focus on a Wednesday night prayer meeting in a non-affiliated black church. The study centers on the church service as a model for a therapeutic group. (Sociological Abstracts AN: 80K7899)

Gruner, Leroy. "The Correlation of Private, Religious Devotional Practices and Marital Adjustment." *Journal of Comparative Family Studies* 16, no. 1 (Spring 1985): 47– 59.
This study indicates a positive relationship between prayer and marital adjustment. (Sociological Abstracts AN: 85Q0587)

Henning, Grant. "An Analysis of Correlates of Perceived Positive and Negative Prayer Outcomes." *Journal of Psychology and Theology* 9, no. 4 (1981): 352–358.
An examination of the relation between "perceived binary outcome" (answered or unanswered prayer) and various independent prayer variables, such as fasting, thanksgiving, repetition, and urgency.

Homan, Roger. "Interpersonal Communications in Pentecostal Meetings." *Sociological Review* 26 (1978): 499–518.
Homan describes his paper as a "survey of the schemes within which interpersonal relations are developed in Pentecostal meetings. Expressions of sympathy and appreciation and the recognition of individual merit are made not directly between persons but indirectly in the form of public prayer and testimony. The indirectness of the interpersonal transactions accords well with the theocentricity of the Pentecostal world-view and the conscientious denial of personal competence." (cf. Homan, 1986, p. 122)

Homan, Roger. *The Sociology of Religion: A Bibliographical Survey.* New York: Greenwood Press, 1986.

Horton, P. C. "The Mystical Experience as a Suicide Preventative." *American Journal of Psychiatry* 130 (1973): 294–297.

Linden, W. "Practicing of Meditation by School Children and Their Levels of Field Dependence-Independence, Test Anxiety, and

Reading Achievement." *Journal of Consulting and Clinical Psychology* 41 (1973): 139–143.

Marinier, P. *Reflexions sur la priere: Ses causes et ses effets psychophysiologiques.* Geneva: Cailler, 1952.

Matthews, Dale A., and David B. Larson. *A Bibliography of Research by Scientists on Spiritual Subjects.* Philadelphia: John Templeton Foundation, 1991.

McDonagh, John M. "Working Through Resistance by Prayer and the Gift of Knowledge: A Case Study of Anger." *Journal of Psychology and Christianity* 4, no. 2 (Summer 1985): 26–28.
McDonagh "presents the case of a devout Christian woman whose rage was ruining her life. Psychotherapy that focused on dreams and their interpretation and spiritual symbolism, decreases in the subject's resistance, and spiritual counseling helped her regain a normal emotional balance." (PsycLIT Database AN: 73-17850)

McGuire, Meredith B. "Words of Power: Personal Empowerment and Healing." *Culture, Medicine, and Psychiatry* 7, no. 3 (1983): 221–240.
McGuire examines instances of the ritual use of words in a diverse selection of alternative healing groups in modern society. These words are distinguished by their users' beliefs that they are endowed with a power, an effectiveness separate from and in addition to their literal meaning. It is argued that one of the key factors in healing illness is mobilizing resources of power, especially enhancing the ill person's sense of personal empowerment. Ritual language use in alternative healing is one of the foremost elements in this empowerment, because it both represents and objectifies power. Within a belief system in which they are significant, words of power indeed have the power to effect healing. (PsycLIT Database AN: 71-26642)

McKenzie, N. C. "Prayer, Meditation and Religious Experience: An Empirical Study." Master's thesis, King's College, London, 1979.

Moore, Richard H. "Changes in Psychological Functioning Through

Contemplative Meditation." Ph.D. diss., Nova University, 1984. Abstract in *Dissertation Abstracts International* 43 (1983): 2319B.

Overall, Christine. "The Nature of Mystical Experience." *Religious Studies* 18 (1981): 47–54.

Pagano, R. R., and W. S. Warrenburg. "Meditation and Hemispheric Specialization." *Biofeedback and Self-Regulation* 6, no. 3 (1981): 406.

Poloma, Margaret M., and Brian F. Pendleton. "The Effects of Prayer and Prayer Experiences on Measures of General Well-Being." *Journal of Psychology and Theology* 19, no. 1 (1991): 71–83.

Propst, L. "The Comparative Efficacy of Religious and Non-Religious Imagery for the Treatment of Mild Depression in Religious Individuals." *Cognitive Therapy and Research* 4 (1980): 167–178.

Sacks, H. L. "The Effect of Spiritual Exercises on the Integration of Self-Esteem." *Journal for the Scientific Study of Religion* 18 (1979): 46–50.

Sajwaj, T., and D. Hedges. "A Note on the Effects of Saying Grace on the Behavior of an Oppositional Retarded Boy." *Journal of Applied Behavior Analysis* 6 (1973): 711–712.

Schlientz, Margarett A. "A Study on the Decrease of Unresolved Anger Through a Teaching Protocol and Healing Prayer as a Nursing Intervention in Spiritual Care." *Dissertation Abstracts International* 42, 8-B (February 1982): 1167.

Sensky, Tom. "Religiosity, Mystical Experience and Epilepsy." In *Research Progress in Epilepsy*, edited by F. Clifford Rose, 214–220. London: Pitman, 1983.

Surwillo, W. W., and D. P. Hobson. "Brain Electrical Activity During Prayer." *Psychological Reports* 43 (1978): 135–143.

Sutton, T. D., and S. P. Murphy. "Stressors and Patterns of Coping in Renal Transplant Patients." *Nursing Research* 38, no. 1 (January–February 1989): 46–49.

Swatos, William H. "The Power of Prayer: A Prolegomenon to an Ascetical Sociology." *Review of Religious Research* 24, no. 2 (1982): 153–163.

A sociological analysis of an ascetic community based on participation observation data. Swatos proposes an initial taxonomy.
Sociofile notes that functions of prayer in various types of societies are analyzed and suggestions made concerning the theoretical and applied issues that might be addressed by a sociology of
prayer. (Sociological Abstracts AN: 83N3147)

Tappeiner, D. A. "A Psychological Paradigm for the Interpretation of
the Charismatic Phenomenon of Prophecy." *Journal of Psychology
and Theology* 5, no. 1 (1977): 23–29.

Thomson, A. "A Comparison of Scientific Research with Worship."
Bulletin of Science, Technology, and Society 9, no. 5 (1989): 302–
311.
Sociofile lists this article as a study "relying heavily" on the research of Michael Polanyi, where Thomson argues that research
done in the scientific community is comparable to the inquiry
done in the religious community during worship and prayer. Scientific theories arise out of research just as theological beliefs
grow out of worship and prayer. (Sociofile AN: 90V8581)

Tisdale, John R. "Mystical Experience: Normal and Normative." In
Growing Edges in the Psychology of Religion. Chicago: Nelson-Hall,
1980.
A short essay in which Tisdale argues that the human capacity for
mystical experience "is universal to the species, seems to have
clear physiological roots, and is necessary to man's fullest human
development" (p. 239). Appropriate literature and empirical
studies are cited.

Wallace, R. K., and H. Benson. "The Physiology of Meditation." *Scientific American* 226 (1972): 89–90.

Welford, A. T. "A Psychological Footnote to Prayer." *Theology Today,*
3 (1947a): 498–501.
"Results of a test given to 45 male university and seminary students on the relation of emotional stability and tendency to pray.
Results indicate a reliable tendency for emotional stability to increase with the number of situations in which the subjects would
pray. 'Praying in a situation is not, in most cases at any rate, an

acknowledgment of defeat in the face of difficulty, but a means whereby a person seeks to overcome it'" (Meissner, 27).

Witt, L. A. "Religion and Delay of Gratification." *Psychological Reports* 62, no. 2 (1988): 426.

Worten, Susan A., and Steven J. Dollinger. "Mothers' Intrinsic Religious Motivation, Disciplinary Preferences, and Children's Conceptions of Prayer." *Psychological Reports* 58, no. 1 (1986): 218.

2

Faith Healing

IN THE POPULAR CULTURE, Katherine Kuhlmann, Oral Roberts, and now Benny Hinn embody the best or perhaps the worst examples of what is generally considered to be "faith healing." They, along with a host of imitators, have taken a decidedly "nonscientific" approach to healing. In fact, whatever limited scientific study has been done in examining these "faith healers" has usually resulted in attempts to debunk the claims of those who claim to have been healed.

Faith healing has been construed to be at odds with modern medical systems in our technologically driven society. Faith healing has generally been regarded as the "remnant of primitive or peasant, old country traditions, or as characteristic of uneducated, lower class persons who cannot afford modern 'scientific' medical treatment" (McGuire, 1983, p. 221).

Typical of the scientific perspective on faith healing is the conclusion of Pattison, Lapins, and Doerr (1973):

> The primary function of faith healing is not to reduce symptomatology, but to reinforce a magical belief system that is consonant with the sub-culture of these subjects. Faith healing in contemporary America is part of a continuum of magical belief systems ranging from witchcraft to Christian Science. The psychodynamics are similar in all such systems, the variation is in the abstractness of the magical belief system. Within the framework of the assumptive world view in which faith healing subjects live, their

personality structure and magical belief systems are not abnormal, but are part of a coping system that provides ego integration for the individual and social integration for the subculture (p. 397).

McGuire (1983) provides an excellent context for our discussion by grouping various approaches to faith healing into five distinct categories. They are (1) Christian healing groups, particularly those involving Pentecostal Christian healing, (2) meditation and human potential groups, (3) traditional metaphysical groups, (4) occult and eclectic groups including Christian Science, and (5) manipulation/technique practitioners including chiropractic, shiatsu, and reflexology.

Glik (1990a), who has studied faith healing as much as anyone, concluded that ritual healing groups in urban America attract persons whose illnesses are the reflection of the stresses and strains of modernization. Glik defined charismatic Christian faith healing groups as groups that stress intense personal religious experiences such as speaking in tongues, baptism of the Holy Spirit, and prophesying with words of knowledge. These groups are generally considered to be a part of the Pentecostal movement within Christianity, which promotes "spiritual renewal" in both Protestant and Catholic denominations. Glik contended that healing rituals within charismatic Christian groups "elicit ecstatic or dissociative states in members" (p. 160).

Dissociation is a psychological construct defined as a separation or in some cases an isolation of one group of mental processes in such a way that the processes become split off from the main personality. It is a disruption of integration in the personality, which affects consciousness, memory, identity, or perception. The most common forms of dissociation are amnesia and dissociative identity disorder (DID), formerly known as multiple personality disorder (MPD). Hypnosis, trance, and daydreaming are also forms of dissociation.

It is thought that dissociative states are produced by various self-hypnotic phenomenon and include the ecstasies and trances often

found in mystical and religious rituals. The capacity to enter hypnotic trance is considered to be a genetic predisposition most likely
distributed normally over the population. According to Bliss (1985),
a conservative estimate is that 10 percent of all people would be excellent hypnotic subjects and another 20 percent would be considered good hypnotic subjects.

It seems clear that "suggestibility" may be familiar to fundamen-
talist/evangelical Christianity where dynamic, powerful evangelistic
preaching has a rich tradition of purposefully utilizing the fear of
hell and hope of salvation and eternal life to create anxiety, which
sometimes leads to a sense of emotional disequilibrium, which the
evangelist hopes will eventuate in a conversion experience. Perhaps
the best example is American evangelist and revivalist Jonathan Edwards (1997) and his famous eighteenth-century hell-fire-and-
brimstone sermon "Sinners in the Hands of Angry God." The
heightened emotional frenzy of a revival meeting or charismatic
healing service seems to create the context for hypnotic trance
among participants, particularly those who are good hypnotic
subjects.

According to Glik, new age or metaphysical groups emphasize the
power of the mind in the healing process, the mind-body interaction, and its approaches to physical manifestations of the healing
process, including the laying on of hands, remote prayer, therapeutic touch, positive imaging, and affirmations. Techniques differ between groups, but a primary common activity is meditation, which
elicits meditative states among participants.

Glik (1990b) found that the members of charismatic Christian
groups tend be drawn from working or lower middle class backgrounds while the members of new age metaphysical groups tend
to be drawn from middle and upper middle class socioeconomic
strata. According to Glik (1990a) "adherence to systems of knowledge and meaning supportive of intense religiosity may be most
common within certain social strata" (p. 161). Glik maintains that
within the working class and the lower middle class the concern is
for personal salvation as well as with social or self-transformation
themes (a compensatory function), while within the upper socio-

economic classes the focus is on a religiosity of good fortune and self-actualization (an enriching function).

Csordas (1988) examined Catholic Pentecostalism and charismatic faith healing. He suggested that Catholic Pentecostals have participated in a recent shift among Christians away from an emphasis on suffering and self-mortification to an emphasis on the possibility and benefit of divine healing. He further suggested that the process of healing is necessarily related to spiritual growth in that illness is typically regarded as an obstacle to spiritual growth. In this context, healing becomes a necessary ingredient for persons who seek spiritual growth and spiritual growth is in turn regarded as conducive if not necessary to good health. "The healing system is holistic in that it aims in principle to integrate all aspects of the person, conceived as a tripartite composite of body, mind, and spirit" (p. 123).

Glik (1986) undertook a study to examine the relationship between degrees of religiosity and mental health within three types of faith healing groups comprised of a) charismatic Christians, b) new age, and c) persons representing the general population of HMO patients. The charismatic Christian faith healing group was comprised of 83 volunteers. The so-called "new age" or metaphysical group was comprised of 93 individuals and the 117 HMO patients were randomly obtained from a comprehensive list of adult patients enrolled in a local HMO. Glik found that the illnesses across all three groups were mainly chronic and not life threatening nor were there significant differences on an illness severity scale. Her findings suggest that there is a relationship between religiosity and mental health, which is influenced by the religious context of the respondents. Her findings show that while age and physical well-being explain most of the variance in mental health, religiosity remains significant when sociodemographics and health predictor variables are controlled.

In her 1990b study, Glik reexamined her 1986 research to determine just how participants in the various faith healing groups regarded their health problems and how and if these health problems were resolved or "healed" over a six-month period of time. She found that the majority of respondents in fact did claim some degree of faith healing, which was generally associated with symptom reduction rather than with cure. She also found that the respondents seemed to redefine their problems in order to be able to testify to an actual faith-healing experience. She concluded that this process of redefinition, or what she called the "psychologization" of problems, suggests that the healing experience can be conceived as a socially constructed event. Her attempt was to examine the rhetoric of healing, that is the testimonies about successful faith healings offered by persons obviously strongly committed to a belief in faith healing who claimed actual positive changes in their health or illness experiences. She noted that such healing experiences have previously been linked to the placebo effect, to suggestion, to altered states of consciousness, to the relaxation response, and to social support of certain lifestyles.

Glik's (1990) approach was to ask what was actually healed. She also asked the respondents to explain how the faith healing was experienced. Glik found that 20 percent claimed that they were "completely healed"; 24 percent claimed that they were "almost completely healed"; 27 percent claimed that they were "partially healed"; 6 percent claimed that they were "very slightly healed"; and 13 percent claimed that they were "not at all healed"(pp. 155–156).

Glik determined that it was psychological, physical, and religious problems that tended to be healed as opposed to behavioral, social, and moral problems, which proved more difficult and intransigent. She found that there was little change in the actual health status of the respondents overall; in fact the majority of the persons in her study were generally healthy and not ill. She concluded that the healing experienced was "often described as process of symptom alleviation, relief from distress, acceptance of some health or life situation, or adoption of another perspective of one's situation" (p. 157).

Upon further analysis, she found a discrepancy between the problems expressed initially and the problems for which healing was ultimately claimed. This process of "redefining their problems" occurred with slightly more than half of the respondents in her study and with both the Christian and the new age groupings.

In the end, her study, which was designed to document how persons who have engaged in faith healing construct their "clinical reality," found that most persons claimed that their healing had been complete and most cited improvements in some health or life situation. And she found that there was an obvious trend for symptoms to be redefined rather than healed, a process that she calls "becoming psychologized." A greater degree of healing was claimed among those who psychologized their problems. This phenomenon was construed by Csordas (1983) as the process of socialization into a religious world view. An alternate explanation is that faith healing represents a process of denial, repression, and rationalization. The process of redefining one's health problems may not be significantly different from how psychotherapy works as well. Glik (1990) concluded that her social constructionist approach to the study of faith healing helps us understand how individuals "view their illnesses or life situations, and how they interpret their resolution, transformation or continuation. Thus social context influences cognitive representations, which in turn may help persons in such groups 'get well'" (p.165).

McGuire (1987) studied the use of ritual language and other religious symbols as important elements in the dynamics of faith healing. McGuire defined ritual language as consisting of speech and words that the individual believes have a special efficacy or an inherent power. This belief in the power of ritual language and religious symbolism for Christian groups includes the ritual use of words such as "heal" or naming the name of Jesus. Symbolism includes the Bible, the use of candles, oils, crosses, religious icons, and pictures. According to McGuire, the use of ritual language as well as nonverbal symbols can be important aspects of how Christian groups produce a sense of order and control, as well as personal empowerment for their adherents.

Csordas (1986) conducted a fascinating study of faith healing in the context of Catholic Pentecostalism. Seventy-five healing ministers were interviewed in the first phase of his research. Six of the seventy-five were studied in the second phase in much more depth and intensity. The six were observed and recorded in up to five healing sessions. At the conclusion, Csordas determined that the faith healings reported apparently fell rather short of anything close to a "cure." It was Csordas's view that the process of faith healing is in-cremental and does not appear to become integrated into the per-sonalities of the subjects. In fact, Csordas believed that it is the pro-cess of faith healing that has the greatest impact and the most meaning; therefore, the cure is secondary.

Csordas defined Catholic Pentecostal healing as serving four specific types of healing:

(1) Spiritual healing that involves both repentance from sin and forgiveness of others.
(2) Physical healing as a present-day manifestation of the heal-ing tradition of Jesus.
(3) Inner healing that is psychologically oriented but has a basis in the theological doctrine of sin.
(4) Deliverance in which a person is "delivered" from the op-pression of demon possession.

Ness (1980) conducted a review of the literature in which he found that both positive and negative outcomes are possible from participation in the very same religious healing rituals depending on the psychological, emotional, and spiritual resources of the par-ticular individual. According to Ness, the research indicates that "for some individuals, participation in non-medical, healing activ-ity may be emotionally and behaviorally disorganizing" (p. 168).

Ness went on to conduct a study in which he looked at the rela-tionship between religious participation and emotional stability within two "fundamentalist" churches in a Newfoundland coastal community. The first church was a Pentecostal church in which the members shared a common world view about the causes and proper treatment of various illnesses. In the first church, the Pentecostal preacher was a member of the community and maintained close personal relationships with the church members. A characteristic of the Pentecostal preacher was a certain charisma derived from his reputation as a "healer." In the first church, the members expected to received a "blessing"; they expected to be healed. Ritual healing activities included anointing with oil, laying on of hands, and speaking in tongues (glossolalia).

The second church, which Ness described as also fundamentalist, was affiliated with a mainline Protestant group in Canada. This church was actually the "mother church" of the Pentecostal church. Differences between the churches include the fact that members of the Pentecostal church spent thirteen hours on average per week in their church while members of the mainline Protestant group spent about six hours a week in their church. Also, the minister of the mainline church was not a member of the community and he had additional pastoral responsibilities for churches elsewhere. The pastor of the mainline church did not have a reputation as a healer and the members of his church did not stress the possibility or even likelihood of faith healing.

Ness found that people who are active in faith healing are likely to report fewer symptoms of psychological distress than individuals who are less active. Ness concluded, based on his research, that it is the diagnosis and realignment of anxiety-provoking and conflictual interpersonal relationships that are the primary healing outcomes practiced by faith healers. Related to this would be the practice of some Pentecostal churches in offering crisis intervention cures for homosexuals. It may be that it is not so much the homosexual's basic orientation that is being "cured" by faith healing rituals as much as it is his or her definition of self and self-conscious identity as homosexual.

It is only in the last twenty years or so that "faith healing" has begun to be examined by social science research (Poloma, 1991). According to Poloma, the few studies that have addressed this issue indicate that spiritual healing is not as "marginal" as most persons in our popular culture would believe. For example, a 1984 telephone survey of more than five hundred adults in Richmond, Virginia, conducted by Johnson, Williams, and Bromley (1986), found that 14 percent of the respondents reported that they had experienced "healing of a serious disease or physical condition" (p. 72) as a result of prayer.

A study that also dealt with faith healing utilized data from an Akron, Ohio study of 560 randomly chosen respondents. In analyzing the data, Poloma (1991) reported that 72 percent claimed to believe that people sometimes experience physical healing as a result of prayer; an additional 44 percent reported that they had participated in "special healing rituals," and nearly 32 percent of the sample claimed to have had a personal experience of healing (p. 337). Poloma concluded that faith healing is not concentrated among economically deprived populations as is commonly assumed. Rather, the belief in and practice of spiritual healing is widely diffused through a broad range of the general population.

References

Bliss, J. and Bliss, E. (1985). *Prism: Andrea's World*. Briarcliff Manor, NY: Stein and Day, Inc.

Csordas, T. (1983). "The Rhetoric of Transformation in Ritual Healing." *Culture, Medicine and Psychiatry*, 7, 333–375.

Csordas, T. J. (1988). "Elements of Charismatic Persuasion and Healing." *Medical Anthropology Quarterly*, 2, 121–142.

Edwards, J. (1997). *Sinners in the Hands of an Angry God*. New Kensington, PA: Whitaker House.

Glik, D. C. (1986). "Psychosocial Wellness Among Spiritual Healing Adherents." *Social Science and Medicine*, 22, 579–586.

Glik, D. C. (1990a). "Participation in Spiritual Healing, Religiosity, and Mental Health." *Sociological Inquiry*, 60(2), 158–176.

Glik, D. C. (1990b). "The Redefinition of the Situation: The Social Construction of Spiritual Healing Experiences." *Sociology of Health and Illness*, 12(2), 151–168.

Johnson, D. M., Williams, J. S., and Bromley, D. G. (1986). "Religion, Health, and Healing: Findings from a Southern City." *Sociological Analysis*, 47, 66–73.

McGuire, M. B. (1983). "Words of Power: Personal Empowerment and Healing." *Culture, Medicine, and Psychiatry*, 7, 221–240.

McGuire, M. B. (1987). "Ritual, Symbolism and Healing." *Social Compass*, 34(4), 365–379.

Ness, R. C. (1980). "The Impact of Indigenous Healing Activity: An Empirical Study of Two Fundamentalist Churches." *Social Science and Medicine*, 14, 167–180.

Pattison, E. M., Lapins, N. A., and Doerr, H. A. (1973). "Faith Healing: A Study of Personality and Function." *The Journal of Nervous and Mental Disease*, 157(6), 397–409.

Poloma, M. M. (1991). "A Comparison of Christian Science and Mainline Christian Healing Ideologies and Practices." *Review of Religious Research*, 32(4), 337–349.

Bibliography

Achterberg, J. *Imagery in Healing: Shamanism and Modern Medicine.*
Boston and London: Shambhala, 1985.
A book that contains helpful chapters on "Science and the Imagination," the relation between imagery in healing and the behavioral and social sciences, and the effect of imagery on the immune system. The book is weaker, however, in its attempt to
construct a metaphysic or world view around its empirical observations and discoveries. Once again, as in Bernard Siegel's work,
we find an openness to occultic practices that many Christian
readers would find worrisome.

Bourguignon, Erika. "The Effectiveness of Religious Healing Movements: A Review of the Literature." *Transcultural Psychiatric Research Review* 13 (1976): 5–21.

Bradley, D. E. "Religious Involvement and Social Resources: Evidence from the Data Set 'Americans' Changing Lives.'" *Journal
for the Scientific Study of Religion* 34 (1995): 259–267.

Calestro, Kenneth. "Psychotherapy, Faith Healing and Suggestion."
International Journal of Psychiatry 10 (1972): 83–113.

Charuty, Girodana. "Guérir la mémoire: L'Intervention rituelle du
catholicisme pentecotiste francais et italien" (Healing memory:
The ritual intervention of Pentecostalist Catholicism in France
and Italy). *Social Compass* 34, no. 4 (1987): 437–463.
According to Sociofile, this study sheds light on the multiple
facets of the notion of a specialized cure for psychic suffering,
which certain communities of worship claim as their specificity.
Comparisons between the medical model of psychotherapy and
the religious model of exorcism are explored. (Sociological Abstracts AN: 88U0658)

Court, John C. "A Case of Congregational Healing." *Journal of Psychology and Christianity* 4, no. 2 (1985): 98–102.
Court reports the case of a depressed and dissociated pastor's
wife "to illustrate how personal and congregational relationships

can be healed by the spiritual resources of prayer. The patient's willingness to share her personal experience with the 'family' of her local church led to others coming forward and seeking similar help." (PsycLIT Database AN: 73-18217)

Csordas, Thomas. "Health and the Holy in African and Afro-American Spirit Possession." *Social Science and Medicine* 24, no. 1 (1987): 1–12.

Csordas, Thomas J. and Steven Cross. "Healing of Memories: Psychotherapeutic Ritual Among Catholic Pentecostals." *Journal of Pastoral Care* 30 (1976): 245–257.

Frazier, Claude A. *Faith Healing: Finger of God? or Scientific Curiosity?* Camden, NJ: Thomas Nelson, 1973.

Glik, Deborah C. "Symbolic, Ritual and Social Dynamics of Spiritual Healing." *Social Science and Medicine* 27, no. 11 (1988): 1197–1206.
A two-year study of the organizational characteristics, leadership patterns, ideological systems, and ritual processes of Christian Pentecostal and Neo-Pentecostal groups and new age or metaphysical groups. (PsycLIT Database AN: 89U6618)

Griffith, E. "The Impact of Sociocultural Factors on a Church-Based Healing Model." *American Journal of Orthopsychiatry* 53, no. 2 (1983): 291–302.

Griffith, E., T. English, and V. Mayfield. "Possession, Prayer, and Testimony: Therapeutic Aspects of the Wednesday Night Meeting in a Black Church." *Psychiatry* 43 (1980): 120–128.

Griffith, E., and G. E. Mahy. "Psychological Benefits of Spiritual Baptist 'Mourning.'" *American Journal of Psychiatry* 141, no. 6 (1984): 769–773.

Griffith, E., G. E. Mahy, and J. L. Young. "Psychological Benefits of Spiritual Baptist 'Mourning,'" II: An Empirical Assessment." *American Journal of Psychiatry* 143 (1986): 226–229.

Griffith, E., J. L. Young, and D. L. Smith. "An Analysis of the Therapeutic Elements in a Black Church Service." *Hospital and Community Psychiatry* 35, no. 5 (1984): 464–469.

Hahn, Robert A., and Arthur Kleinman. "Belief as Pathogen, Belief as Medicine: 'Voodoo Death' and the 'Placebo Phenomenon' in Anthropological Perspective." *Medical Anthropology Quarterly* 14 (1983): 3, 16–19.
A study of the causal role of belief and expectation in both pathogenesis ("voodoo death") and therapeutics (the "placebo effect" and "faith healing"). Sociofile comments that the study argues that beliefs have physiological concomitants and consequences through neuroendocrine and autonomic nervous system incorporation in perceptual and motor processes. (Sociological Abstracts AN: 8401944)

Kiev, Ari. "Psychotherapeutic Aspects of Pentecostal Sects Among West Indian Immigrants to England." *British Journal of Sociology* 15 (1964): 129–138.

Kleinman, Arthur. *Patients and Healers in the Context of Culture.* Berkeley: University of California Press, 1980.

Kleinman, Arthur, and J. L. Gale. "Patients Treated by Physicians and Folk Healers: A Comparative Outcome Study in Taiwan." *Culture, Medicine, and Psychiatry* 6 (1982): 405–423.
Supported by a grant from the National Institute of Mental Health.

Kleinman, Arthur, and Lillian H. Sung. "Why do Indigenous Practitioners Successfully Heal?" *Social Science and Medicine* 13B (1979): 7–26.

Lapins, N. A. "The Personal Meaning of Faith Healing." In *Faith Healing: Finger of God? Or Scientific Curiosity?* edited by Claude Frazier, 105–115. New York: Thomas Nelson, 1973.

Lewis, David C. "Signs and Wonders in Sheffield: A Social Anthropologist's Analysis of Words of Knowledge, Manifestations of the Spirit, and the Effectiveness of Divine Healing." In *Power Healing*, by John Wimber and Kevin Springer, Appendix F. New York: Harper & Row, 1987.

Lewis, David C. *Healing: Fiction, Fantasy or Fact?* London: Hodder & Stoughton, 1989.

A sympathetic analysis of the healing ministry of John Wimber by a medical anthropologist. Statistical analysis of healings as a result of prayer, follow-up to reported healings, statistical analysis of various "words of knowledge," and sociological background analysis are included in the study. This is a report that might easily be overlooked, but should be taken into account by research scientists interested in physical and mental healing by spiritual means.

Matthews, Dale A., and David B. Larson. *A Bibliography of Research by Scientists on Spiritual Subjects*. Philadelphia: John Templeton Foundation, 1991.

McGuire, Meredith B. *Ritual Healing in Suburban America*. New Brunswick, NJ: Rutgers University Press, 1988.

McGuire, Meredith B. and Debra J. Kantor. "Belief Systems and Illness Experiences: The Case of Non-Medical Healing Groups." *Research in the Sociology of Health Care* 6 (1987): 221–248.
A study of three different alternative healing groups. Interviews reveal the different belief systems of the groups, particularly regarding the meaning of healing and definitions of health and illness. Varying notions about the nature, source, and appropriate channeling of healing power are examined. (Sociological Abstracts AN: 88T1412)

Ness, R., and R. M. Wintrob. "The Emotional Impact of Fundamentalist Religious Participation: An Empirical Study of Intragroup Variation." *American Journal of Orthopsychiatry* 50 (1980): 302–315.
Research support provided by a NIH training grant and administered by the Social Sciences and Health Services Training Program in the Department of Community Medicine and Health Care, University of Connecticut Health Center.

Ness, R., and R. M. Wintrob. "Folk Healing: A Description and Synthesis." *American Journal of Psychiatry* 138, no. 11 (1981): 1477–1481.

Ngokwey, M. "On the Specificity of Healing Functions: A Study of Diagnosis in Three Faith Healing Institutions in Feira Bahia, Brazil." *Social Science and Medicine* 29, no. 4 (1989): 515–529.

O'Regan, Brendan. "Inner Mechanisms of the Healing Response." *Saybrook Review* 5, no. 1 (Summer-Fall 1985): 10–31.
O'Regan reviews recent healing research and outlines ideas for future research. The author comments on psychoneuroimmunology and research into the nature of attention and dissociation, multiple personality disorders, the placebo effect, and spiritual healing.

Pattison, E.M., N.A. Lapins, and Hans Doerr. "Faith Healing: A Study of Personality and Function." *Journal of Nervous and Mental Disease* 157 (1973): 397–409.

Pattison, E.M., and R. M. Wintrob. "Possession and Exorcism in Contemporary America." *Journal of Operational Psychiatry* 12, no. 1 (1981): 13–20.
The phenomena of possession states and exorcism practices are reviewed in cross-cultural perspective and a taxonomy of four types is presented. The effectiveness of different healing systems is also discussed. (Sociological Abstracts AN: 82M6740)

Paulsen, Alice. "Religious Healing: A Preliminary Report." *Journal of the American Medical Association* 86 (1926): 1519–1524.

Peacock, James. "Symbolic and Psychological Anthropology: The Case of Pentecostal Faith Healing." *Ethos* 12, 1 (1984): 37–53.
Concepts from symbolic and psychological anthropology are used in an analysis of faith healing as practiced in Pentecostal fundamentalist churches in the United States. Sociofile notes that the model proposed by Arthur Kleinman in *Patients and Healers in the Context of Culture* (Berkeley: University of California Press, 1980) suggests a synthesis of psychological and symbolic models that avoids biological and psychological reductionism. (Sociological Abstracts AN: 8506895)

Poloma, Margaret M. "Religious Domains and General Well-Being." *Social Indicators Research* 22 (1990): 255–276.

Rose, Louis. *Faith Healing.* Harmondsworth, England: Penguin Books, 1971.
A somewhat dated, objectively written account of Rose's search for empirically valid evidence for the efficacy of faith healing. After close to twenty years of searching, he has yet to discover "one miracle cure."

Tambiah, Stanley J. "The Cosmological and Performative Significance of a Thai Cult of Healing Through Meditation." *Culture, Medicine and Psychiatry* 1 (1977): 97–132.

Turner, B. S. "The Body and Religion: Towards an Alliance of Medical Sociology and Sociology of Religion." *Annual Review of the Social Sciences of Religion* 4 (1980): 247–286.

Uyanga, J. "The Characteristics of Patients of Spiritual Healing Homes and Traditional Doctors in Southeastern Nigeria." *Social Science and Medicine* 13A (1979): 323–329.
A connection between faith healing and the report of material benefit from both somatic and psychogenic symptoms is discussed.

Wardwell, Walter I. *Patients and Healers in the Context of Culture: An Exploration of the Borderline Between Anthropology, Medicine and Psychiatry.* Berkeley: University of California Press, 1980.

Wolfe, D. Richard. "Faith Healing and Healing Faith." *Journal of the Indiana Medical Association* 53 (April 1959).
A follow-up study by a group of physicians to a healing mission of faith healer Charles S. Price in Vancouver, BC. Of the 350 people who professed to be healed, 301 demonstrated little or no physical change, 39 died within six months, 5 became insane, and 5 who suffered from various nervous disorders were apparently healed.

PART TWO

The Relationship of Realized Religion to Well-Being

3

Mental Health

THE RESEARCH EXAMINING the relationship between religion and mental health is complex and often contradictory. For example, Dittes (1969) concluded that a fair reading of the research pertaining to religion and mental health reveals that they are negatively related, even while Becker (1971) believed that the literature is actually saying that religion and mental health are positively related. Richards and Bergin (1997) claimed the middle ground, asserting that the relationship between religion and positive mental health or adjustment is not ". . . a uniform phenomenon. There are diverse, broadly defined measures of both religiousness and mental functioning. When so many inconsistently defined indexes of religion and pathology are correlated in different studies, they have yielded different results" (p. 78). Worthington and colleagues (1996) suggested that religion may have a positive affect on mental health primarily because religion provides a sense of meaning as well as a sense of hope and optimism. Religion gives people a sense of control as well as an opportunity to give up control to a beneficent God. Religion prescribes a healthier lifestyle. Religion sets up positive social norms that elicit approval, nurturance, and acceptance from others while providing a social support network. Religion gives a person a sense of the supernatural and an opportunity to fulfill one's spirituality.

Defining Terms: Religiosity

A significant problem in the attempt to measure and understand the nature of the relationship between mental health and religion begins with the surprisingly difficult task of simply defining terms. Religiosity is by definition, a subjective, personal experience and therefore very difficult to define with anything approaching scientific precision. However, Duke and Johnson (1984) asserted that there now appears to be a growing consensus in both scientific and religious communities on the importance of at least five dimensions contained in any working definition of religiosity. They are: a) belief system or ideology, b) intellectual knowledge or doctrinal system, c) public devotion or church attendance, d) private devotion such as prayer or Scripture reading, and e) spiritual or religious experience.

Duke and Johnson were actually arguing for a distinction between the consequence of religion and the correlates of religiosity. They suggested that the consequences of religiosity include what they called (not so originally) the beatitudes: integrity, loving service, and spiritual well-being. They cited other variables that they called correlates of religiosity, which would include quality of life, prejudice, marital satisfaction, mental health, economic development, self-esteem, job satisfaction, and political conservatism. These matters are considered to be correlates of religiosity because they are primarily secular and not religious variables, whereas the consequential dimensions involve aspects of social life that "are inherently religious and [that] are included in Christian (and some non-Christian) theology as moral precepts that faithful followers are urged to follow" (p. 60).

Defining Terms: Mental Illness

Even the commonly used terms "mental health," "mental illness," "psychopathology," and "abnormal behavior" have proven surprisingly difficult to define. The history of the *Diagnostic and Statistical Manual of Mental Disorders (DSM-IV)* published by the American Psychiatric Association (1994) is an example of the challenge to social science research in developing commonly understood and agreed-upon terms for what constitutes mental illness, psychopathology, and abnormal and maladaptive behavior. "The need for a classification of mental disorders has been clear throughout the history of medicine, but there has been little agreement on which disorders should be included and the optimal method for their organization" (p. xvi).

Nonetheless, Rosenhan and Seligman (1995) have suggested a definition of abnormality that includes: 1) personal suffering; 2) maladaptiveness, applied to both individual and social contexts; 3) irrationality or incomprehensibility; 4) unpredictability and/ or loss of control; 5) unconventionality; 6) observer discomfort; or 7) violation of moral or ideal standards.

Psychopathology has been defined as the study of mental disorders. A working definition of psychopathology involves impairments, deviance, and distress. However, as Maxman and Ward (1995) suggested in their book, *Essential Psychopathology and Its Treatment*, not all impairments, deviance, and distress are psychopathological.

Defining Terms: Mental Health

Malony (1998) answered the question, How should mental health be conceived? in a chapter outlining the Protestant perspective on mental health in Koenig's recent *Handbook of Religion and Mental Health* (1998). Malony described the struggle to examine religious variables empirically when there is so much diversity among and between religions and religious traditions. Malony notes that within the Christian tradition "many churches are defined as 'Protestant,' because they are 'not Catholic' " (p. 203). He summarized the diversity of Protestantism by providing the follow typology:

> *Fundamentalist Protestant churches* in which the Bible is the prime source of authority and obedience to biblical commands is the criterion of judgment as to who is religious or not.
> *Evangelical Protestant churches* in which experience is the prime

source of authority and having undergone an event that resulted in emotional assurance of salvation is the criterion of judgment as to who is religious or not.

Traditional Protestant churches in which historical tradition is the prime source of authority and active involvement in a particular religious group is the criterion of judgment as to who is religious or not.

Liberal Protestant churches in which rational thinking is the prime source of authority and ethical behavior is the criterion of judgment as to who is religious or not (p. 205).

Malony suggested that for some Protestants, spiritual health and mental health are distinctions that should not be confused. According to Malony, fundamentalist Christians define a spiritually healthy person as one who is obedient to "God's commands, as derived from the Bible" (p. 205). For these Protestants, mental health is synonymous with spiritual health. However, Malony contended that liberal Protestants for whom spiritual health is paramount and determinative define mental health as obedience to the scriptural mandate to love thy neighbor and pursue social justice, while evangelical Christians see "joy" as the goal of spiritual health and "happiness" as the indicator of mental health. "Joy refers to the assurance that one has been 'born again' and that God is available for companionship in daily living. Happiness is the experience of being well-adjusted and productive" (p. 206).

Batson and colleagues (1993) in a review of the literature, provided the following helpful list of seven different aspects of mental health in an attempt to clarify the often conflicting operational definitions of mental health: 1) absence of mental illness, 2) appropriate social behavior, 3) freedom from worry and guilt, 4) personal competence and control, 5) self-acceptance or self-actualization, 6) unification and organization of personality, and 7) open-mindedness and flexibility.

In their review of the literature, encompassing studies from the last century through 1991, Batson and colleagues (1993) summarized 115 findings based on 91 different studies and concluded that

47 findings showed a negative relationship between religiosity and mental health, 31 showed no clear relationship between religiosity and mental health, and the remaining 37 reported a positive relationship between religion and mental health. Hence, the difficulty of studying the relationship between religion and mental health begins with the use of terminology often understood differently by researchers, subjects, and the various communities of faith and science.

Religion and Mental Health

In 1989 Crawford, Handal, and Wiener examined the relationship between religion and mental health and distress. Their primary finding indicated that religion not only does not appear to be harmful to mental health, but rather, "high religious subjects were significantly less distressed and manifested better psychological adjustment than medium and low religious subjects" (p. 16). In a related study, Williams and colleagues (1991) found that religion is indeed an effective coping strategy in adjusting to the stresses of life. They defined religious behavior as religious attendance and religious affiliation. Both attendance and affiliation were found to be inversely associated with psychological distress. They also found that religious affiliation was unrelated to mental health status. Worthington and colleagues (1996) conducted a ten-year review of empirical research dealing with religion and psychotherapeutic processes and outcomes. They concluded that "religion does not affect mental health negatively" (p. 451). To the contrary, they believe that there appears to be a positive relationship between religion and mental health overall.

Bergin (1983) conducted a meta-analysis of twenty-four studies completed between the years 1951 and 1979. He found that 23 percent of the studies indicated that religious measures were associated with poor mental health. However, 47 percent indicated that religion was associated with better mental health and 30 percent showed no significant relationship.

In an extensive analysis of the literature, which includes more than two hundred studies, Gartner, Larson, and Allen (1991) reviewed the published empirical research dealing with religion and mental health and reported:

1. A positive effect of religion on mental health was found regarding such issues as depression, suicide, marital satisfaction, divorce, drug and alcohol use, delinquency, and well-being.
2. Ambiguous associations relative to religion and mental health were found in the areas of anxiety, sexual disorders, self-esteem, prejudice, and psychosis.
3. Religion was associated with psychopathology in such areas as authoritarianism, suggestibility/dependence, dogmatism/tolerance of ambiguity.

Gartner, Larson, and Allen concluded that low levels of religiosity are most often associated with psychological disorders related to low impulse control while high levels of religiosity are associated with disorders related to over-control. They also concluded that behavioral measures of religiosity (i.e., church attendance) are indeed more powerfully associated with mental health than are attitudinal measures.

Judd (1985) examined 116 studies and found results similar to Bergin's meta-analysis; 30 percent showed a positive relationship between religion and mental health, 30 percent showed a negative relationship, and 33 percent showed no relationship. We are left to conclude that generally the positive results are mitigated by the negative results taken together with the neutral results.

Intrinsic and Extrinsic Religious Orientation

Allport (1937, 1950a, 1955) has made important contributions to psychology through his eclectic theory of personality, which deemphasized Freudian views on the unconscious and the role of the past in determining one's future. In contrast to Freud, Allport emphasized rational and conscious functioning of normal persons. He argued that personality theory should focus on the uniqueness of the individual. His concept of functional autonomy is based on individuality, conscious motivation, and behavior that is oriented in the present and internally consistent.

Allport (1950b) has also made significant contributions to the psychology of religion. His concept of religious orientation refers to what faith means to the individual with respect to motivation and maturity. Allport developed the concept of religious orientation that includes both intrinsic and extrinsic orientation.

Extrinsically motivated individuals approach religion from an instrumental or utilitarian perspective. Extrinsic religiosity suggests a "what's in it for me?" utilitarianism. Extrinsic religiosity infers that a person is religious as a way to achieve status, power, influence, or social acceptance. According to Allport,

> Persons with this orientation are disposed to use religion for their own ends. . . . Extrinsic values are always instrumental and utilitarian. Persons with this orientation may find religion useful in a variety of ways—to provide security and solace, sociability and distraction, status and self-justification. The embraced creed is lightly held or else selectively shaped to fit more primary needs. In theological terms the extrinsic type turns to God, but without turning away from self (Hunt and King, 1971, p. 341).

Tisdale (1966) observed that extrinsic religious orientation is likely to be found in individuals "whose childhood has been marked by suspicion, distrust, insecurity, and feelings of inferiority" (p. 82). His research indicates that extrinsic males attend church relatively regularly, pray often, perceive themselves to be more serious about religion than most other people, feel comfortable in belonging to groups, accept religious doctrine without much question or criticism, and avoid conflict and the expression of anger. Extrinsic females exhibit many of these same characteristics, but are less likely to formally belong to a church. Females are more apt to use religion to provide "a sense of order and regularity in living, a perceptual space in which [they] may hold a rather passive, self-abasing position" (p. 83).

In contrast, intrinsically motivated individuals conduct their religious lives as ends in themselves, apart from utilitarian or instrumental considerations. According to Allport, intrinsic religiosity provides life with meaning and motivation. It is not limited to self-interest as is the case with extrinsic religiosity. Intrinsic religion creates or leads to a motivation to serve others as an expression of one's inner religiosity whereas extrinsic religiosity seems to provide a motivation for self-serving utilitarianism, religion where self-interest pervades and serves the individual rather than the individual serving religion.

Jalali-Tehrani (1985) conducted research on a sample of thirty Christian males and thirty Muslim males and discovered a positive correlation between religious commitment, purpose of life, and personality integration. In summarizing Jalali-Tehrani's work King noted that those "individuals who were more intrinsically (genuinely) committed to their religious beliefs also had higher degrees of purpose of life and possessed more integrated personalities" (King, 1990, pp. 101–102).

Bergin, Masters, and Richards (1987) studied the correlation between religiousness and mental health in an intrinsically religious sample. They concluded that the intrinsic orientation is negatively correlated with anxiety and positively correlated with self-control as well as with "better" personality functioning. They found the opposite to be the case with the extrinsic orientation. As a caveat, Matthews, Larson, and Barry (1993) observed that this study used a more highly religious sample than most studies and that the sample was comprised of college students. Still, they noted, "the significant benefit of the intrinsic form of religiosity over its extrinsic form is clearly evident" (p. 24). Three later studies affirm this observation by showing a correlation between higher levels of intrinsic orientation with lower levels of depression, anxiety, dysfunctional attention-seeking, and higher levels of self-esteem (Gartner, Lawson and Allen, 1991; Mickley, Carson and Soeken, 1995; and Ventis, 1995).

Religiosity and Loneliness, Self-Esteem

Schwab and Petersen (1990) looked at the relationship between loneliness and religious beliefs, religious behavior, neuroticism, and subjective well-being and found that what a person believes, that is, the content of one's religious belief system, is important in determining the relationship of religion to loneliness. Schwab and Peterson conclude that belief in God appeared to have little or no influence on loneliness; however, perceiving God as wrathful tended to be positively correlated with more loneliness, while viewing God as supportive and caring tended to be correlated with less loneliness.

Similarly with respect to content of belief, Benson and Spilka (1973) saw a relationship between a person's image of God and his or her self-esteem. They found that "self-esteem is related positively to loving God-images and negatively to rejecting-impersonal-controlling definitions of God" (p. 306). Hence they argue that self-esteem might be the source or major determinant of our God-images.

Preston and Viney (1986) explored the relationship between a person's perceived interaction with God and his or her emotional experience and reported that their research supported the findings of Benson and Spilka. Their investigation was conducted within an Australian context and suggested that cultural and historical constructs can affect individual perceptions of God as well as the emotional responses related to these perceptions. Many Australian Christians, for example, were found to picture God as a stern overseer, an image perhaps related to Australia's history as an English penal colony. Preston and Viney observed that this image was "less likely to be associated with positive feelings about oneself and the world" (p. 328). Alternatively, constructions of God as loving and supportive, "were more likely to be associated with positive emotional experience" (p. 328). Preston and Viney concluded that people tend to interact with more than one image of God, "on a one-to-one basis and in company with other people, and thus construed God as having more than one role in their lives" (p. 328).

Does religion have an impact on an important aspect of mental health such as self-esteem? Smith, Weigert, and Thomas (1979) found a positive relationship between adolescent self-esteem and religiosity. However, when Bahr and Martin (1983) set out to test the hypothesis "that religiosity, however measured, has a positive effect on self-esteem as well as attitudes toward others," (p. 132) their findings "reveal little relationship between religiosity and self-esteem" (p. 132).

Aycock and Noaker (1985) compared self-esteem levels in evangelical Christians to that of the general population. They administered the Self-Esteem scale of the Coping Resources Inventory for Stress to 351 evangelical Christians and 1,115 general volunteers comprised of students, administrators, and government employees. Variation in self-esteem levels appeared to be related to educational level, but no significant differences in self-esteem were observed between the evangelical and volunteer groups. However, according to Aycock and Noaker,

> Christian faith did not seem to impact self-esteem levels in the evangelical population studied. This nonsignificant difference between the self-esteem levels of Christians and others is of import to the evangelical community. At issue is the effect of religious faith and redemption on the perceived personal value, life satisfaction, and behavior of the believer. Does a relationship with Christ impact the self-esteem of the Christian in practical ways? Christian theoreticians present a biblical basis for positive self-esteem which is available to all believers, yet Christians apparently do not readily translate their positional acceptance into attitudinal and behavioral evidences of high self-esteem. Is this a function of their inadequate knowledge (or appropriation) of the full meaning of redemption or is it merely a magnification of the limitations of cognitive change alone? (p. 204)

Matthews, Larson, and Barry (1993) noted that in Aycock and Noaker's study, evangelical males with college degrees had significantly higher self-esteem scores than evangelical females with a graduate education. Evangelical males and females over the age of fifty had lower self-esteem scores than any other subgroup, evangelical or general. Matthews, Larson, and Barry hypothesized that the lower self-esteem scores for evangelical women might be related to "the lack of a significant role in the church hierarchy for women" (p. 14) and called for further research on lower self-esteem in older evangelicals.

Interestingly, Hjelle (1975) reported a negative correlation between active involvement in religious activity and self-actualization in Catholic males. Sixty-three male undergraduates enrolled in a Catholic coeducational institution reported on the extent of their religious activity and completed the Personal Orientation Inventory. Hjelle hypothesized that "self-actualizing students construe involvement in religious activities as being detrimental to their psychosocial development" (p. 179). In other words, it may not be "cool" to be regarded as being actively religious if you are male in a Catholic college.

Watson and colleagues (1985) have also studied the functioning of the self in religious persons in an ambitious five-part series. They found small, predictable correlations between religiosity and self-esteem.

In another study that dealt with religious values and self-actualization, Watson, Hood, and Morris (1984) examined the relationship between sin, humanist values, and narcissism. A number of scales were employed to determine whether humanistic values were associated with narcissism and whether religious values were compatible with self-actualization. They concluded that "both religious and non-religious persons can express humanistic values reflecting actualization" (p. 262), a result that they believe undercuts the notion that religiosity negatively affects psychological well-being. They further concluded that the claim by some religious persons that humanistic values guarantee narcissistic self-interest appears unwarranted.

Church Membership and Mental Health

Does the social impact of membership in religious denominations, groups, or cults promote mental health? Galanter and Buckley (1978) examined reports that members of the Divine Light

Mission (a religious group we believe to have been inaccurately classified as "evangelical" Christian by Galanter and Buckley) experienced significant psychological benefits from membership in the group as well as relief from alcohol and drug abuse. The responses from 119 members to a multiple-choice questionnaire indicated "a significant decline" in frequency of neurotic symptoms and of alcohol and drug use. Galanter and Buckley observed that this lower incidence "persisted over the course of membership, an average of 21 months" (p. 685). Symptom decline appeared to be related to various group activities and to a form of ritual meditation practiced within the group.

Tamburrino and colleagues (1990) reported in a similar study that recovery from post-abortion dysphoria was related to new involvement in fundamentalist or evangelical denominations. Christiano (1986) analyzed data from a nationally representative sample of Americans and observed that church involvement was not associated with feelings of anomie. It seems possible if not likely that it is the social benefits of group membership that promote mental health rather then the doctrines or specific beliefs of the group itself.

Sharkey and Malony (1986) concluded that religious affiliation had no discernible effect on mental health. Sharkey and Malony referenced Ellis's claim that being religious is antithetical to being mentally healthy, which he made in his 1971 book *The Case Against Religion: A Psychotherapist's View*, when they undertook a study (with Ellis's assistance) to assess the validity of the contention that being religious was negatively correlated with mental health.

The authors were given access to the records of clients of the Ellis-sponsored Institute for the Advanced Study of Rational Psychotherapy in New York. The authors divided the 440 clients into three groups 1) very religious, 2) atheist, and 3) neither very religious nor atheist. The groups were compared by way of the average number of problems reported under the categories of acceptance, frustration, injustice, achievement, self-worth, control, certainty, and catastrophizing.

Sharkey and Malony found no significant differences among the three groups. They therefore concluded that there was no significant tendency for the "very religious" to report higher incidences of problems and their evidence "does not warrant Ellis's continuing claim that religion and psychopathology are positively related" (p. 641).

Masters and colleagues (1991) published the results of a three-year follow-up on a group of religious young adults who were studied to discover "more about the relations between religious involvement and mental health" (p. 211). Their data demonstrated "no overall evidence, for the group as a whole, of a link between orthodox religiosity and pathology" (p. 221). This finding was particularly interesting because participants in the sample held to "absolute values," a stance psychologists such as Ellis associate with emotional disturbance. Ellis (1980), known as the founder of RET or Rational Emotive Psychotherapy, asserts that "religiosity is in many respects equivalent to irrational thinking and emotional disturbance" (p. 635). Young adults in the sample appeared to be "distinctly intrinsic in their religious orientation" and became more intrinsic in their orientation as the three years passed. Masters and colleagues (1991) noted that this finding had "not been previously presented and deemed it worthy of replication on other samples of differing faiths in order to determine if this is a typical developmental pattern for highly religious persons" (p. 221).

Morris (1982) investigated and assessed the levels of anxiety, depression, and religious attitudes in a group of physically sick men and women planning to go on a religious pilgrimage to Lourdes. Morris then measured levels of depression and anxiety one month after the pilgrimage had been completed. A "significant lessening" of state and trait anxiety was observed in both males and females after their visit to Lourdes, and "this was sustained over the year" (p. 292). Levels of depression were also significantly lessened after the pilgrimage. Morris attributed this improvement to the opportunity to take a holiday, the companionship, and the change of environment related to the pilgrimage, but "most of all to the spiritual atmosphere of the shrine, which engendered hope in the pilgrims for the future, both in this life and the life hereafter" (p. 294).

Bergin (1983) reviewed the issue of religiosity and mental health in a meta-analysis conducted in 1993. He cited Rokeach's 1960 study as an example of "how much research results in behavioral science conformed to the intellectual ethos of the time" (p. 172). Rokeach found that believers compared with nonbelievers were more tense, anxious, and symptomatic. After citing numerous examples of conflicting results, Bergin reasoned that they were due to the different views of investigators as well as the utilization of different personality and religiosity measurements. For example, "one researcher views a worshipful-style positively in terms of reverence, humility, and constructive obedience to universal moral laws, whereas another researcher views the same life-style negatively, as self-abasing, unprogressive, and blindly conforming" (p. 174).

Stark (1971) compared the degree of religious involvement among one hundred mentally ill persons and one hundred similarly matched controlled persons and found that the mentally ill were distinctly less religious on several measures. Payne and colleagues (1991) concluded that it is safe to say that religion is positively correlated with adjustment while the relationship with mental illness is far more elusive.

It seems clear that actively committed religious persons have better overall psychological adjustment. We might infer that it is likely that religious organizations, churches, and denominations that foster the development of an intrinsic religious orientation do in fact contribute to the psychological well-being of their members. Perhaps it should also be noted that an alternative explanation is that it is possible that high functioning well-adjusted persons are more apt to be actively committed to their religions.

In any case, it can be said with some confidence that religion is positively associated with a sense of well-being, healthier self-esteem, and better personal adjustment. We might infer from this that religiosity has the potential for the prevention of problems associated with mental illness and disorders. However, it is impossible at this point to conclude that serious mental disorders are affected by religiosity.

As Payne concluded, "Mental health workers need to be aware of the positive potential of religious involvement. Theories of pathology and psychotherapy are secular and do not lead naturally to thinking of religion as a health-promoting agent. In fact, early research and theory portrayed religion as anti-health" (pp. 33–34).

References

Allport, G. W. (1937). *Personality: A Psychological Interpretation.* New York: Holt.

Allport, G. W. (1950a). *The Nature of Personality: Selected Papers.* Cambridge, MA: Addison-Wesley. (Includes the most important of Allport's papers published prior to this date.)

Allport, G. W. (1950b). *The Individual and His Religion.* New York: Macmillan.

Allport, G. W. (1955). *Becoming: Basic Considerations for a Psychology of Personality.* New Haven: Yale University Press.

American Psychiatric Association. (1994). *Diagnostic and Statistical Manual of Mental Disorders,* 4th ed. Washington, DC: American Psychiatric Association.

Aycock, D. W., and Noaker, S. (1985). "A Comparison of the Self-Esteem Levels in Evangelical Christian and General Populations." *Journal of Psychology and Theology, 13*(3), 199–208.

Bahr, H. M., and Martin, T. K. (1983). " 'And Thy Neighbor as Thyself': Self-Esteem and Faith in People as Correlates of Religiosity and Family Solidarity Among Middletown High School Students." *Journal for the Scientific Study of Religion, 22*(2), 132–144.

Batson, C. D., Schoenrade, P., and Ventis, W. L. (1993). *Religion and the Individual: A Social-Psychological Perspective.* New York: Oxford University Press.

Becker, R. J. (1971). "Religion and Psychological Health." In M. Strommen (Ed.), *Research on Religious Development: A Comprehensive Handbook* (pp. 391–421). New York: Hawthorn.

Benson, P., and Spilka, B. (1973). "God Image as a Function of Self-Esteem and Locus of Control." *Journal for the Scientific Study of Religion, 12,* 297–310.

Bergin, A. E. (1983). "Religiosity and Mental Health: A Critical Reevaluation and Meta-Analysis." *Professional Psychology: Research and Practice, 14*(2), 170–184.

Bergin, A. E., Masters, K. S., and Richards, P. S. (1987). "Religiousness and Mental Health Reconsidered: A Study of an Intrinsically Religious Sample." *Journal of Counseling Psychology, 34*(2), 197–204.

Christiano, K. J. (1986). "Church as a Family Surrogate: Another Look at Family Ties, Anomie, and Church Involvement." *Journal for the Scientific Study of Religion, 25*(3), 339–354.

Crawford, M. E., Handal, P. J., and Wiener, R. L. (1989). "The Relationship Between Religion and Mental Health/Distress." *Review of Religious Research,* *31*(1), 16–22.

Dittes, J. E. (1969). "Psychology of Religion." In G. Lindzey and E. Arronson (Eds.), *The Handbook of Social Psychology* (vol. 5, pp. 602–659). Reading, MA: Addison-Wesley.

Duke, J. T., and Johnson, B. L. (1984). "Spiritual Well-Being and the Consequential Dimension of Religiosity." *Review of Religious Research,* *26*(1), 59–72.

Ellis, A. (1971). *The Case Against Religion: A Psychotherapist's View.* New York: Institute for Rational Living.

Ellis, A. (1980). "Psychotherapy and Atheistic Values: A Response to A. E. Bergin's 'Psychotherapy and Religious Values.'" *Journal of Consulting and Clinical Psychology, 48,* 635–639.

Galanter, M., and Buckley, P. (1978). "Evangelical Religion and Meditation: Psychotherapeutic Effects." *The Journal of Nervous and Mental Disease, 166*(10), 685–691.

Gartner, J., Larson, D. B., and Allen, G. B. (1991). "Religious Commitment and Mental Health: A Review of the Empirical Literature." *Journal of Psychology and Theology, 19*(1), 6–25.

Hjelle, L. A. (1975). "Relationship of a Measure of Self-Actualization to Religious Participation." *The Journal of Psychology, 89,* 179–182.

Hunt, R. A., and King, M. (1971). "The Intrinsic-Extrinsic Concept: A Review and Evaluation." *Journal for the Scientific Study of Religion, 10,* 339–356.

Jalali-Tehrani, S. (1985). "Religious Commitment as a Factor in Personality Integration: A Factor in Mental Health." *Dissertation Abstracts International, 46*(10B), 3629.

Judd, D. K. (1985). "Religiosity and Mental Health: A Literature Review 1928–1985." Master's thesis, Brigham Young University.

King, D. G. (1990). "Religion and Health Relationships: A Review." *Journal of Religion and Health, 29*(2), 101–109.

Malony, H. N. (1998). "Religion and Mental Health from the Protestant Perspective." In H. G. Koenig (Ed.), *Handbook of Religion and Mental Health* (pp. 203–210). San Diego: Academic Press.

Masters, K. S., Bergin, A. E., Reynolds, E. M., and Sullivan, C. E. (1991). "Religious Life-Styles and Mental Health: A Follow-Up Study." *Counseling and Values, 35,* 211–224.

Matthews, D. A., Larson, D. B., and Barry, C. P. (1993). *The Faith Factor: An Annotated Bibliography of Clinical Research on Spiritual Subjects.* Washington, DC: National Institute for Healthcare Research.

Maxman, J. S., and Ward, N. G. (1995). *Essential Psychopathology and Its Treatment.* New York: Norton.

Mickley, J. R., Carson, V., and Soeken, K. L. (1995). "Religion and Adult Mental Health: State of the Science in Nursing." *Issues in Mental Health Nursing, 16,* 345–360.

Morris, P. A. (1982). "The Effect of Pilgrimage on Anxiety, Depression, and Religious Attitude." *Psychological Medicine, 12,* 291–294.

Payne, I. R., Bergin, A. E., Bielema, K. A., and Jenkins, P. H. (1991). "Review of Religion and Mental Health: Prevention and the Enhancement of Psychosocial Functioning." *Prevention in Human Services, 9*(2), 11–40.

Preston, C. A., and Viney, L. L. (1986). "Construing God: An Exploration of the Relationships Between Reported Interaction with God and Concurrent Emotional Experience." *Journal of Psychology and Theology, 14*(4), 319–329.

Richards, P. S., and Bergin A. E. (1997). *A Spiritual Strategy for Counseling and Psychotherapy.* Washington, DC: American Psychological Association.

Rokeach, M. (1960). *The Open and Closed Mind: Investigations into the Nature of Belief Systems and Personality Systems.* New York: Basic Books.

Rosenhan, D. L., and Seligman, M. E. (1995). *Abnormal Psychology.* New York: W. W. Norton.

Schwab, R., and Petersen, K. U. (1990). "Religiousness: Its Relation to Loneliness, Neuroticism, and Subjective Well-Being." *Journal for the Scientific Study of Religion, 29*(3), 335–345.

Sharkey, P. W., and Malony, H. W. (1986). "Religiosity and Emotional Disturbance: A Test of Ellis's Theory in His Own Counseling Center." *Psychotherapy, 23,* 640–641.

Smith, C. B., Weigert, A. J., and Thomas, D. L. (1979). "Self-Esteem and Religiosity: An Analysis of Catholic Adolescents from Five Cultures." *Journal for the Scientific Study of Religion, 18*(1), 51–60.

Stark, R. (1971). "Psychopathology and Religious Commitment." *Review of Religious Research, 12*(3), 165–176.

Tamburrino, M. B., Franco, K. N., Campbell, N. B., Pentz, J. E., Evans, C. L., and Jurs, S. G. (1990). "Post-Abortion Dysphoria and Religion." *Southern Medical Journal, 83,* 736–738.

Tisdale, J. R. (1966). "Selected Correlates of Extrinsic Religious Values." *Review of Religious Research, 7,* 78–84.

Ventis, W. L. (1995). "The Relationships Between Religion and Mental Health." *Journal of Social Issues, 51*(2), 33–48.

Watson, P. J., Hood, Jr., R. W., and Morris, R. J. (1984). "Religious Orientation, Humanistic Values, and Narcissism." *Review of Religious Research, 25*(3), 257–264.

Watson, P. J., Hood, Jr., R. W., Morris, R. J., and Hall, J. R. (1985). "Religiosity, Sin and Self-Esteem." *Journal of Psychology and Theology, 13*(2), 116–128.

Williams, D. R., Larson, D. B., Buckler, R. E., Heckmann, R. C., and Pyle, C. M.

(1991). "Religion and Psychological Distress in a Community Sample." *Social Science and Medicine, 32*(11), 1257–1262.

Worthington, E. L., Kurusu, T. A., McCullough, M. E., and Sandage, S. J. (1996). "Empirical Research on Religion and Psychotherapeutic Processes and Outcomes: A 10-Year Review and Research Prospectus." *Psychological Bulletin, 119*(3), 448–487.

Bibliography

Agnor, D.W. "Christian and Non-Religious Sociopaths Compared: Self-Concept, Locus of Control, Guilt, and Quality of Religious Experience." Ph.D. diss., Western Conservative Baptist Seminary, 1986. Abstract in *Dissertation Abstracts International* 48 (1986): 3713B.

Albrecht, S. L., B. A. Chadwick, and D. S. Alcorn. "Religiosity and Deviance: Application of an Attitude-Behavior Contingent Consistency Model." *Journal for the Scientific Study of Religion* 16 (1977): 263–274.

Allison, J. "Adaptive Regression and Intense Religious Experiences." *Journal of Nervous and Mental Disease* 145, no. 6 (December 1967): 452–463. Supported by a grant from the National Institute of Mental Health.

Alter, Margaret G. "Religious Experience Inventory: An Empirical Study of Christian Religious Maturity and Its Relationship to Mental Health." Ph.D. diss., Graduate Theological Union. Abstract in *Dissertation Abstracts International* 46, 7-A (January 1986): 1973.

Andreason, N. J. C. "The Role of Religion in Depression." *Journal of Religion and Health*, 11 (1972): 153–166.

Arceneaux, Cathann. "Religious Life-Styles and Mental Health: A Follow-Up Study—Comment." *Counseling and Values* 35, no. 3 (April 1991): 225–227.

Armstrong, R. C., G. L. Larsen, and S. A. Mourer. "Religious Attitudes and Emotional Adjustment." *Journal of Psychological Studies* 13 (1962): 35–47.

Bainbridge, William Sims. "The Religious Ecology of Deviance." *American Sociological Review* 29 (1989): 288–295.

Baither, R. C., and L. Saltzberg. "Relationship Between Religious Attitude and Rational Thinking." *Psychological Reports* 43 (1978): 853–854.

Baker, M., and R. Gorsuch. "Trait Anxiety and Intrinsic-Extrinsic Religiousness." *Journal for the Scientific Study of Religion* 21 (1981): 119–122.

Baker, Mark W., and Richard L. Gorsuch. "Anxiety and Values: Anxiety as Caused by the Frustration of a Major Value—Religion." *Southern Psychologist* 2, no. 4 (Spring-Summer 1985): 35–41.

Barkman, P. F. "The Relationship of Personality Modes to Religious Experience and Behavior." In *Current Perspectives in the Psychology of Religion*, edited by H. N. Malony, 201–208. Grand Rapids, MI: Eerdmans, 1977.

Barton, K., and G. M. Vaughn. "Church Membership and Personality: A Longitudinal Study." *Social Behavior and Personality* 4, no. 1 (1976): 11–16.

Bateman, Mildred M., and Joseph S. Jensen. "The Effect of Religious Background on Modes of Handling Anger." *The Journal of Social Psychology* 47 (1958): 133–141.

Bergin, A. E., K. S. Masters, R. D. Stinchfield, T. A. Gaskin, C. E. Sullivan, E. M. Reynolds, and D. W. Greaves. (in press). "Religious Life-Styles and Mental Health." In *Religion, Personality, and Mental Health*, edited by L. B. Brown. New York: Springer. Also found in *Journal of Counseling Psychology* 35 (1988): 91–98.

Bergin, A. E., R. D. Stinchfield, T. A. Gaskin, K. S. Masters, and C. E. Sullivan. "Religious Life-Styles and Mental Health: An Exploratory Study." *Journal of Counseling Psychology* 35 (1988): 91–98.
Funded by the Department of Psychology, the Counseling and Development Center, the Comprehensive Clinic, and the Dean's Research Fund, College of Family, Home, and Social Sciences, Brigham Young University.

"Bibliography on Religion and Mental Health 1960–1964." Public Health Service Publication 159, Department of Health, Education and Welfare. Washington, DC: U. S. Government Printing Office, 1967.

Bishop, L.C., D. B. Larson, and W. P. Wilson. "Religious Life of Individuals with Affective Disorders." *Southern Medical Journal* 80, no. 9 (1987): 1083–1086.

Broen, W. E. "Personality Correlates of Certain Religious Attitudes." *Journal of Consulting Psychology* 19 (1955): 64–68.

Brown, D. G., and W. L. Lowe. "Religious Beliefs and Personality Characteristics of College Students." *Journal of Social Psychology* 33 (1951): 103–129.

Brown, Kenneth B. "Relationship Between Personal Religious Orientation and Positive Mental Health." *Dissertation Abstracts International* 35, 3-B (September 1974): 1376.

Brown, L. B. "A Study of Religious Belief." *British Journal of Psychology* 53 (1962): 259–272. Zero relationship between religiosity and mental health (Bergin, 1983).

Bruun, C. V. "A Combined Treatment Approach: Cognitive Therapy and Spiritual Dimensions." *Journal of Psychology and Christianity* 4, no. 2 (1985): 9–11.

Bryant, Fred B., and Joseph Veroff. "Dimensions of Subjective Mental Health in American Men and Women." In *Research on the Quality of Life*, edited by Frank M. Andrews, 117–146. Ann Arbor: Survey Research Center, Institute for Social Research, University of Michigan, 1986.

Buckalew, L. W. "A Descriptive Study of Denominational Concomitants in Psychiatric Diagnosis." *Social Behavior and Personality* 6 (1978): 239–242.

Burgess, J. H., and R. L. Wagner. "Religion as a Factor in Extrusion to Public Mental Hospitals." *Journal for the Scientific Study of Religion* 10 (1971): 237–240.

Burkett, S. R., and M. White. "Hellfire and Delinquency: Another Look." *Journal for the Scientific Study of Religion* 13 (1974): 455–462.

Carr, L. G., and W. J. Hauser. "Anomie and Religiosity: An Empirical Re-examination." *Journal for the Scientific Study of Religion* 15 (1976): 69–74.

Carr, L. G., and W. J. Hauser. "Class, Religious Participation, and Psychiatric Symptomatology." *International Journal of Social Psychiatry* 27 (1981): 133–142.

Cavenar, J. O., and J. G. Spaulding. "Depressive Disorders and Religious Conversions." *Journal of Nervous and Mental Disease* 165 (1977): 200–212.

Chambers, J. L., W. T. Wilson, and B. Barger. "Need Differences Between Students With and Without Religious Affiliation." *Journal of Counseling Psychology* 15 (1968): 208–210. Cf. Bergin, 1983.

Childs-Clarke, Adrian, and John Sharpe. "Keeping the Faith: Religion in the Healing of Phobic Anxiety." *Journal of Psychosocial Nursing* 22, no. 2 (1991): 22–24.

Cohen, Eric J. "Holiness and Health: An Examination of the Relationship Between Christian Holiness and Mental Health." *Journal of Psychology and Theology* 5, no. 4 (Fall 1977): 285–291.

Cothran, M. M., and P. D. Harvey. "Delusional Thinking in Psychotics: Correlates of Religious Content." *Psychological Reports* 58 (1986): 191–199.

Crumpler, N. J.G. *The Relationship Between Spiritual Well-Being and Reported Self-Actualization Among College Students.* Master's thesis, East Carolina University, 1989.

Donahue, M. J., and A. E. Bergin. "Religion, Personality, and Lifestyle: A Meta-Analysis."
Paper presented at the meeting of the American Psychological Association, Anaheim, CA.

Dufton, Brian D., and Daniel Perlman. "The Association Between Religiosity and the Purpose in Life Test: Does It Reflect Purpose or Satisfaction? *Journal of Religion and Theology* 14 (1986): 42–48.

Dunn, R. F. "Personality Patterns Among Religious Personnel: A Review." *Catholic Psychological Record* 3 (1965): 125–137.

Ellison, C. W., ed. *Your Better Self: Christianity, Psychology, and Self-Esteem.* New York: Harper & Row, 1983.

Fazel, Mohammed K., and David M. Young. "Life Quality of Tibetans and Hindus: A Function of Religion." *Journal for the Scientific Study of Religion* 27, no. 2 (1988): 229–242.

Fitz, Allan. "Religious and Familial Factors in the Etiology of Obsessive-Compulsive Disorder: A Review." *Journal of Psychology and Theology* 18, no. 2 (1990): 141–147.

Forst, Edmund C., and Rose M. Healy. "Relationship Between Self-Esteem and Religious Faith." *Psychological Reports* 67, no. 2 (October 1990): 378.

Francis, L. J., and P. R. Pearson. "Psychoticism and Religiosity Among 15-Year-Olds." *Personality and Individual Differences* 6 (1985): 397–398.

Francis, Leslie J., and Paul R. Pearson. "Personality Characteristics of Mid-Career Male Anglican Clergy." *Social Behavior and Personality* 18, no. 2 (1990): 347–351.

Funk, R. A. "Religious Attitudes and Manifest Anxiety in a College Population." *American Psychologist* 2 (1956): 375–377.

Galanter, Marc, David Larson, and Elizabeth Rubenstone. "Christian Psychiatry: The Impact of Evangelical Belief on Clinical Practice." *The American Journal of Psychiatry* 148 (1991): 90–95. This report indicates the need for greater attention and sensitivity to the religious needs of patients seeking psychiatric care. It also reports that empirical evidence fails to uphold or indicate Freud's contention that religious belief is a sign of neurosis. The question remains as to what degree a psychiatrist should incorporate a religious perspective into clinical practice.

Gallemore, J. L., W. P. Wilson, and J. M. Rhoads. "The Religious Life of Patients with Affective Disorders." *Diseases of the Nervous System* 30 (1969): 483–486.

Gardella, Peter. "From Possession to Compulsion: Religion, Sex, and Madness in Popular Culture." *Social Research* 53, no. 2 (1986): 311–326.

Garrison, V. "Sectarianism and Psychosocial Adjustment: A Controlled Comparison of Puerto Rican Pentecostals and Catholics." In *Religious Movements in Contemporary America*, edited by

I. Zaretsky and M. Leone. Princeton, NJ: Princeton University Press, 1974.

Geist, Charles R., and Cynthia M. Daheim. "Religious Affiliation and Manifest Hostility." *Psychological Reports* 55 (1984): 493–494.

Gill, Newell T., and Linda H. Thornton. "Religious Orientation and Self-Esteem Among High School Students." *High School Journal* 73, no. 1 (October–November 1989): 47–60.

Gorsuch, Richard L. "Psychology of Religion." *Annual Review of Psychology* 39 (1988): 201–221.

Gregory, W. E. "The Orthodoxy of the Authoritarian Personality." *Journal of Social Psychology* 45 (1957): 217–232.

Groesch, S. J., and W. E. Davis. "Psychiatric Patients' Religion and MMPI Responses." *Journal of Clinical Psychology* 33 (1977): 168–171.

Guntrip, H. "Religion in Relation to Personal Integration." *British Journal of Medical Psychology* 42 (1969): 323–333.

Gupta, A. "Mental Health and Religion." *Asian Journal of Psychology Education* 11 (1983): 8–13.

Hanawalt, Nelson G. "Feelings of Security and of Self-Esteem in Relation to Religious Belief." *The Journal of Social Psychology* 59 (1963): 347–353.
Supported in part by the Research Council of Rutgers, The State University of New Jersey.

Hartz, Gary W., and Henry C. Everett. "Fundamentalist Religion and Its Effect on Mental Health." *Journal of Religion and Health* 28, no. 3 (1989): 207–217.

Hassan, M. K., and A. Khalique. "Religiosity and Its Correlates in College Students." *Journal of Psychological Researches* 25 (1981): 129–136.

Heitzelman, M. E., and L. A. Fehr. "Relationship Between Religious Orthodoxy and Three Personality Variables." *Psychological Reports* 38 (1976): 756–758.

Heskestad, S. "Religiosity and Mental Health: An Empirical Study." *Nordisk-Psykiatrisk-Tidsskrift* 38, no. 5 (1984): 353–361.

King notes that Heskestad "studied the correlation between psychiatric morbidity and religiosity (commitment to beliefs) and found that religion can increase psychological stress for some people while serving as a means of self-actualization for others"(King, p. 105).

Hoenig, J., and C. Wijesinghe. "Religious Beliefs and Psychiatric Disorders in Sri-Lanka." *Borderland of Psychiatry* 22, no. 1 (1979): 19–33.

Idler, E. L., and S. V. Kasl. "Religion, Disability, Depression, and the Timing of Death." *American Journal of Sociology*, 97 (1992): 1052–1079.

Jansen, D. G., F. J. Garvey, and E. C. Bonk. "Personality Characteristics of Clergymen Entering a Clinical Training Program at a State Hospital." *Psychological Reports* 31 (1972): 878.

Katchadourian, H. "A Comparative Study of Mental Illness Among the Christians and Moslems of Lebanon." *International Journal of Social Psychiatry* 20, no. 1–2 (Spring-Summer 1974): 56–67.

Kay, W. K. "Psychoticism and Attitude to Religion." *Personality and Individual Differences* 2, no. 3 (1981): 249–252.

Keedy, T. C. "Anomie and Religious Orthodoxy." *Sociology and Social Research* 43 (1953): 34–37.

Keene, J. J. "Religious Behavior and Neuroticism, Spontaneity, and Worldmindedness." *Sociometry* 30 (1967): 137–157. Cf. Bergin, 1983.

Kennedy, E. C., V. J. Heckler, F. J. Kohler, and R. E. Walker. "Clinical Assessment of a Profession: Roman Catholic Clergymen." *Journal of Clinical Psychology* 33 (1977): 120–128.

Kimble, M. A., S. H. McFadden, J. W. Ellor, and J. J. Seeber, eds. *Aging, Spirituality, and Religion: A Handbook.* Minneapolis, MN: Fortress Press, 1995.

Kleiner, R. J., J. Tuckman, and M. Lavell. "Mental Disorder and Status Based on Religious Affiliation." *Human Relations* 12 (1959): 273–276.

Kleiner, R.J., J. Tuckman, and M. Lavell. "Mental Disorder and Status Based on Protestant Subgroup Membership." *Journal of Social Psychology* 58 (1962): 345–348.

Koenig, H. G. *Aging and God: Spiritual Pathways to Mental Health in Midlife and Later Years.* New York: Hawthorn, 1994.

Koenig, H. G. *Is Religion Good for Your Health?: The Effects of Religion on Physical and Mental Health.* New York: Haworth Pastoral Press, 1997.

Kroll, J., and W. Sheehan. "Religious Beliefs and Practices Among 52 Psychiatric Inpatients in Minnesota, USA" *American Journal of Psychiatry* 146, no. 1 (1989): 67–72.

Kupst, Mary J. "Religious Liberalism-Conservatism and Psychological Health in a Study of the Roman Catholic Priesthood." *Dissertation Abstracts International* 32, 12-B (June 1972): 7343.

Larson, D. B., A. A. Hohmann, L. G. Kessler, et al. "The Couch and the Cloth: The Need for Linkage." *Hospital Community Psychiatry* 39 (1988): 1064–1069.

Larson, D. B., K. A. Sherrill, J. S. Lyons, F. C. Craigie, Jr., S. B. Thielman, M. A. Greenwold, and S. S. Larson. "Associations Between Dimensions of Religious Commitment and Mental Health Reported in the *American Journal of Psychiatry* and *Archives of General Psychiatry:* 1978–1989." *American Journal of Psychiatry* 149 (1992): 557–559.

Lea, G. "Religion, Mental Health, and Clinical Issues." *Journal of Religion and Health* 21 (1982): 336–351.

Lee, G. R., and R. W. Clyde. "Religion, Socioeconomic Status, and Anomie." *Journal for the Scientific Study of Religion* 13, no. 1 (1974): 35–47.

Lee, R., and F. P. Piercy. "Church Attendance and Self-Actualization." *Journal of College Student Personnel* 15 (1974): 400–403.

Levin, J. S., and S. S. Tobin. "Religion and Psychological Well-

Being." In *Aging, Spirituality, and Religion: A Handbook*, edited by M. A. Kimble, S. H. McFadden, J. W. Ellor, and J. J. Seeber, 30–46. Minneapolis, MN: Fortress Press, 1995.

Lewis, G. G. (1986). "The Correlations Among Ambivalence, One's Concept of God, and Spiritual Well-Being as Measured in Two Diverse Religious Groups." Ph.D. diss., Western Conservative Baptist Seminary, 1986. Abstract in *Dissertation Abstracts International* 48, 3716B.

Lindenthal, J. J., J. K. Myers, M. Pepper, and M. S. Stern. "Mental Status and Religious Behavior." *Journal for the Scientific Study of Religion* 9 (1970): 143–149.
Funded by a PHS Contract and Research Grant from the National Institute of Mental Health, Public Health Service, Department of Health, Education, and Welfare.

Lindskoog, D., and R. E. Kirk. "Some Life History and Attitudinal Correlates of Self-Actualization Among Evangelical Seminary Students." *Journal for the Scientific Study of Religion* 14 (1975): 51–55.

Lowe, C. Marshall, and Roger O. Braaten. "Differences in Religious Attitudes in Mental Illness." *Journal for the Scientific Study of Religion* 5, no. 3 (1966): 435–445.

MacDonald, C. B., and J. B. Luckett. "Religious Affiliation and Psychiatric Diagnoses." *Journal for the Scientific Study of Religion* 22 (1983): 15–37.

Maranell, G. M. "Religiosity and Personal Adjustment." In *Responses to Religion*, edited by G. M. Maranell, 211–220. Wichita: University Press of Kansas, 1974.

Marto, Reji P. "A Father's Locus of Control, Spiritual Well-Being, and Self-Esteem and Their Relationship to His Child's Self-Esteem in a Catholic Parochial High School Population." *Dissertation Abstracts International* 48, 12-B, Part 1 (June 1988), 3716.

Matthews, Dale A., and David B. Larson. *A Bibliography of Research by Scientists on Spiritual Subjects*. Philadelphia: John Templeton Foundation, 1991.

Mayor, C. M., H. Puryear, and H. Richek. "MMPI Correlates of Religiousness in Late Adolescent College Students." *Journal of Nervous and Mental Disease* 149 (1969): 381–385.

McAllister, R. J., and A. J. Vander Veldt. "Factors in Mental Illness Among Hospitalized Clergy." *Journal of Nervous and Mental Diseases* 132 (1961): 80–88.
Supported by a grant from the National Institute of Mental Health.

McAllister, R. J., and A. J. Vander Veldt. "Psychiatric Illness in Hospitalized Catholic Religious." *Journal of Psychiatry* 121 (1965): 881–884.
Supported by grants from the National Institute of Mental Health.

McClain, E. W. "Personality Differences Between Intrinsically Religious and Nonreligious Students: A Factor Analytic Study." Paper presented at the annual convention of the American Psychological Association, San Francisco, September 1977.

McConahay, J. B., and J. C. Hough, Jr. "Love and Guilt Oriented Dimensions of Christian Belief." *Journal for the Scientific Study of Religion* 12 (1973): 53–64.
Supported by a grant from the Irwin-Sweeney-Miller Foundation of Columbus, IN.

Montague, Havor. "The Pessimistic Sect's Influence on the Mental Health of Its Members: The Case of Jehovah's Witnesses." *Social Compass* 24 (1977): 135–147.
According to Homan, this study indicates that mental disorders among members of this sect are more frequent than in the general population, which is partly attributable to high incidence of mental disturbance among recruits. Homan also notes the pressure to "conform to sect norms and the emotional strain of belief-structures." Members "who suffer are urged to avoid worldly counsel and to consult instead their own Elders whose guidance consists in primitive threats of divine vengeance. Montague suggests that here is the root of a high incidence among Witnesses of aggressive crime" (cf. Homan, 128).

Monteiro, M. G., and M. A. Schuckit. "Alcohol, Drug, and Mental Health Problems Among Jewish and Christian Men at a University." *American Journal of Drug and Alcohol Abuse* 15, no. 4 (1989): 403–412.

Moon, Gary W., and John Fantuzzo. "An Integration: Christian Maturity and Positive Mental Health." *Journal of Psychology and Christianity* 2, no.1 (Spring, 1983): 27–38.

Moore, T. V. "Insanity in Priests and Religious, Part 1: The Rate of Insanity in Priests and Religious." *Ecclesiastical Review* (1936): 485–498.

Mueller, E. E. (1987). "The Relationship Between Religious Beliefs/Attitudes and Psychopathology in an Evangelical Seminary Sample." Ph.D. diss., Western Conservative Baptist Seminary, 1987. Abstract in *Dissertation Abstracts International* 48, 3689B.

Murphy, H. B. M., and G. Vega. "Schizophrenia and Religious Affiliation in Northern Ireland." *Psychological Medicine* 12 (1982): 595–605.

Ndetei, D. M., and A. Vadher. "Cross-Cultural Study of Religious Phenomenology in Psychiatric In-Patients." *Acta Psychiatrica Scandinavica* 72, no. 1 (1985): 59–62.

Olson, Lynette J., Walter R. Schumm, Stephan R. Bollman, and Anthony P. Jurich. "Religion and Anomia in the Midwest." *Journal of Social Psychology* 125, no. 1 (1985): 131–132.

Paloutzian, R. F. *Invitation to the Psychology of Religion*, 2nd ed. Needham Heights, MA: Allyn and Bacon, 1996.

Panton, J. H. "An MMPI Item Content Scale to Measure Religious Identification Within a State Prison Population." *Journal of Clinical Psychology* 35 (1979): 588–591.

Propst, L. R. "The Comparative Efficacy of Religious and Nonreligious Imagery for the Treatment of Mild Depression in Religious Individuals." *Cognitive Therapy and Research* 4, no. 2 (1980): 167–178.

Propst, L. R. *Psychotherapy in a Religious Framework: Spirituality in the Emotional Healing Process*. New York: Human Sciences, 1988.

Propst, L. R. "Religious Values in Psychotherapy and Mental Health: Empirical Findings and Issues." Presentation given at the meeting of the Society for Psychotherapy Research, Wintergreen, VA, June 1990.

Purdy, B. A., C. G. Simari, and G. Colon. "Religiosity, Ethnicity, and Mental Health: Interface the 8os." *Counseling and Values* 27, no. 2 (1983): 112–122.
King writes that Purdy studied Puerto Ricans, blacks, and whites in New York City "to discover the relation among religiosity, ethnicity, and mental health. It was found that the church and pastor exercised a very important role in the consultation process of parishioners. The study . . . concluded that if clinicians are to serve everyone, they need to come to some understanding of the role of religious beliefs and must establish relationships with the pastors, with whom clinicians have much in common"(King, 106).

Ranck, J. G. "Some Personality Correlates of Religious Attitude and Belief." *Dissertation Abstracts* 15 (1955): 878–879.

Ranck, J. G. "Religious Conservatism-Liberalism and Mental Health." *Pastoral Psychology* 12 (1961): 34–40.

Reglin, R. (1976). "A Study of Self-Actualization Factors in Individuals with a Conservative Evangelical Religious Background." Ph.D. diss., United States International University. *Dissertation Abstracts International*, 37, 690B.

Reynolds, M. M. "Religious Institutions and the Prevention of Mental Illness." *Journal of Religion and Health* 21, no. 3 (1982): 245–253.

Rice, C. A. "The Relationship of Intrinsic and Extrinsic Religious Orientations to Selected Criteria of Mental Health." *Dissertation Abstracts International* 32, 4-A (1971): 2194.

Richards, P. S., S. A. Smith, and L. F. Davis. "Healthy and Unhealthy Forms of Religiousness Manifested by Psychotherapy Clients: An Empirical Investigation." *Journal of Research in Personality* 23 (1989): 506–524.

Roberts, B. H., and J. K. Myers. "Religion, National Origin, Immigration, and Mental Illness." *American Journal of Psychiatry* 110 (1954): 759–764. Funded by a grant from the United States Public Health Service.

Roberts, Carl W. "Imagining God: Who Is Created in Whose Image?" *Review of Religious Research* 30, no. 4 (June 1989): 375–386.

Rodriguez, K. (1988). "Predictors of Spiritual Well-Being and Self-Esteem Among Sexually Abused Women." *Dissertation Abstracts International* 49, 2872B (University Microfilms International, no. 88-11007).

Rohrbaugh, J., and R. Jessor. "Religiosity in Youth: A Control Against Deviant Behavior." *Journal of Personality* 43 (1975): 136–155.

Ross, M. "Mental Health in Hare Krishna Devotees: A Longitudinal Study." *American Journal of Social Psychiatry* 5 (1985): 65–67.

Schumaker, John F. *Religion and Mental Health.* New York: Oxford University Press, 1992.

Scott, E. M. "Presumed Correlation Between Religion and Mental Health." *Guild of Catholic Psychiatrists Bulletin* 8 (1961): 113–121.

Sharma, Savitri. "A Comparison of Neurotic and Normal Individuals on Certain Important Variables: Faith in Religion as a Successful Method of Counseling." *Indian Journal of Psychometry and Education* 9, no. 1–2 (1978): 40–46.

Sheehan, W., and J. Kroll. "Psychiatric Patients' Belief in General Health Factors and Sin as Causes of Illness." *American Journal of Psychiatry* 147, no. 1 (1990): 112–113.

Sherman, D. B. (1986). "A Comparison of Interpersonal Behavior Traits and Spiritual Well-Being Among Eating-Disordered Patients and Medical Outpatients." *Dissertation Abstracts International* 47, 4680B (University Microfilms International, no. 87-04722).

Shields, Joseph J. (1984). "Religion and Delinquent Behavior: A Study of Adolescents." *Dissertation Abstracts International* 45, Sec. A, 03-08.

Shrauger, J. S., and R. E. Silverman. "The Relationship of Religious Background and Participation to Locus of Control." *Journal for the Scientific Study of Religion* 10 (1971): 11–16.

Smith, Archie. "Religion and Mental Health Among Blacks." *Journal of Religion and Health* 20, no. 4 (1981): 264–287.

Spellman, C. M., G. D. Baskett, and D. Byrne. "Manifest Anxiety as a Contributing Factor in Religious Conversion." *Journal of Consulting and Clinical Psychology* 36 (1971): 245–247.

Spencer, J. "The Mental Health of Jehovah's Witnesses." *British Journal of Psychiatry* 126 (1975): 556–559.

Spendlove, D. C., D. W. West, and W. M. Stanish. "Risk Factors in the Prevalence of Depression in Mormon Women." *Social Science Medicine* 18 (1984): 491–495.

Spilka, B. "Some Personality Correlates of Interiorized and Institutionalized Religious Belief." *Psychological Newsletter* 9 (1958): 103–107.

Spilka, B., and P. H. Werme. "Religion and Mental Disorder: A Research Perspective." In *Research on Religious Development: A Comprehensive Handbook*, edited by M. Strommen, 461–481. New York: Hawthorn, 1971.

Stack, Steven. "Religion and Anomia: Regional Versus National Specifications." *Journal of Social Psychology* 125, no. 1 (1985): 133.

Stark, R., L. Kent, D. P. Doyle, and J. G. Weis. "Religion and Delinquency: The Ecology of a Lost Relationship." Paper prepared for the National Institute for Juvenile Justice and Delinquency Prevention, Law Enforcement Assistance Administration, U.S. Department of Justice, Washington, DC, 1979.

Stewart, R. A. C., and A. C. Webster. "Scale for Theological Conservatism and Its Personality Correlates." *Perceptual and Motor Skills* 30 (1970): 867–870.

Stoudenmire, J. "The Role of Religion in the Depressed Housewife." *Journal of Religion and Health* 15, no. 1 (1976): 62–67.

Strunk, O. "Interest and Personality Patterns of Pre-Ministerial Students." *Psychological Reports* 5 (1959): 740.

Sturgeon, R. S., and R. W. Hamley. "Religiosity and Anxiety." *The Journal of Social Psychology* 108 (1979): 137–138.

Summerlin, F. A. *Religion and Mental Health: A Bibliography.* Washington, DC: U.S. Government Printing Office, 1980.

Swindell, D. H., and L. L'Abate. "Religiosity, Dogmatism, and Repression Sensitization." *Journal for the Scientific Study of Religion* 9 (1970): 249–251. Cf. Bergin, 1983.

Tennison, J. C., and W. U. Snyder. "Some Relationships Between Attitudes Toward the Church and Certain Personality Characteristics." *Journal of Counseling Psychology* 15 (1968): 187–189.

Thorne, B., ed. "Spiritual Dimensions in Counseling." *British Journal of Guidance and Counseling* 18, no. 3 (1990).

Thyer, Bruce A., Marie K. Kramer, John Walker, and James D. Papsdorf. "Religious Orthodoxy and Rational Thinking." *Psychological Reports* 49 (1981): 802.

Tilley, Sharon E. "Religious Maturity and Mental Health: Verification for the Religious Status Interview." *Dissertation Abstracts International* 46, 8-B (February 1986): 2826.

Tuckman, J., and R. J. Kleiner. "Mental Disorder and Status: A Research Note." *Journal of Social Psychology* 65, no. 1 (1965): 85–87.

Ullman, C. "Cognitive and Emotional Antecedents of Religious Conversion." *Journal of Personality and Social Psychology* 43 (1982): 183–192.

Ullman, C. "Psychological Well-Being Among Converts in Traditional and Nontraditional Religious Groups." *Psychiatry* (New York) 51, no. 3 (1988): 312–322.

Vergote, A., A. Tamayo, L. Pasquali, M. Bonami, A. Pattyn, and A. Custers. "Concept of God and Parental Images." *Journal for the Scientific Study of Religion* 8 (1969): 79–87.

Walters, O. S. "Religion and Psychopathology." *Comprehensive Psychiatry* 101 (1964): 24–35.

Watson, P. J., Ralph W. Hood, Jr., Shelly G. Foster, and Ronald J. Morris. "Sin, Depression, and Narcissism." *Review of Religious Research* 25 (1988): 295–305.

Watson, P. J., Ralph W. Hood, Jr., Ronald J. Morris, and James R. Hall. "The Relationship Between Religiosity and Narcissism." *Counseling and Values* 31 (1987): 179–184.

Watson, P. J., Ronald J. Morris, and Ralph Hood, Jr. "Antireligious Humanistic Values, Guilt, and Self Esteem." *Journal for the Scientific Study of Religion* 26, no. 4 (1987): 535–546.

Watson, Paul J., Ronald J. Morris, and Ralph W. Hood. "Sin and Self-Functioning, Part II: Grace, Guilt, and Psychological Adjustment." *Journal of Psychology and Theology* 16 (1988): 270–281.

Watson, P. J., Ronald J. Morris, and Ralph W. Hood, Jr. "Intrinsicness, Religious Self-Love, and Narcissism." *Journal of Psychology and Christianity* 8, no. 1 (Spring 1989a): 31–37.

Watson, Paul J., Ronald J. Morris, and Ralph W. Hood. "Sin and Self-Functioning, Part 4: Depression, Assertiveness, and Religious Commitments." *Journal of Psychology and Theology* 17, no.1 (1989b): 44–58.
Intrinsicness, grace, and self-guilt "seemed to operate within a more-or-less integrated matrix of orthodox perspectives that produced beneficial psychological effects."

Watson, P. J., Ronald J. Morris, and Ralph W. Hood, Jr. "Sin and Self-Functioning, Part 5: Antireligious Humanistic Values, Individualism, and the Community." *Journal of Psychology and Theology* 17, no. 2 (1989c): 157–172.

Watson, Paul J., Ronald J. Morris, and Ralph W. Hood. "Intrinsic Self-Actualization, and the Ideological Surround." *Journal of Psychology and Theology* 18 (1990): 40–53.

Watson, P. J., Ronald J. Morris, Ralph W. Hood, Jr., and Michael D. Biderman. "Religious Orientation Types and Narcissism." *Journal of Psychology and Christianity* 9, no. 1 (1990): 40–46.

Webster, A. C. "Patterns and Relations of Dogmatism, Mental Health, and Psychological Health in Selected Religious Groups." *Dissertation Abstracts International* 27 (1967): 4142-A.

Webster, A. C., and R. A. C. Stewart. "Psychological Attitudes and Beliefs of Ministers." *Anvil Quarterly* 1 (1969): 11–16.

Weiss, A. S., and R. H. Mendoza. "Effects of Acculturation into the

Hare Krishna Movement on Mental Health and Personality." *Journal for the Scientific Study of Religion* 29 (1990): 173–184.

Weltha, D. A. (1969). "Some Relationships Between Religious Attitudes and the Self-concept." Ph.D. diss., Iowa State University, 1969. Abstract in *Dissertation Abstracts International* 30, 2782B (University Microfilms International, no. 69-20, 684). Cf. Bergin, 1983.

Wheeler, M. S. *The Nature of the Relationship Between the Style of Parenting and the Religiosity and Spiritual Well-Being of College Students.* Master's thesis, International School of Theology, 1985.

Wickstrom, D. L., and J. R. Fleck. "Missionary Children: Correlates of Self-Esteem and Dependency." *Journal of Psychology and Theology* 11 (1983): 226–235.

Wiebe, Ken F., and J. Roland Fleck. "Personality Correlates of Intrinsic, Extrinsic, and Nonreligious Orientations." *The Journal of Psychology* 105 (1980): 181–187.

Wilson, W., and H. L. Miller "Fear, Anxiety, and Religiousness." *Journal for the Scientific Study of Religion* 7 (1968): 111–115.

Wilson, W., and W. Kawamura. "Rigidity, Adjustment, and Social Responsibility as Possible Correlates of Religiousness: A Test of Three Points of View." *Journal for the Scientific Study of Religion* 6 (1967): 279–280.

Wilson, W. P. "Mental Health Benefits of Religious Salvation." *Journal of Diseases of the Nervous System* 36, no. 6 (1972): 382–386.

Wilson, W. P., D. B. Larson, and P. D. Meier. "Religious Life of Schizophrenics." *Southern Medical Journal* 76 (1983): 1096–1100.

Witztum, E., D. Greenberg, and H. Dasberg. "Mental Illness and Religious Change." *British Journal of Medical Psychology* 63, no. 1 (1990): 33–42.

Wong, Elsa. "Correlations Between Spiritual Well-Being, Self-Esteem, and Social Desirability for Chinese-Americans in the Northwest." *Dissertation Abstracts International* 50, 9-A (March 1990): 3071.

4

Life Satisfaction

IN A PARTICULARLY helpful article, Myers and Diener (1995) discussed the always provocative question, Who is happy? A casual review of the self-help section of any bookstore reveals that in our curious culture the quest for happiness appears to be nearly consuming. According to Myers and Diener, during the 1980s, the *Psychological Abstract* citations for "well-being," "happiness," and "life satisfaction" quintupled to nearly 780 annually (p. 10).

Defining happiness has always been challenging. "Aristotle regarded happiness as the *summum bonum*, the supreme good. Virtue, he believed, is synonymous with happiness" (p. 10). Unlike Aristotle, however, psychologists need a tool with which to define and measure this abstract term.

Subjective Well-Being (SWB) is a psychological construct that has been developed by researchers to measure happiness. Diener and Myers defined SWB as an individual's cognitive and affective assessment of his or her own relative degree of satisfaction with life. It is how people think and feel about their lives. Earlier, Moberg (1984) suggested that SWB can be described as "the human need to deal with sociocultural deprivations, anxieties and fears, death and dying, personality integration, self images, personal dignity, social alienation and philosophy of life" (p. 351). In practice, SWB is a more scientific-sounding term for what people usually mean by happiness.

Hunter (1983) suggested in his book *American Evangelism: Conservative Religion and the Quandary of Modernity*, that for the 22 percent of Americans who regard themselves as "evangelicals," religion has a definite positive impact on their sense of well-being and life satisfaction. Hunter also reported that 82 percent of evangelical Christians and 55 percent of Catholics receive "a lot" of consolation from their faith versus 18 percent of non-Christians and 23 percent of secularists.

Pfeifer and Waelty (1995) conducted a controlled study dealing primarily with the relationship of psychopathology and religious commitment, and found there was a positive correlation between life satisfaction and religious commitment. They concluded that the primary factor in explaining neurotic functioning in religious patients is not their personal religious commitment but their underlying psychopathology.

Myers (2000) cites data from the National Opinion Research Center surveys that has three in ten Americans saying that they are "very happy," one in ten saying they are "not too happy," and the remaining six in ten describing themselves as "pretty happy." In effect, Myers is saying that almost all of us are happy individually and that collectively we are actually happier than we think we are.

Myers also reports that a Gallup Poll (1984) found that people with the highest scores on a spiritual commitment scale were twice as likely as those with the lowest scores to identify themselves as "very happy." Myers reports National Opinion Research Center Surveys show higher levels of "very happy" people among those who feel "extremely close to God."

The popular culture holds that happiness is related to a never-ending materialistic life quest. Education and educational attainment have also been cast as the royal road to happiness. However, as early as 1976, Campbell, Converse, and Rogers pointed out in their book, *The Quality of American Life*, that there seems to be a shift from "a concentration on being well-off to a concern with a sense of well-being" (p. 1). In fact, some studies indicate that when happiness is studied and when other social and psychological variables are controlled, "the effects of educational and income levels are reduced almost to the point of being inconsequential" (Hadaway and Roof, 1978, p. 295). In contrast, LaBarbera and Gurhan (1997) cited a number of studies that suggest that "materialistic people generally have been found to be unhappy" (p. 74). One look at Belk's materialism scale would help us understand why. Belk (1984) has proposed a scale that includes possessiveness, nongenerosity, and envy and he has found each to be negatively associated with happiness. We might presume that persons who would score high on a so-called "greed scale" would be unlikely to be truly happy. In fact, Belk suggests that research findings demonstrate that materialistic people have generally been found to be unhappy.

As researchers have explored the various dimensions of life satisfaction and quality of life, they have measured a full range of variables that go beyond income and education and include race, age, sex, marital status, perceived health, social participation, social class, and religion. For example, Myers and Diener (1995) answered the question, Who is happy? and concluded that the flood of new studies exploring people's subjective well-being (SWB) reveal that happiness and life satisfaction are similarly available to the young and the old, women and men, blacks and whites, the rich and the working-class. They assert that a better understanding of the derivation of well-being and happiness would come from knowing about a person's traits, close relationships, work experiences, and most significantly for our purpose, religiosity.

Perhaps we should not be surprised that "religiosity" would be thought to help us understand who is happy; however, we might indeed be surprised with Hadaway and Roof's observation (1978) that "remarkably little attention has been given to religious variables in this line of research, although the issue would seem important to the study of both religion and subjective indicators of the quality of life" (p. 296). In a study that analyzed data from the Quality of American Life survey conducted by the Survey Research Center at the University of Michigan, Hadaway determined that religious commitment, conceptualized as "meaning" and "belonging," positively related to subjective feelings of satisfaction with life. "Consistent with our expectation that religious commitment acts as [a] resource, it was found that those who feel that their religious faith is important and those who participate in religious activities also tend to feel their lives are more worthwhile" (p. 295). Hadaway also found that religion was the best of eight predictors for quality of life, ranking higher than health, race, marital status, or number of friends. The research of Hadaway and Roof indicated that 50 percent of persons who belong to a church or synagogue rated their lives as extremely worthwhile compared to 39.4 percent of unaffiliated or nonmembers.

Gallup (1984) compared people low in "spiritual commitment" to highly spiritual people, people who consistently agree with statements such as "my religious faith is the most important influence in my life." The highly spiritual were twice as likely to say they were "very happy."

Poloma and Pendleton (1990) found that religious satisfaction is important for general life satisfaction. They found that frequency of prayer, prayer experience, and relationship with God were important predictors of general life satisfaction, existential well-being, and overall happiness. Markides (1983) and Markides, Levin, and Ray (1987) also found that religious attendance is a significant predictor of life satisfaction.

After reviewing the literature, Ellison, Gay, and Glass (1989) suggested that three dimensions of religiosity are related to subjective well-being: (1) individual belief or personal religious experience or both, (2) level of participation in organized religious activity, and (3) the type and strength of personal identification with a religious community. They concluded that devotional or private religiosity as well as participating in public religiosity have relatively small but persistent positive relationships to life satisfaction.

Ellison's research examined whether multiple dimensions of religiosity, secular forms of social involvement, and demographic covariance were associated with subjective reports of life satisfaction. Ellison concluded that prayer and frequency of attendance at religious services form small, but persistently positive, statistically significant, direct effect on life satisfaction. Ellison actually developed a life satisfaction measurement, the Overall Life Satisfaction Scale (1989), which contains four items: satisfaction with family life, finances, friendships, and health.

Moberg (1979) studied spiritual well-being from a sociological perspective and suggested that spiritual well-being is an important contributor to a more general sense of well-being for many people. Moberg concluded that finding meaning in life, having harmony with one's self, happiness, and being good to others were either "essential" or "most likely to be present if one has spiritual well-being" (Moberg, p. 9).

Ross (1990) found a correlation between strength of religious belief and low levels of psychological distress; however, he also discovered low levels of psychological distress in persons with no religious belief, "thus, there was a curvilinear effect of religious belief on distress" (p. 236). Protestants had the lowest levels of distress, followed by Catholics, Jews, and others. Differences in belief systems did not explain the differences in levels of distress. Rather, the strength of religious belief seemed "to be more important than content in explaining the effect of religion on psychological distress" (p. 236).

Harmon (1985) reviewed empirical and theoretical literature illustrating connections between religious value systems, health, and quality of life. Her research indicated positive health results among Mormons due to their abstinence from alcohol, tobacco, tea, and coffee. The Mormon emphasis on a close network of communal and family support also appeared to be linked to health. Church attendance was linked to lower levels of death anxiety, and being "born again" was correlated with stronger family relationships and increased family communication.

Fehring, Brennan, and Keller (1987) investigated the relationship between spirituality and psychological mood states in response to life change in two separate correlational studies. In the first study ninety-five freshman nursing students were administered a spiritual well-being index, a spiritual maturity scale, a life-change index, and a depression scale. In the second study seventy-five randomly selected college students were administered a spiritual-outlook scale and the Profile of Mood Index, in addition to the tests taken by the first group. Life change and depression demonstrated a weak positive relationship. Spiritual well-being, existential well-being, and spiritual outlook "showed strong inverse relationships with negative moods, suggesting that spiritual variables may influence psychological well-being" (p. 391).

Berkman and Breslow (1983) investigated the relationship between church attendance and health, and reported that a number of factors could influence this relationship. Such factors include religious belief, health-related behavior associated with religious belief, health status, social and demographic factors, and church support.

Race, Life Satisfaction, and Well-Being

The black church has historically been at the center of community, political, social, and religious life in the African American community and has played a significant role in the broader American social, cultural context. There is ample evidence that religion, and in particular Christianity, is especially significant to the lives of African Americans. According to Lincoln and Mamiya (1990) the religious beliefs of African Americans and their expressions are "uniquely oriented and adapted to the amelioration, buffering and/ or abolishment of conditions that are deleterious to the well-being of Blacks" (Levin, Chatters, and Taylor, 1995, p. S161).

St. George and McNamara (1984) employed the NORC (National Opinion Research Center) general survey to explore the relationship between religiosity and well-being, with particular emphasis on a "deeper exploration of the differences in religiosity-life-satisfaction relationships by race" (p. 353). They report that black Americans "differ from other Americans in their degree of reliance on church and religious beliefs" for their sense of well-being (p. 362).

Perhaps more significantly, St. George and McNamara address important methodological issues. They argue that the apparent "bland" relationship between quality of life, religiosity, and a sense of well-being is at least partially related to the way religiosity is defined. "What is essential is to measure the degree of engagement of individual's beliefs with the way they look at life and feel about it.

To do this requires questions that go beyond frequency of church attendance and strength of religious preference" (p. 361).

Levin and Vanderpool (1989) have suggested several ways in which the religious beliefs, attitudes, and behaviors of African Americans have influenced both the physical health and psychological well-being of individual African Americans. First, the black church and its attendant religious experiences provide a critical social support role by promoting stability and continuity in both personal and family relationships. The church also provides a social infrastructure that centers on community cohesiveness, integration, participation, and inclusiveness. Second, specific doctrinal beliefs, that is, original sin, belief in a personal God, the free will of the believer, and the sovereignty of God, can and do engender the ability to explain cognitively and affect emotionally the health and well-being of the individual. Third, the public rites and rituals of the church, including baptism, communion, confession, and prayer, give active expression to religious beliefs that can promote various affective states (e.g., peacefulness, belonging, anxiety, fear, and loneliness). They may also promote the functioning of the immune system.

Levin, Chatters, and Taylor (1995) studied the religious effects on health status and life satisfaction among black Americans in a 1995 study and found that "organizational religiosity maintains a strong, significant effect on life satisfaction" (p. S154). They also found that the association between religion and well-being is consistent over the life course. They drew on data from the National Survey of Black Americans, a nationally representative sample of blacks at least eighteen years old.

Levin, Chatters, and Chambers also suggested that the effect of "organizational religiosity" on well-being may well extend beyond social support and health issues. As they pointed out, all religious traditions share various forms of public religious behavior and community involvement that provide a) existential coherence and personal integration, b) the affirmation of shared beliefs, and c) the development of personal and communal social bonds. However, they emphasized that "distinctive to Black American religious traditions is the continuing and principal role that religious institutions have played as the arbiter of the spiritual and secular life of Blacks" (p. S161).

Blaine and Crocker (1995) examined the question of religious- ness, race, and psychological well-being among a group of sixty-six black and fifty-nine white university students. Their findings sug- gest that blacks are generally more religious than whites, that blacks regard religion as more important to them on a personal level, that blacks are more likely to be church members, and finally that blacks are more intrinsically religious. "These findings imply that the gen- eral relationship between religion and psychological well-being may be more positive among blacks than whites" (p. 1032). Their findings support the conclusion that religious commitment is more strongly associated with global happiness among blacks than whites. Blaine and Crocker speculated that religious belief seems to have a greater psychological benefit to blacks because it "provides a frame- work of coping strategies, and these strategies appear to be more functional for black than white individuals" (p. 1037).

Ellison and Gay (1990) published a study based on data from the National Survey of Black Americans, which directly addressed the question of geography, religious commitment, and life satisfaction among black Americans. They reported that religion influenced subjective well-being only among non-southern blacks. They also found that private religiosity was not related to well-being "in any analysis" (p. 123). Ellison and Gay also observed important "de- nominational effects" (p. 123). Non-southern Methodists and Bap- tists and southern Catholics reported high levels of life satisfaction. Age was related to life satisfaction among non-southerners only.

Brown, Ndubuisi, and Gary (1990) also included the geographic/ demographic factor in their study of religion in the lives of eastern, urban blacks. They noted that higher levels of religiosity were cor- related with less depression in both men and women.

Handal, Black-Lopez, and Moergen (1989) tested 114 black women to determine whether religion affects mental distress. The Integration Scale of the Personal Religiosity Inventory and the Langner Symptom Survey was administered to a sample of 750 women, of whom 114 responded. The researchers discovered that a high religious level did not lead to mental distress, while low levels were associated with significant mental difficulties. However, according to Matthews, Larson, and Barry (1993), the low response rate and sample of convenience limited the generalizability of this study; nevertheless, "the finding, using a conservative statistical procedure (Tukey's), that for black women, the lack of religious commitment is a better predictor of poor mental health than is socioeconomic status, is important" (pp. 149–150).

Taylor (1986) examined religious participation among elderly blacks and found that "neither age nor health disability significantly decreased church attendance among respondents of the sample" (p. 635). Taylor believed this was particularly striking because of the number of serious illnesses, bed disability, and restricted activity days among the black elderly. "The absence of significant relationships between church attendance and age and health disability gives an indication of the importance of religion in the lives of elderly blacks" (p. 635).

Age and Life Satisfaction

Ortega, Crutchfield, and Rushing (1983) produced findings indicating that while aging minority populations suffered in terms of objective conditions such as income or housing, they are "at least as well off as older whites in terms of subjective well-being" (p. 101). Multiple regression analysis revealed "that frequency of contact with church-related friends is the critical factor in accounting for race differences in well-being" (p. 101).

Steinitz (1980) used four measures of religiosity from the NORC Survey to determine how well they predicted reports of personal well-being, life satisfaction, and world-view of elderly persons. She had observed that most empirical studies reporting a positive correlation between religion and well-being in older populations had relied upon religious activities such as church attendance and had not incorporated other dimensions of religiosity. Steinitz cross-tabulated the four religiosity variables from the NORC Social Survey for the years 1972–1977 with six well-being variables on a sample of 1,493 persons sixty-five years of age or older. Among other things, she discovered that church attendance seems to be more a measure of activity than religiosity. Its correlation with well-being was among people reporting poor or fair health, indicating that if people with poor health were able to attend church, their sense of well-being would increase. Interestingly, church attendance seemed to make little difference in the sense of well-being in healthy older people. Steinitz argued that belief in life after death is a better measure of religiosity, because "it is not directly influenced by physical health and environmental factors" (p. 64). She discovered scant evidence of any consistent correlation between world view and religiosity. Steinitz accentuated the need for recognizing "potential intervening factors" (p. 66) that might influence religiosity in older people, such as health, age, and economic situation, and also called for better measures for identifying both dimensions and "levels of intensity of religious identification" (p. 66). Koenig, however, critiqued Steinitz for repeating an error he encountered in much research on religion and well-being: "The religious variable here is once again treated in a relatively superficial manner, with little attention given to religiosity as a multi-dimensional variable" (Koenig, Smiley, and Gonzales, 1988, p. 28).

Research to be noted on well-being and aging populations includes Johnson and Mullins's (1989) study of religion and loneliness among the healthy elderly, and Willits and Crider's (1988) analysis of religion and well-being in men and women in their middle years. Johnson and Mullins observed that the social dimension of religiosity was "significantly related" to low levels of loneliness among the healthy elderly, while Willits and Crider's findings "indicated that religious attitudes positively related to overall well-being, community and marital satisfaction of both men and women, and to the job satisfaction of men" (p. 281).

Koenig, meanwhile, highlighted a result from the 1982 Gallup poll on religion in America. In response to the statement "I receive a great deal of comfort and support from my religious beliefs,"

58 percent of those sixty-five or over answered completely true and 29 percent mostly true. Those under thirty responded completely true 23 percent of the time. Gallup also measured the religious commitment of 1,485 Americans, 39 percent of whom were fifty or older. Twelve percent were categorized as having a very high spiritual commitment (VHSC) and 15 percent as having a very low spiritual commitment (VLSC). What is particularly striking is the difference in level of reported life satisfaction and happiness between these two groups. Sixty-five percent of the people with VHSC reported being very satisfied with life, while 36 percent of the people with VLSC reported the same response (Koenig, Smiley, and Gonzales 1988, p. 29; cf. Princeton Religion Research Center, 1982).

Research by Witter and colleagues (1985) summarized twenty-eight studies in a meta-analysis that examined the relationship between religiosity and well-being and found positive correlation between religiosity and subjective well-being. Witter and colleagues performed a quantitative research synthesis (meta-analysis) and found that religion was significantly, positively related to subjective well-being and that religion accounts for between 2 and 6 percent of the variance in adult subjective well-being.

Cutler's (1976) research indicated that church involvement could be linked to higher levels of life satisfaction and happiness among older persons. Cutler examined the relationships between membership in volunteer associations and life satisfaction and happiness in a sample of 438 respondents, sixty-five years of age and older. A multiple regression analysis demonstrated that "life satisfaction and happiness were related to membership in only one type of association—church-affiliated groups—after controlling for health, socioeconomic status, and membership in the remaining types of associations" (p. 338). Cutler concluded that membership in most voluntary associations is apparently not related to psychological well-being for older persons, that to the extent that well-being is related to membership in voluntary associations it is "confined primarily to membership in church-affiliated associations" (p. 338), and finally that membership in church-related associations, while statistically significant, accounts for only 1 to 2 percent of the variance in measures of psychological well-being.

Blazer and Palmore (1976) conducted an eighteen-year longitudinal study investigating religion and aging. Their analysis indicated that although religious activities decline as people grow older, their interest in religion remains stable. They observed no correlation of religious activity or attitude with longevity, but "they were correlated with happiness, feelings of usefulness and personal adjustment, especially among men, those from manual occupations, and those over 70" (p. 85). These correlations tended to increase over time, and supported the theory "that religion becomes increasingly important for personal adjustment in the later years" (p. 85).

Hunsberger (1985) also studied the relationship between religion and life satisfaction. He investigated the responses of eighty-five elderly volunteers and found a significant correlation between subjects reporting religious beliefs and those indicating high levels of personal adjustment. The importance of religious beliefs was also related to happiness and health. Hunsberger noted, however, that "although highly religious older persons tended to report an increase in religiousness over the course of their lives, respondents who were low in religiosity tended to report a decrease" (p. 615). In response to Hunsberger's discovery, Matthews, Larson, and Barry (1993) commented that an association between religious orthodoxy and greater life satisfaction is "particularly important, because of an often-assumed idea that increasing orthodoxy leads to increasing rigidity and decreased happiness" (p. 168).

Perkins (1991) studied the relationship between religious commitment and well-being, and the values of young urban professionals. Young adults with greater religious commitment were both less oriented to "yuppie values" and demonstrated fewer problems with alcohol abuse. Young people who had absorbed the yuppie value system failed to score higher on any measure of healthy lifestyle, smoked more often, and among women in the sample, "consumed more alcohol and were more likely to report a possible eating disorder" (p. 244). Perkins concluded that religiosity not only promoted a healthy lifestyle, but discouraged a materialistic value structure divorced from a "larger moral orientation" such as concern about family or social relationships.

Frankel and Hewitt (1994) conducted a study that dealt with religion and well-being among Canadian university students and found a positive relationship between faith-group involvement and various aspects of health status. They concluded that the students in the faith group seemed to be more satisfied with their lives and able to express more positive psychological states than the control group.

In a provocative article dealing with religion and the well-being of adolescents, Donahue and Benson (1995) explored what is known about the relationship between religiosity and the well-being of adolescents in the United States. They concluded that American adolescents are indeed religious and that their religiosity has not declined over time. However, the religiosity of individual adolescents does appear to decline across the years of their adolescence. Donahue and Benson also concluded that blacks are more religious than whites and that girls are more religious than boys. They noted that adolescents who are religious score higher in altruism and engage more often in community service projects. They also found that religiousness is a strong inhibitor of both suicide ideation and suicide attempts for adolescents. Finally, they observed that religiosity is a strong negative predictor of alcohol use and sexual involvement as well as interpersonal violence. They therefore concluded that "the weight of empirical evidence suggests that religiousness is associated with positive developmental outcomes" (p. 156).

In a study that attempted to measure personality functioning in college students, Richards (1994) administered measures of religious devoutness, impression management, and personality adjustment to 178 undergraduate college students. He found that greater religiousness was associated with greater existential well-being, self-control, and social desirability, suggesting that students who are more religious "tended to feel more satisfaction and purpose in their lives and to feel more loved and valued by God compared to the less religious persons" (p. 21).

Readers should note carefully the excellent suggestions made by Ellison and Gay (1990) in their article regarding future research on religion, life satisfaction, and mental health. First, Ellison and Gay contended that research on religion and life satisfaction was vulnerable to critique in two areas:

1. The causal effect of religion on life satisfaction has yet to be demonstrated. "While the problem of causality is central to most research in this area, its definitive resolution awaits the collection and analysis of longitudinal data on religion and well-being" (p. 139).
2. Some indicators of life satisfaction might be biased toward maintaining the status quo. Greater attention to psychiatric symptoms and clinical diagnoses might serve to overcome the influence of "the generally conservative personal and social orientations of religious persons" (p. 139).

Ellison and Gay (1990) also commented on the religion-stress link. Most studies have focused on the role of religion in buffering the effects of life stress. Ellison and Gay, however, called for more research exploring the role of religion in managing chronic stress and studies distinguishing "more carefully among various types of life events and stressors" (p. 139). Is religion, for example, more effective in buffering the effect of bereavement than of financial difficulties?

Finally, Ellison and Gay singled out three areas for future theoretical and empirical research on the links between religion, stress, and mental health. Religion may influence the outcome of the stress process by (1) leading individuals to interpret various events in less threatening terms from the outset, (2) channeling various forms of support through church programs and fellowship, and (3) encouraging specific coping styles and strategies in response to stress. Further work is needed in all these areas.

In an earlier article Ellison, Gay, and Glass (1989) reported "small but statistically significant relationships between affiliative, participatory, and devotional aspects of religiosity and general life satisfaction" (p. 117). Multiple dimensions of religiosity were examined in relationship with secular forms of social involvement, demographic covariates, and subjective reports of life satisfaction. Results indicated that both devotional (private) and participatory (public) aspects of religiosity were correlated with life satisfaction. Certain denominational affiliations (e.g., Southern Baptist) were also positively associated with life satisfaction.

These associations are both statistically and theoretically significant. They remain despite efforts to control for the effects of both qualitative and quantitative measures of nonreligious social ties. This research indicates that the links between religiosity and psychological well-being in previous studies do not reflect merely the effects of high levels of social participation (p. 100).

Ellison (1991) published a helpful article on religious involvement and subjective well-being in the *Journal of Health and Social Behavior.* Ellison's research indicated that previous correlations between religious attendance, religious devotion, and subjective well-being are a result of attendance and devotion serving to "strengthen religious belief systems" (p. 80). Interestingly, he found a direct correlation between religious certainty and well-being. Individuals exercising strong religious faith reported "higher levels of life satisfaction, greater personal happiness, and fewer negative psychosocial consequences of life events" (p. 80). The positive influence of religion was "especially pronounced for older persons and persons with low levels of formal education" (p. 80).

Ellison called for further empirical research in several specific areas:

1. Subsequent research on religiosity and well-being "should consider the relationships between the strength of religious beliefs and other aspects of physical and psychological well-being" (p. 91). For example, the links between religiosity and "various aspects of self-concept and personality (e.g., self-esteem, personal efficacy)" should be researched in greater depth. Measures should be developed analyzing "not only the

strength of faith, but also the centrality of religious interpretations of life experiences" (p. 92).

2. More research is needed on the "determinants and varieties"
   of religious coping strategies. What nontheological factors
   (i.e., gender, age, region, socioeconomic status) might influence or increase the possibility that individuals will use
   religion as a coping device? Are certain life events such as
   bereavement "particularly amenable" to religious coping behaviors? Further, what evidence can be gathered "regarding
   the use and the effects of religion in coping with chronic
   (as opposed to acute) stressors and in altering patterns of
   perceived stress or worry?" (p. 92). According to Ellison,
   ". . . future research in the social psychology of religion
   should work toward linking varieties of stress, attributional
   patterns, and types of divine interaction . . . with an array
   of mental health outcomes" (p. 92).

3. Further research is needed to "clarify the precise links between collective participation, private devotion and belief,
   and various dimensions of personal well-being" (p. 92).

Researchers responding to Ellison's call for deeper investigation
into the relationship between religiosity, physical well-being, and
psychological well-being have a solid foundation on which to build.
Petersen and Roy (1985) analyzed the correlation between two types
of psychological well-being (anxiety together with meaning and
purpose) and different aspects of religious commitment. They
found only one religious variable (religious salience) to have an independent effect on meaning and purpose, and only church attendance had a significant effect on anxiety. Peterson and Roy believed
their study could help to guide future research in two ways:

1. Future research "should be sensitive to the fact that aspects
   of religious commitment which affect one dimension of well-
   being do not necessarily affect another" (p. 59). In their
   study, religious salience was predictive of meaning and purpose but not of anxiety. The opposite proved to be true for
   anxiety.

2. Future religiosity measures should involve multiple controls. When Petersen and Roy introduced their multiple controls, "only religious salience had a significant independent effect" (p. 59).

The millennial issue of *American Psychologist* (January 2000) is a special issue dealing with topics pertaining to happiness, excellence, and optimal human functioning. In their introduction, Seligman and Csikszentmihalyi suggest that the exclusive focus on pathology that has dominated psychology and psychiatry has resulted in a model of the human being that is bereft of the positive characteristics that make life worth living, including hope, wisdom, creativity, future-mindedness, courage, responsibility, perseverance, and spirituality. They call for a positive psychology that would document "what kind of families result in children who flourish, what work settings support the greatest satisfaction among workers, what policies result in the strongest civic engagement, and how people's lives can be most worth living" (p. 5).

Seligman and Csikszentmihalyi further suggest that positive psychology is concerned with the "subjective human experiences of well-being, contentment, and satisfaction (in the past); hope and optimism (for the future); and flow and happiness (in the present)" (p. 5).

References

Belk, R. W. (1984). "Three Scales to Measure Constructs Related to Materialism: Reliability, Validity, and Relationships to Measures of Happiness. In T. Kinnear (Ed.), *Advances in Consumer Research* (vol. 11, pp. 291–297). Provo, UT: Association for Consumer Research.

Berkman, L. F., and Breslow, L. (1983). *Health and Ways of Living: The Alameda County Study.* New York: Oxford University Press.

Blaine, B., and Crocker, J. (1995). "Religiousness, Race, and Psychological Well-Being: Exploring Social Psychological Mediators." *Personality and Social Psychology Bulletin, 21*(10), 1031–1041.

Blazer, D., and Palmore, E. (1976). "Religion and Aging in a Longitudinal Panel." *The Gerontologist, 16*(1), 82–85.

Brown, D. R., Ndubuisi, S. C., and Gary, L. E. (1990). "Religiosity and Psychological Distress Among Blacks." *Journal of Religion and Health, 29*(1), 55–68.

Campbell, A., Converse, P. E., and Rogers, W. (1976). *The Quality of American Life: Perceptions, Evaluations, and Satisfactions.* New York: Russell Sage.

Cutler, S. J. (1976). "Membership in Different Types of Voluntary Associations and Psychological Well-Being." *The Gerontologist, 16*(4), 335–339.

Donahue, M. J., and Benson, P. L. (1995). "Religion and the Well-Being of Adolescents." *Journal of Social Issues, 51*(2), 145–160.

Ellison, C. G. (1991). "Religious Involvement and Subjective Well-Being." *Journal of Health and Social Behavior, 32,* 80–99.

Ellison, C. G., and Gay, D. A. (1990). "Region, Religious Commitment, and Life Satisfaction Among Black Americans." *The Sociological Quarterly, 31*(1), 123–147.

Ellison, C. G., Gay, D. A., and Glass, T. A. (1989). "Does Religious Commitment Contribute to Individual Life Satisfaction?" *Social Forces, 68*(1), 100–123.

Fehring, R. J., Brennan, P. F., and Keller, M. L. (1987). "Psychological and Spiritual Well-Being in College Students." *Research in Nursing and Health, 10,* 391–398.

Frankel, B. G., and Hewitt, W. E. (1994). "Religion and Well-Being Among Canadian University Students: The Role of Faith Groups on Campus." *Journal for the Scientific Study of Religion, 33*(1), 62–73.

Gallup, G., Jr. (1984). "Religion in America." *Gallup Report.*

Hadaway, C. K., and Roof, W. C. (1978). "Religious Commitment and the Quality of Life in American Society." *Review of Religious Research, 19*(3), 295–307.

Handal, P. J., Black-Lopez, W., and Moergen, S. (1989). "Preliminary Investigation of the Relationship Between Religion and Psychological Distress in Black Women." *Psychological Reports, 65,* 971–975.

Harmon, Y. (1985). "The Relationship Between Religiosity and Health." *Religiosity and Health, 9*(3), 23–25.

Hunsberger, B. (1985). "Religion, Age, Life Satisfaction, and Perceived Sources of Religiousness: A Study of Older Persons." *Journal of Gerontology, 40*(5), 615–620.

Hunter, J. D. (1983). *American Evangelism: Conservative Religion and the Quandary of Modernity.* New Brunswick, NJ: Rutgers University Press.

Johnson, D. P., and Mullins, L. C. (1989). "Subjective and Social Dimensions of Religiosity and Loneliness Among the Well Elderly." *Review of Religious Research, 31*(1), 3–15.

Koenig, H. G., Smiley, M., and Gonzales, J. A. (1988). *Religion, Health, and Aging: A Review and Theoretical Integration.* New York: Greenwood Press.

LaBarbera, P. A., and Gurhan, Z. (1997). "The Role of Materialism, Religiosity, and Demographics in Subjective Well-Being." *Psychology and Marketing, 14*(1), 71–97.

Levin, J. S., Chatters, L. M., and Taylor, R. J. (1995). "Religious Effects on Health Status and Life Satisfaction Among Black Americans." *Journal of Gerontology, 50B*(3), S154–S163.

Levin, J. S., and Vanderpool, H. Y. (1989). "Is Religion Therapeutically Significant for Hypertension?" *Social Science and Medicine, 29*(1), 69–78.

Lincoln, C. E., and Mamiya, L. H. (1990). *The Black Church in the African American Experience.* Durham, NC: Duke University Press.

Markides, K. S. (1983). "Aging, Religiosity, and Adjustment: A Longitudinal Analysis." *Journal of Gerontology, 38*(5), 621–625.

Markides, K. S., Levin, J. S., and Ray, L. A. (1987). "Religion, Aging, and Life Satisfaction: An Eight-Year, Three-Wave Longitudinal Study." *The Gerontologist, 27*(5), 660–665.

Matthews, D. A., Larson, D. B., and Barry, C. P. (1993). *The Faith Factor: An Annotated Bibliography of Clinical Research on Spiritual Subjects.* Washington, DC: National Institute for Healthcare Research.

Moberg, D. O. (1979). *Spiritual Well-Being: Sociological Perspectives.* Washington, DC: University Press of America.

Moberg, D. O. (1984). "Subjective Measures of Spiritual Well-Being." *Review of Religious Research, 25*(4), 351–363.

Myers, D. G. (2000). "The Funds, Friends, and Faith of Happy People." *American Psychologist, 55(1),* 56–67.

Myers, D. G., and Diener, E. (1995). "Who Is Happy?" *Psychological Science, 6*(1), 10–19.

Ortega, S. T., Crutchfield, R. D., and Rushing, W. A. (1983). "Race Differences in Elderly Personal Well-Being." *Research on Aging, 5*(1), 101–118.

Perkins, H. W. (1991). "Religious Commitment, Yuppie Values, and Well-Being in Post-Collegiate Life." *Review of Religious Research, 32*(3), 244–251.

Petersen, L. R., and Roy, A. (1985). "Religiosity, Anxiety, and Meaning and Purpose: Religion's Consequences for Psychological Well-Being." *Review of Religious Research, 27*(1), 49–62.

Pfeifer, S., and Waelty, U. (1995). "Psychopathology and Religious Commitment: A Controlled Study." *Psychopathology, 28*(2), 70–77.

Poloma, M. M., and Pendleton, B. F. (1990). "Religious Domains and General Well-Being." *Social Indicators Research, 22,* 255–276.

Richards, P. S. (1994). "Religious Devoutness, Impression Management, and Personality Functioning in College Students." *Journal of Research in Personality, 28,* 14–26.

Ross, C. E. (1990). "Religion and Psychological Distress." *Journal for the Scientific Study of Religion, 29*(2), 236–245.

Seligman, M., and Csikszentmihalyi, M. (2000). "Positive Psychology: An Introduction." *American Psychologist, 55(1),* 5–14.

St. George, A., and McNamara, P. H. (1984). "Religion, Race, and Psychological Well-Being." *Journal for the Scientific Study of Religion*, 23(4), 351–363.

Steinitz, L. Y. (1980). "Religiosity, Well-Being, and *Weltanschauung* Among the Elderly." *Journal for the Scientific Study of Religion*, 19(1), 60–67.

Taylor, R. J. (1986). "Religious Participation Among Elderly Blacks." *The Gerontologist*, 26(6), 630–635.

Willits, F. K., and Crider, D. M. (1988). "Religion and Well-Being: Men and Women in the Middle Years." *Review of Religious Research*, 29(3), 281–294.

Witter, R. A., Stock, W. A., Okun, M. A., and Haring, M. J. (1985). "Religion and Subjective Well-Being in Adulthood: A Quantitative Synthesis." *Review of Religious Research*, 26(4), 332–342.

Bibliography

Beck, Rubye Wilkerson. "The Subjective Well-Being of Widowed Men and Women: The Influence of Social Support, Social Interaction and Religion (Bereavement Overload)." *Dissertation Abstracts International* 48, no. 04, Sec. A, 1026.

Belyea, M., J. Barefoot, I. Siegler, and K. Hooker. "Religion, Well-Being, Social Contacts, and Survival: A Conceptual Replication." *American Journal of Epidemiology* 128, no. 4 (1988): 927.

Blaikie, N. W. H., and G. P. Kelsen. "Locating Self and Giving Meaning to Existence: A Typology of Paths to Spiritual Well-Being Based on New Religious Movements in Australia." In *Spiritual Well-Being: Sociological Perspectives*, edited by D. O. Moberg, 133–152. Washington, DC: University Press of America, 1979.

Bolt, M. "Purpose of Life and Religious Orientation." *Journal of Psychology and Theology* 3 (1975): 116–118.

Bortman, R.W. and D. F. Hultsch. "A Multivariate Analysis of Correlates of Life Satisfaction in Adulthood." *Journal of Gerontology* 25 (1970): 41–47.

Bufford, R. K. "Empirical Correlations of Spiritual Well-Being and Spiritual Maturity Scales."
Paper presented at the annual meeting of the Christian Association for Psychological Studies, Dallas, TX, April 1984.

Bufford, R. K., and T. G. Parker, Jr. "Religion and Well-Being: Concurrent Validation of the Spiritual Well-Being Scale." Paper presented at the annual meeting of the American Psychological Association, Los Angeles, CA, 1985.

Capps, Donald. "Religion and Psychological Well-Being." In *The Sacred in a Secular Age: Toward Revision in the Scientific Study of Religion*, edited by P. E. Hammond, 237–256. Berkeley: University of California Press, 1985.

Chamberlain, K., and S. Zika. "Religiosity, Life Meaning and Well

Being: Some Relationships in a Sample of Women." *Journal for the Scientific Study of Religion* 27 (1988): 411–420.
Supported in part by a grant from the Social Science Research Fund.

Champagne, K.E. *The Relationship Between Nurses' Spiritual Well-Being and Nurses' Perception of Patients' Spiritual Needs.* Master's thesis, The Catholic University of America, 1986.

Clarke, D. E. (1986). "Predictors of Spiritual Well-Being Among Full-Time Youth for Christ/USA Staff Members." *Dissertation Abstracts International* 47, 4680B (University Microfilms International, 87-04710).

Crumpler, N.J.G. "The Relationship Between Spiritual Well-Being and Reported Self-Actualization Among College Students." Master's thesis, East Carolina University, 1989.

Diener, E. "Traits Can Be Powerful, but Are Not Enough: Lessons from Subjective Well-Being. *Journal of Research in Personality* 30 (1996): 389–399.

Dufton, Brian D., and Daniel Perlman. "Loneliness and Religiosity: In the World but Not of It." *Journal of Psychology and Theology* 14 (1986): 135–146.

Duke, James T., and Barry L. Johnson. "Spiritual Well-Being and the Consequential Dimension of Religiosity." *Review of Religious Research* 26, no. 1 (September 1984): 59–72. Funded by the Institute for Studies in Values and Human Behavior, Brigham Young University.

Edwards, J. N., and D. L. Klemmack. "Correlates of Life Satisfaction: A Reexamination." *Journal of Gerontology* 28 (1973): 497–502.

Ellison, C. W. "Spiritual Well-Being: Conceptualization and Measurement." *Journal of Psychology and Theology* 11 (1983): 330–340.

Ellison, C. W., and R. F. Paloutzian. "Religious Experience and Quality of Life." Paper presented at the meeting of the American Psychological Association, New York, 1979.

Guy, R. F. "Religion, Physical Disabilities and Life Satisfaction in Older Age Cohorts." *International Journal of Aging and Human Development* 15, no. 3 (1982): 225–232.

Hadaway, Christopher Kirk. "Life Satisfaction and Religion: A Reanalysis." *Social Forces* 57 (1978): 636–643.

Hall, Margaret C. "Crisis as Opportunity for Spiritual Growth." *Journal of Religion and Health* 25, no. 1 (1986): 8–17.

Huggins, S. M. (1988). "The Effect of Small Group Attendance, Personal Devotions and Church Attendance on Spiritual Well-Being." *Dissertation Abstracts International* 49, 1943B (University Microfilms International 88-14665).

Matthews, Dale A., and David B. Larson. *A Bibliography of Research by Scientists on Spiritual Subjects.* Philadelphia: John Templeton Foundation, 1991.

McClure, R.F., and M. Loden. "Religious Activity, Denomination Membership and Life Satisfaction." *Psychology, A Quarterly Journal of Human Behavior* 19 (1982): 13–17.

McNamara, P. H., and A. St. George. "Measures of Religiosity and the Quality of Life: A Critical Analysis." In *Spiritual Well-Being: Sociological Perspectives*, edited by D. O. Moberg, 229–236. Washington, DC: University Press of America, 1979.

Paloutzian, R., and C. W. Ellison. "Loneliness, Spiritual Well-Being and the Quality of Life." In *Loneliness: A Sourcebook of Current Theory, Research and Therapy*, edited by A. Peplau and D. Perlman, 224–237. New York: John Wiley and Sons, 1982.

Paloutzian, R. F., and L. A. Kirkpatrick. "Introduction: The Scope of Religious Influences and Personal and Society Well-Being." *Journal of Social Issues* 51 (1995): 1–12.

Princeton Religion Research Center. *Religion in America.* Princeton, NJ: The Gallup Poll, 1976.

Princeton Religion Research Center. *Religion in America.* Princeton, NJ: The Princeton Religious Center, 1982.
    A survey of a random sample of Americans sixty-five and over, seeking responses, agreement, or disagreement with the follow-

ing statement: "I receive a great deal of comfort and support from my religious beliefs." Fifty-eight percent reported completely true and 29 percent mostly true. People under thirty years of age responded completely true 23 percent of the time (Koenig,17). "The Gallup organization measured religious commitment (in terms of belief, ritual, and experience) among 1,485 Americans, 39 percent of whom were over 50 years of age. Twelve percent of the total sample were categorized as having a very high level of spiritual commitment (VHSC), based on responses to a seven-item religious commitment scale. Fifteen percent of the sample were categorized as having a very low level of spiritual commitment (VLSC). There were significant differences between these two groups in terms of life satisfaction and happiness. Sixty-five percent of the VHSC group compared to 36 percent of the VLSC group reported being very satisfied with life, while 68 percent of the VHSC and 36 percent of the VLSC claimed to be very happy" (Koenig, 29).

Princeton Religion Research Center. *1985 Religion in America.* Princeton, NJ: The Gallup Poll, 1985.

Soderstrom, G. D. "Religious Orientation and Meaning in Life." Ph.D. diss., Utah State University, 1977.

Weinstein, L., A. De Man, and L. Almaguer. "Purpose in Life as a Function of Religious Versus Secular Beliefs." *Perceptual and Motor Skills* 67, no. 1 (1988): 335–337.

5

Mental Disorders

IN ATTEMPTING TO understand the obviously complex relationship between religion and psychopathology, researchers have frequently compared psychiatric patients with control groups of normal adults, reasoning that if psychiatric patients who were religious
responded differently to various measures than "normal" persons
who also were religious, then perhaps religiosity could be isolated as
a causal factor in the etiology of psychopathology, thereby confirm-
ing the theoretical point-of-view of various psychologists from
Freud through Ellis who regarded religion itself as psychopathological and who believed that religion played a primary role in causing
mental disorders. Such studies have yielded a fascinating array of
results.

Armstrong, Larsen, and Mourer (1962) undertook a study to determine whether a relationship exists between one's religious beliefs and one's emotional adjustment, self-concept, interests, education, and age. They found that the religious attitudes and practices
of psychiatric patients compared with "normal" individuals were
actually quite similar.

Kroll and Sheehan (1989) investigated the beliefs and religious
practices of psychiatric inpatients in Minnesota. They discovered
that their sample of psychiatric patients had religious beliefs and
practices similar to nonpatients as reported in national and state
surveys. Matthews, Larson, and Barry (1993) noted that this study
of depression "was correlated with gender, but not with greater religiosity, except that belief in individual sin was associated with
higher levels of self-reported depressive symptoms" (p. 203).

Lowe and Braaten (1966) measured the religious ideas of psychiatric patients and reported that their findings disproved "several traditional beliefs of the psychiatric folklore" (p. 437) and concluded that paranoid schizophrenics were no more religious than other patients as measured by frequency of church attendance, Bible reading, and praying. In an earlier study, Roberts and Myers (1954) noted that rates of schizophrenia, affective disorders, psychosis with mental deficiencies, and illnesses of aging (senescence) were the same for Catholic, Protestant, and Jewish groupings as they were for the general population. The inference drawn from these studies taken together is that religion does not seem to be a causal factor in the development of mental disorders.

Furthermore, Wilson, Larson, and Meier (1983) conducted research on the religious life of schizophrenics, which evaluated the methods used by parents of schizophrenics in raising their children. They found that the homes of schizophrenics were characterized by a family culture based primarily on obligation and threat and a fairly limited religious emphasis rather than a pervasively religious culture. In these families, the father had less of a religious commitment than the mother. Mothers of schizophrenics tended to be more domineering than the "emotionally and geographically absent father" (p. 1096). In addition, schizophrenics saw their religious and developmental upbringing as "lacking in nurture and paternal participation," and they themselves "seldom indulged in personal religious practices" (p. 1096).

Gallemore, Wilson, and Rhoads (1969) studied the religious life of patients with affective disorders to discover what effect the illness might have on religious life and in turn, what effect religious life might have on the illness. The positive or negative effect of religion on patients' affective disorders appeared to be related to the emotional state of the patient. "When ill, patients who have joy, love or awe as a primary affect tend to have strong religious experiences. Patients with depression, fear, confusion or pain tend to doubt their faith or to feel guilty about their lack of faith" (p. 486).

Bishop, Larson, and Wilson (1987) also studied the religious life of patients with affective disorder. They found that these patients were characterized by increase in early life stress, a rejection of religious life during adolescence, and a renewed interest in religious matters in adulthood. Interesting, if somewhat tangential, was the finding that those with a religious commitment remained married longer. However, as Matthews, Larson, and Barry (1993) noted, this study was somewhat hampered by the lack of age and sex matching.

Lindenthal and colleagues (1970) studied nearly one thousand persons in the vicinity of New Haven, Connecticut and found that psychiatric evaluation of the degree of mental impairment showed a negative relationship between impairment and church affiliation and attendance. Stark (1971) also found that survey data from the research center at Berkeley and the National Opinion Research Center at the University of Chicago indicated that mental illness and religious commitment are negatively related. Stark concluded that theories that presume psychopathology to be a primary source of ordinary religious commitment are false. He also found that the mentally ill were less religious than the normal controls.

The net affect of these aforementioned studies is that religiosity cannot be isolated as a causal factor in the development of psychopathology. In fact, the opposite seems more likely to be the case. Numerous studies seem to suggest that psychiatric patients are not anymore religious than so-called normal persons. For example, Payne and colleagues (1991) pointed out that it is possible that persons who are mentally ill naturally fall away from various religious activities and that this could account for the finding that "religiously active sub-groups often show less disturbance on pathology scales" (p. 31). Payne and colleagues concluded that "generally, positive affects of religion are found with variables that are more indirectly related to mental health such as well-being, marital stability, personal adjustment, and social conduct. It is safe to say that religion is positively correlated with adjustment, but the relationship with mental illness is more elusive" (p. 31).

Relationship Between Conversion Experiences and Psychopathology

What about the notion that sudden and intense religious experiences are essentially pathological? That conversion experiences occur because the would-be convert is mentally disordered and is seeking a refuge in religion as a form of self-medication? Or that a sudden, intense conversion experience might actually cause mental disorders?

Allison (1967) investigated the relationship between adaptive regression and intense religious experiences. Adaptive regression is a psychoanalytic term that refers to various psychological benefits, including creativity. Allison noted that other studies had previously linked adaptive regression to greater tolerance for ambiguity, better quality of imaginativeness, increased self-esteem, and an increase in the sense of being a worthwhile individual. He concluded that intense conversion experiences do not necessarily occur "within authoritarian, rigid or pathological contexts, and persons with more intense experiences appear to demonstrate a more pronounced capacity for regressive experiences of an adaptive nature" (p. 458).

Just when it seemed that intense religious experiences may actually lead to positive mental health consequences rather than pathological or negative outcomes, Ullman (1988) found evidence of depression existing in 55 percent of the subjects she studied in the two years preceding their conversions to traditional (Judeo-Christian) and nontraditional (Hare Krishna, Bahai) religions. Furthermore, 53 percent demonstrated a "chaotic lifestyle" and 35 percent reported a history of psychiatric difficulties. Matthews, Larson, and Barry (1993) noted that "psychological benefits of conversion are similar among converts to both types of religion (traditional and non-traditional)" (p. 300). They believed the major question that remained to be answered in Ullman's study concerned "how many of these individuals with severe developmental problems remain converted to their faith over time and experience the relief of psychiatric symptoms and deep healing that they really need?" (p. 300).

Bergin and colleagues (1988) investigated the relationship between values, religion, and mental health, and concluded that subjects with continuous religious development and relatively mild religious experiences appeared to be healthier than those with discontinuous development and intense religious experiences. However, they also noted that intense religious experiences did tend to enhance the adjustment of those who experienced them. They further concluded that there was no evidence of either a negative or positive relationship between religiousness and mental health overall, "but some modes of religious involvement appeared to be related to disturbance, whereas other modes appeared to be related to enhanced stability and resilience" (p. 91). Causality between these relationships remains uncertain.

One more slant on the relationship between religious conversion and mental health is provided by Witztum, Greenberg, and Dasberg (1990), who reported that a higher-than-predicted 12.6 percent of referrals to a community health center were converts to orthodox Judaism. Furthermore, these converts were more likely to be schizophrenic or to be diagnosed with severe personality disorders. They were, however, less likely than other referrals to have anxiety, depressive, or adjustment disorders.

Wooton and Allen (1983) examined the issue of dramatic religious conversions and schizophrenic decompensation in a review of literature and concluded that a conversion experience can appear to be similar to decompensation. Decompensation refers to personality disorganization that occurs under severe stress. Symptoms of decompensation include increased anxiety, distortion of reality, and increase in inappropriate defensive methods of coping. In the extreme, decompensation may be characterized by psychological disorganization that can include delusions and hallucinations.

It may be surprising to some that the empirical literature seems to be finding that religious converts function as well or better than nonconverts, even though the subgroup of sudden converts is sometimes more disturbed than gradual converts or nonconverts (Parker, 1977; Stanley, 1965; Williams and Cole, 1968). It seems safe to conclude that while some converts indeed might become disturbed by the suddenness of their conversion experience, the studies nonetheless seem to be consistent in indicating that conversion and related intense religious experiences can indeed be therapeutic, in part because they seem to reduce pathological symptomatology. In fact, in a study of decreased emotional distress among Pentecostals who experience faith healing, Ness and Wintrob (1980) found that the more frequently people engaged in these intense religious experiences, the less likely they were to report symptoms of emotional distress. Likewise, Bergin (1983) asserted that he has observed that religious converts often have made "fundamental changes and enhanced their reality contact, that the gradual converts to more conventional religiosity are sometimes superior in their life adjustment, and that the effects of psychotherapy are not any better by comparison" (p. 178).

Religiosity and Mental Disorders

Are persons with mental disorders more likely to be religious? And if they are, what conclusions should be made? A 1970 study by Lindenthal and colleagues suggests the answer to the first question may be no. When measurements of psychopathology, institutional behavior, and religious behavior were administered to a cross section of 938 metropolitan area adults, Lindenthal and colleagues found psychopathology to be negatively correlated with church affiliation, church attendance, and increased church attendance at times of crisis. A 1971 study by Burgess and Wagner provides an interesting twist on the relationship between mental disorder and religious belief and practice. Their findings indicate that "members of certain religions and denominations are disproportionately extruded to public mental hospitals" (p. 239). We are left to wonder whether these persons are pushed into hospitals because these denominations are somehow unable to deal with the psychological problems of their membership or whether the teachings and practices of these particular denominations somehow bring on mental illness. Burgess and Wagner provided no definitive answers but called for further research to consider if religion is a potentially precipitative condition of mental illness on the one hand, or if it is a major community mental health resource on the other.

In 1959 Argyle, after reviewing the empirical evidence available, concluded that there is little evidence to support the notions that religion ever causes mental disorders or that religion prevents such disorders. A study by Srole and colleagues (1962) showed more

mental impairment among nonreligious persons as well as some religious subgroups, but less impairment in some other religious sub-
groups.

In a 1987 study that included correlational questionnaire research, Bergin, Masters, and Richards found that religiosity is related to "normality" and is not indicative of emotional disturbance.
They further asserted that they are able to refute the theory that devout religiousness is the equivalent to emotional disturbance as
postulated by Ellis (1980).

Doctrinal Beliefs and Psychopathology

Are the doctrinal beliefs of certain religions or specific Christian
denominations more likely to be associated with psychopathology?
MacDonald and Luckett (1983) examined the relationship between
the religious affiliation and psychopathology of clients at a midwest-
ern psychiatric clinic and found that when under emotional stress
members of major religious groups (i.e., Catholic, Protestant, etc.)
actually seem to experience psychiatric disorders differently. Those
who reported no religious preference were more likely to exhibit
substance abuse and paranoid schizophrenia, as well as socially aggressive and hostile behaviors. Non-mainline Protestants tended to
exhibit neuroses such as anxiety, explosive personality, depression,
and obsessive-compulsive personality disorder. Mainline Protestants tended to exhibit personality disorders and anxiety disorders
such as phobias. Catholics tended to exhibit obsessive-compulsive
personality disorder, hysterical personality disorder, and explosive
personality disorder. MacDonald and Luckett also provided a helpful summary of the research on religious affiliation and mental
status.

Sheehan and Kroll (1990) also studied the belief of psychiatric
patients that sin as well as general health factors might be the cause
of their illnesses. Matthews, Larson, and Barry (1993) noted that
most psychiatric patients in this sample attributed their illnesses
to "general health factors" (p. 263) such as exercise, proper diet,

and the weather, although a smaller group of patients did cite personal sin as the cause of their illnesses. This group (10 percent of the entire sample) was more likely to be female and less likely to be depressed.

In 1986, Cothran and Harvey published a study of the religious correlates of delusional thinking among psychotics. Of interest is the finding that while delusional patients reported high levels of religiosity they also reported "less identification with fundamental beliefs and less support for organized religion than nondelusional patients and normals" (p. 197). This discrepancy between self-ratings of high religiosity and lack of support for doctrinal beliefs was not found in the control group. This result calls into question the notion that psychotic delusions have as their source such factors as religious fundamentalism or other expressions of intense religiosity. Likewise, Francis and Pearson (1985) reported a strong negative correlation between psychoses and religiosity.

Fitz (1990) has written a helpful review of religious and familial factors in the etiology of obsessive-compulsive disorder. He observed that previous studies of obsessive-compulsive disorder had focused on demographic religious factors in analyzing the disease's etiology, but had failed to adequately recognize the multidimensional nature of religious experience.

A possible link between doctrinal beliefs and mental illness is also illustrated in the research of Spencer (1975), who examined the records of all 7,546 inpatients at West Australian psychiatric hospitals. During a thirty-six month period, he found that the ratio of psychiatrically hospitalized Jehovah's Witnesses was nearly twice that of the general population. He further found that the incidence of schizophrenia among Jehovah's Witnesses was about three times as high as for the general population, while paranoid schizophrenia occurred four times as often. Spencer hypothesized that for persons with "extreme religious views" such as those of the Witnesses, the role of religion in preserving the ego and silencing anxiety was somehow bypassed and he speculated that ". . . either the Jehovah's Witnesses sect tends to attract an excess of pre-psychotic individu-

als who may then break down, or else being a Jehovah's Witness is itself a stress which may precipitate a psychosis" (p. 558).

In 1955, Ranck found that while authoritarianism was related to
religious ideology, psychological adjustment as measured by the
Bell Inventory and some of the MMPI Sub-scales was not related to
religious ideology. Hence, specific religious beliefs were found to be
unrelated to psychopathological symptomatology. Rather, beliefs
were found to be primarily a cultural phenomenon.

Groesch and Davis (1997) found that being religious seemed to
influence the MMPI scores of psychiatric patients with respect to
diagnosis, religion, and age. Four groups (eighteen subjects per
group) were randomly selected from the psychiatric population of a
Veterans Administration hospital. All were under sixty years of age,
and there were no significant differences in education among the
four groups. The groups consisted of Protestant schizophrenics,
Protestant drug dependents, Catholic schizophrenics, and Catholic
drug dependents.

In a descriptive study, Buckalew (1978) reported finding an interesting relationship between mental disorders and various Christian denominations. Some denominations tended to be under-
represented while others were over-represented with respect to
specific mental disorders. For example, Buckalew reported low incidences of neuroses among Catholics and Methodists. He also
found a low frequency of personality disorders, drug abuse, and
addiction among members of Episcopalian, Presbyterian, and
Church of God denominations. Alternatively, he found higher proportions of schizophrenia among Catholics, Episcopalians, and
Presbyterians. He also found higher proportions of psychosis among
members of fundamentalist denominations such as Baptist and
Pentecostal.

Earlier, McAllister and Vander Veldt (1961) had studied factors
pertaining to mental illness among Roman Catholic priests, and
discovered that clergy "had notably greater difficulty accepting hos-
pitalization and treatment" (p. 87) than did lay people. A large percentage of clergy subjects also reported psychiatric problems prior
to ordination.

Similarly, when Jansen, Garvey, and Bonk (1972) analyzed the personality characteristics of clergy entering training at a state psychiatric hospital, they observed that the Personal Orientation Inventory scores of these ministers differed "significantly" from a normal adult sample. The clergy sample scored lower "on scales measuring degree of adherence to the values of self-actualizing people and existentiality (flexibility in the application of values), and acceptance of personal feelings of anger or aggression" (p. 1972).

In 1981, Carr and Hauser investigated the possible correlation between religious participation, denomination, authoritarianism, and psychiatric symptomatology. In fact, no correlation was discovered between authoritarianism and religious participation and denomination, nor was religion related to psychiatric symptomatology. Lower position in the class order was found to be "a strong determinant of psychiatric symptomatology," but no support was found for the "essential hypotheses that make up Marx and Freud's theory of religion, authoritarianism, and psychiatric symptomatology" (p. 139).

Alternatively, when Hasson and Khalique (1981) analyzed the relationship between religiosity and personality variables in a sample of 480 Muslim and Hindu college students from Ranchi University, Ranchi, India, they found religiosity to be positively related with "anxiety, authoritarianism, rigidity, and intolerance of ambiguity" (p. 133). The authors developed a religiosity scale that included as content areas faith in God and religion; religious values, conventions, and traditions; and adherence to religious rituals and praying. Hasson and Khalique found that Muslims tended to have a higher degree of religiosity than Hindus. They speculated that "religiosity among Muslims may be related to their minority status and subjective feelings of insecurity and anxiety created by the frequent communal riots" (p. 133).

In a study of 268 undergraduate students, P. S. Richards (1991) concluded that his findings did not support Ellis's (1980) hypothesis that religiously devout and orthodox persons are more emotionally disturbed than less religious persons. Richards's study examined the relationship between religious orientation and mental health. His study included measures of devoutness, depression, shame, guilt, and existential well-being. Richards found that more devout students were not more depressed than less devout students, they were not more prone to shame, and they were no more likely to see themselves as flawed or worthless when they make a mistake or violate their ethical code. They were, however, more prone to guilt, although the levels were not pathological.

Religiosity and Depression

Psychology has "preached" that religiosity in general, and certain religious doctrines that emphasize sin and guilt in particular, inevitably lead to negative psychological consequences such as depression, excessive anger, and repression. For example, Brandon (1969) in his book, *The Psychology of Self Esteem,* contended that "the religious doctrine of original sin . . . is disastrously harmful psychologically" (p. 221). He described the Christian belief in sin as a monstrous injustice and a profound perversion of morality. However, Gartner, Larson, and Allen (1991) concluded that "the preponderance of evidence suggest that religiosity is associated with lower levels of depression" (p. 11). They cited four studies that found a negative relationship between religious commitment and depression (Brown and Lowe, 1951; Hertsgaard and Light, 1984; Mayo, Puryear, and Richek, 1969; McClure and Loden, 1982).

Research by Watson, Hood, Foster, and Morris (1988) on sin, depression, and narcissism has produced interesting findings as well. For example, measures of religious orientation, sin-related beliefs, depression, and narcissism were obtained from students at a state university and at a private Pentecostal college. Watson and colleagues reported that "intrinsic religiosity and associated sin-related beliefs were correlated with less depression and less narcissistic exploitiveness while extrinsic religiosity appeared as a largely maladjusted orientation" (p. 295). Partial correlational evidence also indicated that sin-related beliefs quite possibly exert positive influences apart from intrinsicness. As is noted in the study, empirical results such as these challenge the popular notion that "sin-related beliefs necessarily promote an unhealthy view of the self" (p. 295).

A study by Koenig and colleagues (1997) analyzed a sample of four thousand persons aged sixty-five and over and discovered that frequency of church attendance was positively related to physical health and negatively related to depression. Frequent church goers were about half as likely to be depressed. Private prayer/Bible reading was negatively correlated with physical health and positively correlated with social support, but unrelated to depression. Religious TV/radio listening was unrelated to social support, negatively related to good physical health, and unexpectedly, positively associated with depression.

Wilson (1998) examined the relationship between religion and depression and concluded that while religious experience may trigger a manic episode or play a role in the onset of major depression, nonetheless, religious beliefs do not cause either mania or depression. Wilson maintains that while religion can play a prominent role in depression, "religious beliefs, however, are not etiologic in either mania or depression" (p. 186)."

Grace and Guilt

Watson, Morris, and Hood (1988) turned their attention to the relationship between grace, guilt, and psychological adjustment. "Grace" is a theological term with a variety of connotations. Historically the term has been defined as "unmerited favor," an undeserved blessing freely bestowed on persons by God and a symbol of God's continuing care for His creation. According to theologian Philip E. Hughes (1984), grace is "that which restrains human society from being all together intolerable and ungovernable, and makes it possible for mankind, though fallen, to live together in a generally orderly and cooperative manner, to show mutual forbearance, and to cultivate together the scientific, cultural and economic pursuits of civilization" (p. 480). "It is important always to remember that the operation of God's grace is a deep mystery that is far beyond our limited human comprehension" (p. 482). Watson and colleagues (1998) developed "The Grace Scale" for their study, which "measured orthodox understandings of forgiveness" (p. 272). They concluded that while ideas about guilt may contribute to anxiety, "orthodox notions concerning grace have at least some positive consequences" (p. 278), including less depression and less hopelessness.

In a review of religion and mental health, Payne and colleagues (1991) found little evidence supporting religious influence in the prevention of serious clinical diagnoses like bipolar disorder, major depression, schizophrenia, obsessions, and panic disorders. They concluded therefore that "religious affiliation is not damaging to mental health, nor is it entirely predictive of better mental health." There is now widespread consensus in the field of psychopathology that psychotic illnesses are largely biological in origin and therefore, according to Wilson (1998), "it follows logically that religion could not play a major role in the etiology of schizophrenia, the major affective disorders, delirium, dementia, or other illness with psychotic symptoms" (p. 163). Wilson concluded that religion is but one of the important cultural factors that affect the content of symptoms.

References

Allison, J. (1967). "Adaptive Regression and Intense Religious Experiences." *The Journal of Nervous and Mental Disease, 145*(6), 452–463.

Argyle, M. (1959). *Religious Behavior.* Glencoe, IL: The Free Press.

Armstrong, R.C., Larsen, G. L., and Mourer, S. A. (1962). "Religious Attitudes and Emotional Adjustment." *Journal of Psychological Studies, 13*(1), 35–47.

Bergin, A. E. (1983). "Religiosity and Mental Health: A Critical Reevaluation and Meta-Analysis." *Professional Psychology: Research and Practice, 14*(2), 170–184.

Bergin, A. E., Masters, K. S., and Richards, P. S. (1987). "Religiousness and Mental Health Reconsidered: A Study of an Intrinsically Religious Sample." *Journal of Counseling Psychology, 34*(2), 197–204.

Bergin, A. E., Stinchfield, R. D., Gaskin, T. A., Masters, K. S., and Sullivan, C. E. (1988). "Religious Life-Styles and Mental Health: An Exploratory Study." *Journal of Counseling Psychology, 35*(1), 91–98.

Bishop, L. C., Larson, D. B., and Wilson, W. P. (1987). "Religious Life of Individuals with Affective Disorders." *Southern Medical Journal*, *80*(9), 1083–1086.

Brandon, N. (1969). *Psychology of Self Esteem*. New York: Bantam.

Brown, D. G., and Lower, W. L. (1951). "Religious Beliefs and Personality Characteristics of College Students." *Journal of Social Psychology*, *33*, 103–129.

Buckalew, L. W. (1978). "A Descriptive Study of Denominational Concomitants in Psychiatric Diagnosis." *Social Behavior and Personality*, *6*(2), 239–242.

Burgess, J. H., and Wagner, R. L. (1971). "Religion as a Factor in Extrusion to Public Mental Hospitals." *Journal for the Scientific Study of Religion*, *10*, 237–240.

Carr, L. G., and Hauser, W. J. (1981). "Class, Religious Participation and Psychiatric Symptomology." *International Journal of Social Psychiatry*, *27*, 133–142.

Cothran, M. M., and Harvey, P. D. (1986). "Delusional Thinking in Psychotics: Correlates of Religious Content." *Psychological Reports*, *58*, 191–199.

Ellis, A. (1980). "Psychotherapy and Atheistic Values: A Response to A. E. Bergin's 'Psychotherapy and Religious Values.'" *Journal of Consulting and Clinical Psychology*, *48*, 635–639.

Fitz, A. (1990). "Religious and Familial Factors in Etiology of Obsessive-Compulsive Disorder: A Review." *Journal of Psychology and Theology*, *18*(2), 141–147.

Francis, L. J., and Pearson, P. R. (1985). "Psychoticism and Religiosity Among 15-Year-Olds." *Personality and Individual Differences*, *6*(3), 397–398.

Galanter, M., Larson, D., and Rubenstone, E. (1991). "Christian Psychiatry: The Impact of Evangelical Belief on Clinical Practice." *American Journal of Psychiatry*, *148*(1), 90–95.

Gallemore, J. L., Wilson, W. P., and Rhoads, J. M. (1969). "The Religious Life of Patients with Affective Disorders." *Diseases of the Nervous System*, *30*(7), 483–486.

Gartner, J., Larson, D. B., and Allen, G. D. (1991). "Religious Commitment and Mental Health: A Review of the Empirical Literature." *Journal of Psychology and Theology*, *19*(1), 6–25.

Groesch, S. J., and Davis, W. E. (1997). "Psychiatric Patients' Religion and MMPI Responses." *Journal of Clinical Psychology*, *33*(1), 168–171.

Hassan, M. K., and Khalique, A. (1981). "Religiosity and Its Correlates in College Students." *Journal of Psychological Researches*, *25*(3), 129–136.

Hertsgaard, D., and Light, H. (1984). "Anxiety, Depression, and Hostility in Rural Women." *Psychological Reports*, *55*, 673–674.

Hughes, P. E. (1984). "Grace." In W. A. Elwell (Ed.), *Evangelical Dictionary of Theology* (pp. 479–482). Grand Rapids, MI: Baker Book House.

Jansen, D. G., Garvey, F. J., and Bonk, E. C. (1972). "Personality Characteristics of Clergymen Entering a Clinical Training Program at a State Hospital." *Psychological Reports*, *31*, 878.

Koenig, H. G., Hays, J. C., George, L. K., Blazer, D. G., Larson, D. B., and Lander-
man, L. R. (1997). "Modeling the Cross-Sectional Relationships Between Religion, Physical Health, Social Support, and Depressive Symptoms." *The
American Journal of Geriatric Psychiatry*, *5*, 131–144.

Kroll, J., and Sheehan, W. (1989). "Religious Beliefs and Practices Among
52 Psychiatric Inpatients in Minnesota." *American Journal of Psychiatry*, *146*,
67–72.

Lindenthal, J. J., Myers, J. K., Pepper, M. P., and Stern, M. S. (1970). "Mental
Status and Religious Behavior." *Scientific Study of Religion*, *9*(2), 143–149.

Lowe, C. M., and Braaten, R. O. (1966). "Differences in Religious Attitudes in
Mental Illness." *Journal for the Scientific Study of Religion*, *5*(3), 435–445.

MacDonald, C. B., and Luckett, J. B. (1983). "Religious Affiliation and Psychiatric Diagnoses." *Journal for the Scientific Study of Religion*, *22*(1), 15–37.

Matthews, D. A., Larson, D. B., and Barry, C. P. (1993). *The Faith Factor: An Annotated Bibliography of Clinical Research on Spiritual Subjects*. Washington, DC:
National Institute for Healthcare Research.

Mayo, C. C., Puryear, H. B., and Richek, H. G. (1969). MMPI Correlates of Religiousness in Late Adolescent College Students." *Journal of Nervous and Mental
Disease*, *149*, 381–385.

McAllister, R. J., and Vander Veldt, A. (1961). "Factors in Mental Illness Among
Hospitalized Clergy." *Journal of Nervous and Mental Disease*, *132*, 80.

McClure, R. F., and Loden, M. (1982). "Religious Activity, Denomination Membership and Life Satisfaction." *Psychology, A Quarterly Journal of Human Behavior*, *19*, 13–17.

Ness, R. C., and Wintrob, R. M. (1980). "The Emotional Impact of Fundamentalist Religious Participation: An Empirical Study of Intragroup Variation."
American Journal of Orthopsychiatry, *50*(2), 302–315.

Parker, M. S. (1977). "Dimensions of Religious Conversion During Adolescence." Ph.D. diss., State University of New York at Buffalo, 1977. Abstract in
Dissertation Abstracts International 38 (1978): 3371-B (University Microfilms
no. 72-27, 510).

Payne, I. R., Bergin, A. E., Bielema, K. A., and Jenkins, P. H. (1991). "Review of
Religion and Mental Health: Prevention and the Enhancement of Psychosocial Functioning." *Prevention in Human Services*, *9*(2), 11–40.

Ranck, J. G. (1955). "Some Personality Correlates of Religious Attitudes and Beliefs." *Dissertation Abstracts*, *15*, 878–879.

Richards, P. S. (1991). "Religious Devoutness in College Students: Relations with
Emotional Adjustment and Psychological Separation from Parents." *Journal
of Counseling Psychology*, *38*(2), 189–196.

Roberts, B. H., and Myers, J. K. (1954). "Religion, National Origin, Immigration,
and Mental Illness." *American Journal of Psychiatry*, *110*, 759–764.

Sheehan, W., and Kroll, J. (1990). "Psychiatric Patients' Belief in General Health Factors and Sin as Causes of Illness." *American Journal Psychiatry, 147,* 112–113.

Spencer, J. (1975). "The Mental Health of Jehovah's Witnesses." *British Journal of Psychiatry, 126,* 556–559.

Srole, L., Larger, T., Michael, S. T., Opler, M. K., and Rennie, T. A. (1962). *Mental Health in the Metropolis* (vol. 1). New York: McGraw-Hill.

Stanley, G. (1965). "Personality and Attitude Correlates of Religious Conversion." *Journal for the Scientific Study of Religion, 4,* 60–63.

Stark, R. (1971). "Psychopathology and Religious Commitment." *Review of Religious Research, 12*(3), 165–175.

Ullman, C. (1988). "Psychological Well-Being Among Converts in Traditional and Nontraditional Religious Groups." *Psychiatry, 51,* 312–322.

Watson, P. J., Hood, R. W., Jr., Foster, S. G., and Morris, R. J. (1988). "Sin, Depression, and Narcissism." *Review of Religious Research, 25,* 295–305.

Watson, P. J., Morris, R. J., and Hood, R. W., Jr. (1988). "Sin and Self-Functioning, Part 2: Grace, Guilt, and Psychological Adjustment." *Journal of Psychology and Theology, 16*(3), 270–281.

Watson, P. J., Morris, R. J., and Hood, R. W., Jr. (1989). "Sin and Self-Functioning, Part 4: Depression, Assertiveness, and Religious Commitment." *Journal of Psychology and Theology, 17*(1), 44–58.

Williams, R. L., and Cole, S. (1968). "Religiosity, Generalized Anxiety, and Apprehension Concerning Death." *Journal of Social Psychology, 75,* 111–117.

Wilson, W. P. (1998). "Religion and Psychoses." In H. G. Koenig (Ed.), *Handbook of Religion and Mental Health* (pp. 161–173). San Diego: Academic Press.

Wilson, W. P., Larson, D. B., and Meier, P. D. (1983). "Religious Life of Schizophrenics." *Southern Medical Journal, 76*(9), 1096–1100.

Witztum, E., Greenberg, D., and Dasberg, H. (1990). "Mental Illness and Religious Change." *British Journal of Medical Psychology, 63,* 33–41.

Wooton, R. J., and Allen, D. F. (1983). "Dramatic Religious Conversion and Schizophrenic Decompensation." *Journal of Religion and Health, 22,* 212–220.

6

Marital Satisfaction

THE FIRST MAJOR attempt to empirically examine a wide range of variables associated with marital success or failure came in 1939 with the publication of *Predicting Success or Failure in Marriage* by Burgess and Cottrell. The book cited studies that showed that religiosity, as measured by premarital participation in church activities, church membership prior to and during marriage, the sanctioning of marriage by the church, and regular church attendance, is associated with success in marriage. In another of the earliest studies dealing with religiosity and marital satisfaction, Kirkpatrick (1937) looked at the religious preferences of well-adjusted and poorly adjusted married couples and concluded that religious preference has very little effect on the marital relationship. Since then, researchers have continued to explore the relationship between religiosity and marital satisfaction.

In 1938, Terman studied the relationship between religious training and marital happiness in a sample of one thousand persons. He concluded that there appeared to be a curvilinear relationship in which either too much or too little religious training might affect negatively the happiness of married people, while a moderate amount of religious training appeared to be more likely to correlate with marital happiness.

Burchinal set out to revisit the matter in a study that examined marital satisfaction and religious behavior in 1957. His study sought to test the hypothesis that husbands and wives who are church members or who attend church regularly have significantly higher marital satisfaction than husbands and wives who are not church members or who do not attend church regularly. While he did find that the marital satisfaction scores for both husbands and wives who were church members or who attended church regularly or occasionally were consistently higher than the scores for the husbands and wives who were not church members or who did not attend church, the results failed to reach the level of statistical significance. In a 1960 study, Gurin, Veroff, and Fell also found a positive relationship between church attendance and general happiness as well as marital happiness.

In 1962 Carey, using data from the National Opinion Research Center of the University of Chicago, measured 2,753 Catholics who were between the ages of twenty-three and fifty-seven. Carey (1966) found evidence that supported Burchinal's hypothesis of a positive linear relationship between religious behavior and marital satisfaction. Carey found that devotional practices, ethical attitudes, and religiosity related to the general happiness of married Catholic men and women.

Shrum (1980) set out to assess the influence of religious factors such as religious commitment and religious affiliation on marital stability in the 1970s. Using the 1972–1977 General Social Survey (GSS), conducted by the National Opinion Research Center, Shrum examined a sample of 3,143 adults and found that the relationship between religiosity and marital instability did not change, by which he concluded that "the strength of the relationship between religiosity and instability does not depend on religious affiliation" (p. 135).

Roth investigated the relationship between spiritual well-being and marital adjustment in a 1988 study. This study differs from others in that it attempted to measure spiritual well-being rather than religiosity. Roth defined spiritual well-being as an aspect of one's internal orientation, that "religious and existential orientation which has been well integrated into the inner fiber of the person" (p. 153). Religiosity is generally taken to mean church attendance, denominational affiliation, involvement in church activities, and financial support of church activities. Roth drew a sample of ninety

women and fifty-seven men from three southern California United
Methodist and Baptist churches. She found that for church atten-
ders, spiritual well-being is related to their perception of marital
adjustment. She also found that a rise in spiritual well-being was
frequently accompanied by a similar rise in marital adjustment. She
concluded that there was "empirical support for the hypothesis that
spiritual well-being is an important factor in the perception of marital happiness" (p. 158).

Gruner (1985) hypothesized that the greater the reported number of private religious practices of a devotional nature (specifically
Bible reading and prayer at home), the better the marital adjustment would be. A sample of 208 couples was drawn from four
religious categories: sect, evangelical, liberal, and institutional/
authoritarian. Gruner defined sect as those congregations that are
Pentecostal, including the Assemblies of God and the Four Square
Church. "Evangelical" was defined as conservative churches including Southern and Conservative Baptists, the Nazarenes, and
the Bible and Orthodox Presbyterians. "Liberal" was defined as
the mainline denominations including United Church of Christ,
Methodist, and Lutheran. "Institutional/authoritarian" was limited
to the Roman Catholic Church. Gruner found a positive relationship
between marital adjustment and prayer for all groups. However,
prayer seemed to have the most meaning in terms of marital adjustment for those who are members of the sect and evangelical groups
and the least meaning for members of the liberal group. Bible reading as a substantive religious practice is positively related to good
marital adjustment for the sect and evangelical groups, but the relationship does not exist for the liberal and Catholic groups. The authors conclude that "private religious practices (prayer and Bible
reading) are perceived by sect and evangelical members as highly
important to their handling of marital problems" (p. 57).

Larson and Goltz (1989) examined the relationship between religiosity and marital commitment and found that church attendance
was a major predictor of marital commitment. Larson and Goltz
speculated that the relationship between religious preference and
marital commitment includes the reality that religion serves as a

powerful barrier to leaving marriages and they contended that, "among non-religious couples there are simply fewer barriers to leaving their marriages and they likely sense fewer constraints to stay" (p. 396). The researchers asserted that husbands who are religious conservatives and who are more active in the church are more likely to stay in a marriage, "their feeling of love notwithstanding" (p. 396). Alternatively, they suggested that husbands who are active church members may try harder to make the marriage work.

In a particularly interesting article, Schumm and colleagues (1982) explored the issue of "marital conventionalization" as an explanation for the religiosity-marital satisfaction relationship. Marital conventionalization is defined as the tendency for people to inflate their level of marital adjustment by reporting that their marriages are better and happier than they actually are. Schumm asked whether marital conventionalization might actually explain away the relationship between religiosity and marital satisfaction and found the answer to be inconclusive.

Wilson and Filsinger (1986) conducted a study using a sample of 190 married couples and found support for a broad-based relationship between martial adjustment and religiosity. Specifically, they found that religious ritualism, which they defined as religious experience and religious belief, was related to marital adjustment. The higher the ritualistic involvement, the higher the reported religious experience, and the more conservative the beliefs of the couple, the greater the marital adjustment, including marital consensus, marital satisfaction, and marital cohesion, but interestingly, not marital affection. The 190 couples were white and drawn from a southwestern metropolitan area. They represented Baptist, Nazarene, Charismatic, Seventh-Day Adventist, Methodist, Presbyterian, Lutheran, and Congregational churches.

Recent studies continue to show a relationship between religiosity and marital satisfaction. Kunz and Albrecht (1977) studied the impact of religion on marital stability by examining a range of indicators of marital satisfaction including absence of divorce, willingness to marry the same spouse again, and an absence of disagreement over a range of marital roles. Using a sample of 2,227 adults from the state of Utah, the authors found that church attendance is positively associated with family stability as measured by intact marriages. They further concluded that church attendance is also strongly associated with a willingness to remarry the same spouse again and a decided absence of conflict over central marital roles. Because the study was conducted in Utah, it is reasonable to conclude that a high percentage of those in the sample are Mormon, which may affect the general applicability of the findings.

According to Landis (1963), because religiosity is associated with a general reluctance to divorce, even when people are unhappy in their marriages, it seems possible that religiosity might enhance the likelihood that a marriage would be successful but decrease the probability that at any one time the person would be in a successful marriage. Glenn and Weaver (1978) also noted that some of the positive relationships found in the research between religiosity and marital success are at least partially "spurious" due to a tendency for more conventional people to inflate both their church attendance and their degree of marital happiness. Glenn and Weaver noted that there seems to be "near consensus, at least among authors of family textbooks, that marital happiness varies directly with all four of these variables" (p. 270), the variables being age at marriage, husband's occupational level, family income, and frequency of church attendance. According to Glenn and Weaver, the relationship is causal and not spurious.

Religion and Divorce

The research is clear in its finding that religion operates as a powerful deterrent to divorce. In the 1960s, the divorce rate in the United States began to rise rapidly so much so that 53 percent of American families are now single-parent families. While there is now some indication that the divorce rate may have leveled off, it nonetheless rose by 79 percent between 1970 and 1978. According to Shrum (1980), a variety of explanations have been advanced to explain the increase in divorce, including both the increased influence of the feminist movement, as well as reduced legal and economic barriers to divorce. Religious factors have also been offered to explain this phenomenon. Religious explanations include the assertion of a general decline in religious commitment, various changes in the character of various belief systems, and a blurring vision of differences between Catholicism and Protestantism. Contributions to churches, the value of construction of church buildings, the number of religious books published, and the level of church membership are other factors cited to support the contention that there has been a general decline in religiosity in the United States in the last thirty years. In fact, Wuthnow (1976) cited a decline in church attendance in the United States during the 1960s and 1970s. Gallup polls indicate that in 1967 only 2 percent of the American population reported no religious affiliation whereas in 1990 that figure had risen to 11 percent of the population surveyed. In 1937, 73 percent of the American population reported membership in a church or synagogue while in 1994 that figure had dropped to 70 percent. However, Gallup reports that across a fifty-five-year period from 1939 to 1994 the percentage of Americans who attend church at least weekly has remained remarkably constant at 41 percent in 1939 to 40 percent in 1994.

Kunz and Albrecht (1977) observed that some churches have made it very difficult for their members to dissolve their marriages and therefore low divorce rates may not be good indicators of actual happiness in marriage. Furthermore, they contended that for couples who have a conservative religious value system, divorce is clearly a moral issue of such magnitude that it may be more important to tolerate an unhappy marriage than to terminate it.

For our purposes, the theoretical implications are clear. If religiosity inhibits divorce then presumably a decline in religiosity would suggest an increase in divorce rates. Alternatively, an increase in divorce rates may suggest a decline in religiosity. Furthermore, if churches become more "liberal" in their approach to traditional, social, and moral teachings, including the sanctity of marriage, one would anticipate an increase in the divorce rate. Thus, there may be high levels of religiosity, which would not necessarily be incompatible with justifying the delusion of a happy marriage. Finally, there has been a decline in Catholic religiosity, as some have suggested, particularly since the Second Vatican Council, which has had the effect of blurring the denominational distinctions between Protestantism and Catholicism, and may be related to an increase in the divorce rate among Catholics.

Shrum (1980) set out to assess the influence of religious factors such as religious commitment and religious affiliation on marital stability in the 1970s. He sought to understand whether the decline in marriage stability as measured by increased divorce rates was related to what he believed to be a general decline in institutional religiosity. Using the 1972–1977 General Social Survey (GSS) conducted by the National Opinion Research Center, Shrum examined a sample of 3,143 adults and found that the decline in church attendance was not related to an increased likelihood to be separated from one's spouse. He concluded that these findings discredit the notion of a changing relationship between religiosity and marital stability "at least during the 1970s" (p. 144). He further concluded that the strength of the relationship between religiosity and marital instability does not depend on religious affiliation. Shrum cited Bumpass and Sweet (1972), who found the difference between Protestants and Catholics and rates of separation to be just 3 percentage points, leading him to conclude that "it is plausible that differences in probabilities of divorce by religion have evened out and other factors have gained in relative importance as affiliation matters less" (p. 144).

References

Bumpass, L. L., and Sweet, J. A. (1972). "Differentials in Marital Instability: 1970." *American Sociological Review, 37,* 754–766.1

Burchinal, L. G. (1957). "Marital Satisfaction and Religious Behavior." *American Sociological Review,* 22(3), 306–310.

Bureau of Census. (1978). *Marital Status and Living Arrangement: March 1977.* (Current Population Reports, Series P-20, No. 323). Washington, DC: U.S. Government Printing Office.

Bureau of Census. (1995). *Projections of the Numbers of Households and Families:*

1986—2000. (Current Population Reports, Series P-25, No. 986). Washington, DC: U.S. Department of Commerce.

Burgess, E. W., and Cottrell, L. S. (1939). *Predicting Success or Failure in Marriage.* New York: Prentice-Hall.

Carey, R. G. (1966). "Religion and Happiness in Marriage." *The Review of Religious Research, 8,* 104—112.

Croake, J., and Lyon, R. (1987). "Religion and Measured Marital Adjustment in Army Aviation Officers." *Psychological Reports, 60,* 722.

Gallup, George Jr., and Davies, J. O. III. (1971). *1977—8 Religion in America.* The Gallup Opinion Index.

Glenn, N. D., and Weaver, C. N. (1978). "A Multivariate, Multisurvey Study of Marital Happiness." *Journal of Marriage and the Family, 40,* 269—282.

Gruner, L. (1985). "The Correlation of Private, Religious Devotional Practices and Marital Adjustment." *Journal of Comparative Family Studies, 16*(1), 47—59.

Gurin, G., Veroff, J., and Fell, S. (1960). *Americans View Their Mental Health.* New York: Basic Books.

Kirkpatrick, C. (1937). "Factors in Marital Adjustment." *American Journal of Sociology, 43,* 270.

Kunz, P. R., and Albrecht, S. L. (1977). "Religion, Marital Happiness, and Divorce." *International Journal of Sociology of the Family, 7,* 227—232.

Landis, J. T. (1963). "Social Correlates of Divorce or Non-Divorce Among the Unhappy Married." *Marriage and Family Living, 25,* 178—180.

Larson, L. E., and Goltz, J. W. (1989). "Religious Participation and Marital Commitment." *Review of Religious Research, 30*(4), 387—400.

Prentice Religious Research Center. (1990). *Emerging Trends.* Prentice, NJ: Gallop Poll.

Roth, P. D. (1988). "Spiritual Well-Being and Marital Adjustment." *Journal of Psychology and Theology, 16*(2), 153—158.

Schumm, W. R., Bollman, S. R., and Jurich, A. P. (1982). "The 'Marital Conventionalization' Argument: Implications for the Study of Religiosity and Marital Satisfaction." *Journal of Psychology and Theology, 10*(3), 236—241.

Shrum, W. (1980). "Religion and Marital Instability: Change in the 1970s?" *Review of Religious Research, 21*(2), 135—147.

Terman, L. M. (1938). *Psychological Factors in Marital Adjustment.* New York: McGraw-Hill.

Wilson, M. R., and Filsinger, E. E. (1986). "Religiosity and Marital Adjustment: Multidimensional Interrelationships." *Journal of Marriage and the Family, 48,* 147—151.

Wuthnow, R. (1976). "Recent Patterns of Secularization: A Problem of Generations?" *American Sociological Review, 41,* 850—867.

Bibliography

Bahr, Howard M., and Bruce A. Chadwick. "Religion and Family in Middletown, USA." *Journal of Marriage and the Family* 47, no. 2 (1985): 407–414.

Brutz, Judith L, and Craig M. Allen. "Religious Commitment, Peace Activism, and Marital Violence in Quaker Families." *Journal of Marriage and the Family* 48, no. 3 (1986): 491–502.

Chi, S. K., and K. Houseknecht. "Protestant Fundamentalism and Marital Success: A Comparative Approach." *Sociology and Social Research* 69 (1985): 351–374.

De Neuter, Patrick. "Amour, Sexualité et Religion." *Social Compass* 19 (1972–1973): 365–387.

Dragastin, S. "The Religious Factor in the Structure of Psychological Well-Being." Ph.D. diss., University of Chicago, 1968.

Dudley, Margaret G., and Frederick Kosinski, Jr. "Religiosity and Marital Satisfaction: A Research Note." *Review of Religious Research* 32, no. 1 (September 1990): 78–86.

Filsinger, Erik E., and Margaret R. Wilson. "Religiosity, Socio-economic Rewards, and Family Development: Predictors of Marital Adjustment." *Journal of Marriage and the Family* 46 (1984): 663–670.

Finkelhor, David, Gerald T. Hotaling, I. A. Lewis, et al. "Sexual Abuse and Its Relationship to Later Sexual Satisfaction, Marital Status, Religion and Attitudes." *Journal of Interpersonal Violence* 4, no. 4 (1989): 379–399.
Data analysis supported by funds from the National Center on Child Abuse and Neglect.

Flynn, Ellen E. "Relation of Marital Satisfaction to Transcendent Values and Religious Beliefs in Married Persons." *Dissertation Abstracts International* 48, 11-B (May 1988): 3413.

Hartley, Shirley Foster. "Marital Satisfaction Among Clergy Wives." *Review of Religious Research* 19, no. 2 (Winter, 1978): 178–191.

Hendrick, Susan S., and Clyde Hendrick. "Love and Sex Attitudes and Religious Beliefs." *Journal of Social and Clinical Psychology* 5, no. 3 (1987): 391–398.

Hunt, Richard A., and Morton B. King. "Religiosity and Marriage." *Journal for the Scientific Study of Religion* 17, no. 4 (1978): 399–406.

Johnson, Barry L., Susan Eberly, James T. Duke, et al. "Wives' Employment Status and Marital Happiness of Religious Couples." *Review of Religious Research* 29, no. 3 (1988): 259–270.

Leong, S. B. "Religious Well-Being and Marital Satisfaction Among North American Married Couples of Chinese and European Descent." Ph.D. diss., California Graduate School of Family Psychology, 1990.

Martin, John D., Garland E. Blair, Robert Nevels, and Joyce H. Fitzpatrick. "A Study of the Relationship of Styles of Loving and Marital Happiness." *Psychological Reports* 66 (1990): 123–128.

Matthews, Dale A., and David B. Larson. *A Bibliography of Research by Scientists on Spiritual Subjects.* Philadelphia: John Templeton Foundation, 1991.

McCarthy, J. "Religious Commitment, Affiliation and Marriage Dissolution." In *The Religious Dimension: New Directions in Quantitative Research,* edited by R. Wuthnow, 179–197. New York: Academic, 1979.

Moore, Rosemary. "The Relationship of Religious Beliefs and Values to Adult Adjustment Among Separated and Divorced Roman Catholics." *Dissertation Abstracts International* 49, 4-A (October 1988): 734.

Ortega, Suzanne T., Hugh P. Whitt, and Jallen William. "Religious Homogamy and Marital Happiness." *Journal of Family Issues* 9, no. 2 (1988): 224–239.

Patton, M. S. "Suffering and Damage in Catholic Sexuality." *Journal of Religion and Health* 27, no. 2 (1988): 129–142.

Payne, Barbara P. "Sex and the Elderly: The Religious Response." *Journal of Religion and Aging* 3, no. 1–2 (1986): 165–176.

Rekers, G. A., D. B. Larson, S. White, M. Waller, S. Fields, and J. S. Lyons. "Systematic Analyses: Lack of Attention to Religious Variables in Sex and Marital Journals." Paper presented at the International Congress on Christian Counseling, Atlanta, GA, November 1988.

Schumm, Walter R. "Religiosity and Marital Satisfaction: Can Marital Conventionalization Explain Away the Relationship?" *Journal of Psychology and Christianity* 1, no. 2 (1982): 16—21.

Schumm, Walter R., Felix C. Obiorah, and Benjamin Silliman. "Marital Quality as a Function of Conservative Religious Identification in a Sample of Protestant and Catholic Wives from the Midwest." *Psychological Reports* 64, no. 1 (1989): 124—126. Sponsored in part by the Kansas Agricultural Experimental Station.

Shehan, Constance L., E. Wilbur Bock, and Gary Lee. "Religious Heterogamy, Religiosity, and Marital Happiness: The Case of Catholics." *Journal of Marriage and the Family* 52, no. 1 (1990): 73—79.

Whitaker, R.G. "Comparison of Marital Adjustment and Spiritual Well-Being Among Couples in a Ministry Related Setting." Master's thesis, International School of Theology, 1985.

7

Suicide

SUICIDE HAS BEEN an issue for humanity from the beginning of time. Grollman (1988) traced the historical views on suicide in his helpful book, *Suicide: Prevention, Intervention, Postvention.* He noted that over the course of history attitudes toward suicide have sometimes been permissive and often times harshly restrictive. For example, the ancient Egyptians did not view suicide as a violation of either their spiritual or legal codes and Greek Stoicism suggested that if life became unbearable it could be appropriate to voluntarily withdraw from life by means of suicide. The Epicureans also taught that suicide could be an acceptable choice. Alternatively, Plato insisted that a principled person would find the courage to persist even in the face of great suffering and affliction. Socrates also argued that suicide could never be morally justified.

Historically religion has always played an important role in determining how society views suicide. According to Freedman (1992), the term "suicide" itself is a fairly recent development, which seems to have come into use in 1635. Previously the act of taking one's life had been described by such terms as "self-murder," "self-killing," and "self-slaughter." "The idea that suicide is both a sin and a crime is a relatively late Christian invention taking its impetus from Augustine" (p. 225). This view became canonized in church law in a series of church councils from the sixth and seventh centuries. A review of the biblical literature both from the perspective of the Hebrew Bible and the New Testament finds only six recorded cases of actual suicide.

The first reference is to Abimelech (Judg. 9:54). The second and third reference is to the story of King Saul who, when mortally wounded in a battle with the Philistines, begged his armor bearer to kill him. But his armor bearer refused and Saul took his sword and fell on it, his armor bearer following suit (1 Sam. 31:4–5). The next reference involves Ahithophel (2 Sam. 17:23). The fifth example is Zimri whose account can be found in 1 Kings 16:18. The last example is the story of Samson who deliberately brought the Philistine temple down on his head after being blinded (Judg. 16:29–30).

The New Testament provides only one example of suicide, the infamous story of Judas Iscariot, one of the twelve apostles, who betrayed Jesus for money, and who subsequently hung himself (Matt. 27:3–5).

According to Freedman, "the important point is that none of these biblical figures received censor," suggesting that the biblical literature does not condemn suicide in the same voice as the church after Augustine (p. 228). The only account in which an individual is depressed and considers death as a viable option is the story of Job, who was obviously depressed but who never did commit suicide.

At various times in church history, it has been difficult to distinguish between suicide and martyrdom. Even Paul himself, in Phil. 1:21–22, appears to struggle with the question of martyrdom. "For me to live is Christ and to die is gain. . . . Yet which I shall chose I can not tell." For Paul, clearly death was an option and seemed as a possible "gain" because it would bring him into immediate union with Christ. Nonetheless, even if Paul preferred death, he nevertheless chose life. Martyrdom became a theme of the early Christian era, with Tertullian writing, "We conquer by dying" (Freedman, p. 230).

Suicide came to be regarded as a strong taboo within the Jewish and Christian religions. Religious and community values were such that the taboo was often enforced with remarkable indignities visited upon the corpse of the person who committed suicide while surviving family members were left in disgrace.

For the early Christians, suicide was sometimes equated with martyrdom in that many early Christians apparently chose death in their eagerness to end their earthly ordeals so as to proceed to the joy of heaven. In the New Testament, however, the only reference to suicide is the acknowledgment of the death of Judas.

During the Christian era, it became normative to regard suicide as a hostile act against life itself. However, it was not until Augustine (1993) denounced suicide as a sin in the fourth or fifth century that the church took a position officially opposing suicide. In the thirteenth century, Aquinas (1991) condemned suicide for three reasons: (1) it was contrary to the sanctity of life, (2) it was a trespass against the community, and (3) it was a sin against God. Roman Catholic theology regards suicide as a mortal sin, depriving the soul of the chance of receiving eternal grace. Similarly, Dietrich Bonhoeffer, the great Lutheran pastor imprisoned and then executed by the Nazis, viewed suicide as a sin even in the context of the immense suffering of those extraordinarily bleak times.

In Western countries, theological and moral teachings about suicide found their way into criminal and civil law. For example, early English law penalized the survivors of suicide by confiscating their property. In England suicide was a felony and an unsuccessful suicide was punishable by imprisonment.

It does seem apparent that the prohibitions against suicide have been greatly moderated in the twentieth century. Both the moral and legal prohibitions against suicide have eroded due in part to the influence of social science theory and research. Researchers have wanted to have a better understanding of the dynamics of suicidal behavior, including psychopathological aspects that would lead to such an extreme behavior as suicide.

In attempting to explain suicide psychodynamically, Freud (1957) theorized that the death instinct, or what he called Thanatos, is an instinctual drive that leads to aggressive behavior, destruction, and death. Suicide, according to Freud, is murder of the self in the form of aggression turned against the self. Jung (1964), in contrast, believed that suicide could be explained as an unconscious longing for spiritual rebirth as well as an escape from intolerable living situations.

According to Horney (1950), suicide results from deep-rooted feelings of inferiority that lead to an overwhelming sense of failure in meeting the expectations of society. Menninger (1938), however, theorized that suicide is an extreme form of submission in which the person feels the need to be punished and thereby atone for behavior by being destroyed.

In their 1961 book, *The Cry for Help*, Faberow and Schneidman expanded the understanding of suicide to include other forms of self-destructive behavior such as substance abuse, abuse of prescription medication, criminal and delinquent behavior, and even high-risk sports such as skydiving, hang gliding, and motorcycle racing.

From a sociological perspective, Durkheim (1972), in his classic book on suicide originally published in 1877, stressed the importance of social context and religious integration in accounting for the self-destructive behavior that leads to suicide. According to Durkheim, most suicides are egoistic in that the individual becomes suicidal in reaction to his or her alienation from family, friends, and community. Durkheim's argument was that suicide rates are the highest in the communities in which social integration and social inhibitions are weakest. He observed that it was the Protestant communities that had higher suicide rates as opposed to Catholic communities, which were more structured in terms of promoting social and religious integration through more regulated expectations relative to standards of belief and practice.

Durkheim believed that subordination provides meaning and purpose to life. His theory of suicide was based on an integration model in which integration depends on the subordination of the person's needs, desires, and goals to those of the group. Examples of subordination include subordination to the family, to political causes, and to religion. Durkheim defined religious integration as revolving around shared beliefs and shared practices.

Durkheim examined the sociological context of Protestantism and Catholicism with specific attention given to the differences between the two with respect to belief and practice. He concluded that because Catholicism was more traditional, obligatory, and dogmatic it fostered more religious integration and thereby lowered suicide rates. Because Protestantism was less structured, less dogmatic, and had fewer common beliefs and practices than Catholicism, the suicide rates were commensurately higher for Protestants than for Catholics. Durkheim's one "law" stipulated a negative correlation between suicide rates and the size of the Catholic population; the greater the number of Catholics in a given community, the lower the suicide rate.

Stack (1983a), who has done a great deal of work on the relationship between religion and suicide, discounted somewhat the basis for Durkheim's conclusions. He nonetheless believed that it would be "premature to abandon the religious factor as a possible determinant of suicide" (p. 364).

Stack proposed an alternative theory to explain the impact of religion on suicide. His religious commitment theory includes three basic hypotheses: 1) the greater the religious commitment the lower the rate of suicide, 2) the greater the gender/labor force/equality the greater the suicide rate, and 3) the greater the level of industrialization, the greater the suicide rate.

For our purposes, his first hypothesis bears a fuller explanation. According to Stack, the number of shared beliefs and practices is not significant, rather it is the content of core beliefs and practices that may be a "powerful counteragent against suicide" (p. 364). Belief in an afterlife, particularly an afterlife that is a reward for enduring in the face of significant adversity, is an example of a significant core belief that would naturally have a counter-effect on suicide and thereby reduce the suicide rate accordingly.

Other core beliefs offered by Stack to demonstrate how religion can affect the suicide rate include increasing self-esteem, uniting against a common enemy (i.e., Satan), promoting a belief in prayer, and glorifying the suffering associated with poverty. Job is a biblical example of one who endures terrible suffering but nonetheless perseveres. Stack also contended that belief in a personal or responsive God who hears and answers prayers, particularly those prayers that might alleviate personal suffering, is a strong religious core belief that counteracts the impulse toward suicide.

Stack found that religious commitment is negatively related to the suicide rate. That is, the higher the religious commitment, the lower the suicide rate. He found, however, that the lower suicide rate was only applicable for women, "the group traditionally most committed to religion" (p. 362). It is also well established that more women than men attempt suicide while more men than women are "successful" in their attempts. Lethality of means has always explained the discrepancy, but perhaps religiosity is also a factor. In any case, Stack believed that his findings confirmed his theory that a high level of commitment to a limited number of life-preserving religious beliefs, values, and practices will lead to lower suicide rates.

Stack published another study in 1983 in which he examined the effect of the decline in organized religion, as measured by a decline in church attendance, on suicide rates and concluded that religion appears to be more closely associated with suicide than the rate of employment, "a control taken from one of the dominant paradigms on suicide" (p. 239). Stack found that while the rate of employment and military participation were significant, it is the decline in church attendance that is the primary factor associated with rising suicide rates.

Stack cited Comstock and Partridge's 1972 study, which systematically investigated the effect of church attendance on suicide by examining census data from a county in Maryland. Comstock and Partridge reported that adults who attended church once or more every week had a suicide rate that was less than half of those who did not attend church as regularly.

Stack (1980) also did a study in which he attempted to investigate the relationship between suicide and Catholicism using data from across the United States from the year 1970. This study, which he reported with some caution, hypothesized that while Catholic and Protestant teachings both prohibit suicide with similar passion, Protestants would have a higher suicide rate because Protestantism allows greater intellectual and social freedom than Catholicism. Stack then cited several studies from the early to mid twentieth century, which confirm Durkheim's thesis that Catholics have a lower suicide rate than Protestants. However, Stack concluded that "once we control for divorce, Catholicism has no independent influence on suicide" (p. 69). Stack suggested that because Catholic orthodoxy

has declined at a much greater pace than Protestant orthodoxy in recent years, the result is a convergence of Catholic and Protestant
"normative structure," which accounts for the lack of relationship
between Catholicism and suicide.

Stack and Wasserman (1992) called his approach the religious
commitment perspective, by which he contended that religion effectively lowers suicide risk by fostering commitment to a relatively
small number of core religious beliefs. In a recent study, Stack
hypothesized that churches that encourage social support and networking among the congregation would have lower suicide rates.
Stack analyzed data derived from the General Social Surveys and indeed did find that churches promoting social support were found
to have lower levels of suicidal ideology. Specifically, he found that
it was those churches that were the most conservative in their theology, that distanced themselves from ecumenical unity, and that
regarded the greater culture as a threat that had lower suicidal
ideology.

Stack's (1991) research noted that the impact of religiosity on
suicide has largely been conducted with American samples. In an
attempt to expand the field of study, Stack undertook to explore the
relationship of religiosity on suicide in a study conducted in Sweden. He found no evidence to relate religion to suicide rates in the
general population of Sweden; however, he did find that a decline in
religiosity was associated with the rise of suicide rates of the young.

Stack and Wasserman (1995) also attempted to expand the scope
of studies on religion and suicide by examining the link between
marriage and family ties and suicide ideology among African Americans. Stack asserted that there had been a documented rise in the
suicide rate of African Americans in the 1960s and 1970s. However,
he pointed out that the ratio of suicide rates of blacks relative to
whites in the United States has remained largely the same. Furthermore, any reduction in the difference between whites and blacks
relative to suicide rates is thought to be more the result of a reduction in the rates among whites than an increase in the rates among
blacks. Stack suggested that a "survival solidarity" among African
Americans explains the relatively low rates of suicide in this com-

munity. He cited Early's 1992 study of thirty African American pastors in which evidence was found to indicate a strong condemnation of suicide among black clergy who saw suicide as "unpardonable, unforgivable, and unthinkable for Blacks" (p. 217). Stack cited research indicating that African Americans have a suicide rate that is half that of the white suicide rate. However, Stack's research found that religion lowered suicide ideology more among whites than among blacks. These mixed findings provide more confusion than clarity on the difference between suicide rates by way of race. Nonetheless, Stack did find that church attendance continues to be the most important element for both white and black suicide ideology.

Stack has further extended his interest in the study of suicide to include the impact of feminism on suicide ideology. In a 1994 study, Stack, Wasserman, and Kposowa reviewed the attitudes toward suicide among a national sample of 4,946 women and 4,475 men to determine the influence of feminism/religiosity on the matter of suicide. Citing the earlier work of Feltey and Poloma (1991) Stack, Wasserman, and Kposowa suggested that the greater the feminism, the lower the intensity of religious belief and practice. Feltey and Poloma, in their study, suggested that egalitarian beliefs about women's roles in politics, home, and work are associated with lower levels of religiosity as measured by prayer and church attendance. In this study, Stack, Wasserman, and Kposowa (1994) contended that the greater the exposure to religiosity the lower the feminism. They went on to suggest "to the extent that feminism reduces a nurturant ideology, high feminism should be associated with higher approval of abortion, less approval for childbearing, and more approval of suicide" (p. 111). They concluded that religiosity affects suicide ideology by lowering feminism and that feminism affects suicide ideology by lowering religiosity.

Beit-Hallahmi (1975) conducted a review of the literature dealing with religion and suicidal behavior that led him to conclude that the evidence from clinical studies show that neither religious affiliation nor degree of religious involvement seem related in any significant way to suicide attempts. He speculated that the reason for this was the general trend toward secularization in Western culture, a trend that he believes has led to a reduction in the relative importance of religious factors in determining individual motivation.

Ellison, Burr, and McCall (1997) also sought to extend the research literature on religion and suicide by introducing what they considered to be an overlooked variable, religious homogeneity, which they defined as the extent to which community residents adhere to a single religion or a relatively small number of faiths. They hypothesized that such religious homogeneity would have "protective effect" on suicide rates. They tested their hypothesis using data on 296 metropolitan areas from 1980. They found that religious homogeneity is inversely associated with suicide rates and that religious homogeneity effects are greater than those of other religious variables such as the percentage of Catholics in the population and rate of church membership. They speculated that religious homogeneity increases the likelihood that social integration will occur in a community that consists of neighbors who are similar rather than disparate in their faith backgrounds. In addition to their common theological commitments and faith practices, "many co-religionists tend to hold compatible assumptions regarding morality, family, public affairs, and other domains of life experience" (p. 276).

Burr, McCall, and Powell-Griner (1994) reviewed the literature pertaining to Durkheim's "law," which states there is a negative relationship between suicide rates and size of the Catholic population, and concluded that "many authors who have not found support for the relationship between size of Catholic population and suicide have found support for a negative relationship between rates of church membership and suicide" (p. 301). They asserted that the prevailing view suggests a church membership/suicide relationship but does not suggest a denominational/suicide association. They also found evidence to support the idea that a lower level of family integration as measured by divorce rate is positively associated with suicide rates.

Obviously, Catholic teaching is in strong opposition to divorce (even while annulments are growing at a significant rate), hence some researchers have explored the question of whether divorce could have a mediating effect on suicide, thereby becoming an indirect factor in reducing the suicide rate among Catholics. Stack (1981) had also suggested that Catholicism does not significantly affect suicide when divorce is extruded from the equation. It is this finding that led Stack to conclude that there is no direct relationship between Catholicism and suicide. But Burr, McCall, and Powell-Griner speculated that because divorce is so strongly repudiated as an option for Catholics, divorcing has the effect of destabilizing the individual Catholic, thereby overriding any direct protective effect of Catholicism itself on suicide rates. Using data from the National Center for Health Statistics, Burr, McCall and Powell-Griner (1994) examined and analyzed 294 standard metropolitan statistical areas (SMSAs) from 1980 and found that Catholic church membership has both direct and indirect effects on suicide rates. The indirect effects are mediated through the divorce rate. They also found that Protestant church membership is not related statistically to suicide. "We argue that this evidence supports our central hypothesis that the protective effect of Catholicism is mediated by divorce and that there is an identifiable denominational difference with respect to the religion-suicide relationship" (p. 312).

Domino and Miller (1992) examined the relationship between religiosity and attitudes toward suicide in a sample of 186 Christian adults, which included Protestants, Catholics, and some Mormons, and found "a meaningful and coherent pattern between religiosity and attitudes towards suicide" (p. 278).

Joubert (1994) examined data from the 1990 Census and concluded that those states with higher percentages of persons without religious affiliation tended to have higher suicide rates. Jourbert's findings support the view that being religious reduces the likelihood of suicide.

Martin (1984) reviewed annual variations in the suicide rates of the United States for the years between 1972 and 1978 and compared them to annual variations in church attendance. He found that variations in suicide rates for both whites and blacks were significantly, inversely correlated with variations in church attendance, leading him to conclude that religiosity deters suicide and that religious involvement is an effective deterrent because it enhances group cohesiveness.

Using data from a psychological autopsy study, which examined all suicides in Finland over a period of one year, Sorri, Henriksson, and Lonnqvist (1996) investigated the relative religiosity of suicide victims. Pointing out that most studies have been epidemiological in nature and have generally dealt with differences between religious denominations or changes in religiosity, Sorri, Henriksson, and Lonnqvist attempted to assess actual suicide mortality and conducted their study in Finland because of its relatively high suicide rate compared to other countries. During the time period of April 1, 1997 through March 31, 1998, 13,097 suicides were reported. Data for the psychological autopsies were collected by means of comprehensive interviews of relatives and health care personnel as well as reviews of suicide notes and psychiatric, medical, police, and social agency records. Sorri, Henriksson, and Lonnqvist found overt, active religiosity in 18 percent of the suicides.

Siegrist (1996) used interview data collected in 1986 from a sample of 2,229 West Germans, roughly 50 percent of whom were men. The respondents were between the ages of fifteen and thirty and lived in what was then West Germany. Siegrist found evidence that Catholics reported less approval of suicide than Protestants and that Protestants reported less approval than those who had no religious affiliation at all. According to Siegrist, the data also supported the hypothesis that "religious integration is highest among Catholics and lowest among people without a religious orientation" (p. 564). He also found that suicide ideology was influenced by church attendance as well as by denominational affiliation. Frequent churchgoers were less approving of suicide than those who attended church little or not at all. It is interesting to note that he also found that the suicide of an acquaintance had the effect of decreasing the churchgoers' approval of suicide, but seemed to have the opposite effect on those infrequent churchgoers' attitudes toward suicide.

Lee-Peng Kok (1988) looked at the attempted suicide rate of women among three ethnic groups in Singapore. The overall rate was about 70 per 100,000 according to Kok. For Malaysian women it was 51 per 100,000; for Chinese women it was 112 per 100,000; and for Indian women it was 344 per 100,000.

Kok described Singapore as a multi-racial population in which the Chinese are 75 percent, the Malays 15 percent, the Indians 6 percent, and a mixed group of Eurasians and others 2 percent. Kok suggested that religion may account for the significant discrepancy between these ethnic groups of female suicide attempters. He pointed out that the Malays are Muslims and are subject to a strong Islamic condemnation of suicidal behavior. The Chinese, meanwhile, are influenced by Confucianism, Buddhism, and Christianity. Confucianism is doubtful if not skeptical about the possibility of life after death and does not emphasize the immortality of the soul. Buddhists, in contrast, believe that faith is the determining factor in a person's life and that death leads to a series of reincarnations according to one's karma. The Indians of Singapore are mostly Hindus and Hinduism teaches that there is a cycle of reincarnation and rebirth. In Hindu teaching, suicidal behavior is not strongly condemned. Kok had concluded, therefore, that "the differences in the culture, religion, and outlook of the three major races have led to major differences in suicidal behavior" (p. 239).

Religion, Suicide, and Adolescence

Suicide is a problem of significant proportions for adolescents and young adults as nearly four thousand Americans between the ages of fifteen and twenty-four commit suicide every year. The great majority of these suicides are high school and college students. It is alarming that the rate of suicide among this population doubled in the 1970s from what it was in the 1960s and tripled from what it was in the 1950s. According to the National Center for Health Statistics (1991) cited by Zhang and Jin (1996), suicide is the third leading cause of death among adolescents age fifteen to nineteen. From 1957–1987 the suicide rate for people ages fifteen to twenty-four increased from 4 to 12.9 per 100,000. At the same time, the suicide rate for the general population increased from 9.8 to 12.7 per 100,000.

In a study dealing with adolescent and young adult suicide, Minear and Brush (1980–1981) found that college students who were
less committed to religion were more likely to consider suicide. In
their study, Minear and Brush found that the overwhelming majority of college students reported that they had never thought about
suicide; however, for those students who had contemplated suicide,
there was a weaker religious orientation and "students with weak or
non-existent religious ties have the most favorable, most accepting
attitude towards suicide both for others and themselves" (p. 324).

Minear and Brush (1980–1981) conducted a study of 153 male
and 141 female students drawn from four colleges and universities
in New England. Using the Suicide Belief and Suicide Value Scales
they found that students who stated their religious affiliation as
"atheist" or "agnostic" had the most liberal and accepting attitudes
toward suicide. They also found that of those students who affirmed
a religious commitment, Jews were the most supportive of suicide
followed by Protestants and Catholics respectively. Minear and
Brush concluded that nonreligious students were much more likely
to accept suicide as an option in the event that life became overwhelming, while students who were affiliated with a religious orientation were less accepting of suicide as an option; "the stronger their
attachment to a religion and the more frequently they attend services, the less likely they are to consider suicide as an option for
other people or themselves" (p. 323). In an interesting aspect of
Minear and Brush's study (1980–1981), adolescents who engaged
in more serious suicide ideation seemed to accept suicide as an alternative at a far greater rate than those who had little or no suicide
ideation.

Shagle and Barber (1995) conducted a study dealing with adolescent suicide ideation in which they cited a 1991 Gallup Poll, which
found that 35 percent of nonreligious respondents, compared to 14
percent of Protestant and 13 percent of Catholic respondents,
viewed suicide among healthy individuals as morally acceptable.
Shagle and Barber defined suicidal ideation as ideas or thoughts of
committing suicide.

Greening and Dollinger (1993) conducted a study dealing with
adolescent suicide ideology in which they compared the attitudes

toward suicide of public high school students with those of parochial high school students and found a lower perceived risk of suicide among the parochial school students, which supported their hypothesis that parochial school students may be less vulnerable to suicidal cognitions. Their findings also suggested that ties to religious communities may influence attitudes and perceptions about suicide.

Ellison and Smith (1991) studied one hundred college students, two-thirds of whom were women, from a southern university in order to examine the existence of a relationship between an individual's adaptive cognitive characteristics, which would include moral objections to suicide and which may prevent suicide, and that person's level of spiritual well-being. They found that there was evidence to support their hypothesis that there is a high positive relationship between an individual's faith in God (religious well-being) and the individual's moral objections to suicide.

Zhang and Jin (1996) conducted a fascinating study in which they compared the attitudes of Chinese and American college students with respect to suicide. Their sample included 320 Chinese students from four universities in Beijing and 452 students from the Rocky Mountain area of the United States. In the American sample they found that religiosity is negatively correlated with suicide ideation and that religion is "another buffer between deviant behavior such as suicide ideation for American college students" (p. 464). However, they found that for the Chinese students religiosity was actually positively correlated with suicide ideation, depression, and pro-suicide attitudes. In the case of the Chinese students, the more religious they were, the more likely they were to feel depressed, hold attitudes favorable toward suicide, and engage in thinking about killing themselves. Zhang and Jin speculated that these surprising findings may be an outgrowth of the change of government policy away from the strict repression of religion that began in 1945 to a somewhat liberalized policy that began with the economic reforms instituted in 1978. They suggested that religiosity may promote deviant behavior in China even while it exists as an integrative force in the United States.

Suicide and Depression

Theorists and clinicians have suggested the following psychological motivations for suicide: self-directed hostility (anger turned inward, against oneself), retaliation for some real or imagine slight or offense (payback), a fantasy of rebirth, escape from severe stress, an attempt to rejoin a lost loved one who has died, atonement for some real or imagined sin, a way to control intolerable impulses, and confrontation with a phobic fear of death.

Obviously depression is also a significant factor in suicide. Kay Redfield Jamison is an acknowledged authority on manic depressive illness who holds prestigious academic appointments in the field of psychiatry even while struggling with her own manic depression. She has written a memoir of her battle against depression and suicide in *An Unquiet Mind* (1995) where she concludes that "for someone of my cast of mind and mood, medication is an integral element" in treatment and "without it, I would be constantly beholden to the crushing movement of a mental sea; I would, unquestionably, be dead or insane" (p. 215). Yet, she also acknowledges the role of love and hope in dealing with moods and illness. "After each seeming death within my mind or heart, love has returned to recreate hope and restore life" (p. 215).

Theories dealing with the causes of depression or mood disorders include biological, psychological, and social factors. The best current explanation seems to be a combination of "genetically determined biological vulnerability that can be described as an overreactive neuro-biological response to stressful life events" (p. 209).

Among the psychosocial stressors that can trigger depression is the experience of loss. Fairchild (1980) has identified common losses that cut us off from survival and well-being and that may lead to a generalized loss of life's meaning. Such losses may include failure at work or school, rejection, death of a loved one, physical disability, marital conflict, financial reverses, and falling short in achieving a desired goal.

Fairchild also points out that the loss of faith and the concomitant feeling of being abandoned by God can either lead to depression and suicide or be a result of depression. For example, C. S. Lewis, in his compelling description of his angry response to the death of his wife, described God as a "cosmic sadist," an indication of the extent of his alienation from God.

The biblical account of Job's despair is also a compelling description of loss of hope. Job is depicted as blameless and upright, a man who fears God and shuns evil, who nevertheless suffers through some of the worst calamities known to humankind. Consider his pleas:

> I wish I had died in my mother's womb or died the moment I was born. Why let men go on living in misery? Why give light to men in grief? They wait for death, but it never comes; they prefer a grave to any treasure. They are not happy until they are dead and buried. God keeps their future hidden and hems them in on every side. Instead of eating, I mourn and can never stop groaning. Everything I fear and dread comes true. I have no peace, no rest, and my troubles never end (Job 3:20–26).

The Psalmist also struggles with despair:

> How long, O Lord? Will you forget me forever?
> How long will you hide your face from me?
> How long must I wrestle with my thoughts and every day have
>   sorrow in my heart?
> How long will my enemy triumph over me?
> Look on me and answer, O Lord, My God.
> Give light to my eyes, or I will sleep in death; my enemy will say,
>   "I have overcome him," and my foes will rejoice when I fall.

But he nonetheless rejoices:

> But I trust in your unfailing love; my heart rejoices in your
>   salvation.
> I will sing to the Lord, for He has been good to me (Psalm 13).

Koenig reported on a study that examined the relationship between depression and the use of religion as a coping behavior in a sample of one thousand hospitalized, medically ill men. Koenig's study asked patients open-ended questions about what they did to enable them to cope better. The study included a religious coping index, which was shown to have high inter-rater reliability even when administered by raters from widely divergent religious backgrounds. Patients who used religion as a coping behavior were compared to patients who said they cope in other ways. Koenig found that patients who depended heavily on their religious faith to cope were significantly less depressed than those who did not. Koenig concluded that "the only characteristic that predicted lower rates of depression was not the level of support from family or friends, not physical health status, and not even income or educational level. Rather it was the extent to which patients relied on their religious faith to cope" (p. 57)

In his book, *Finding Hope Again*, Fairchild (1980) suggests a biblical metaphor describing depression as "a wilderness journey, symbolizing the experience of being lost in a desert place, lonely, without water flowing, and in great danger from thorns and beasts. But it is also a place where angels minister, where persons have found transformation, a new identity, and direction. Depression is a painful spiritual condition out of which much growth can come" (p. viii).

References

Aquinas, T. (1991). *Summa Theologiae: A Concise Translation*. Allen, TX: Christian Classics.

Augustine. (1993). *The City of God*. New York: Modern Library.

Beit-Hallahmi, B. (1975). "Religion and Suicidal Behavior." *Psychological Reports*, *37*, 1303–1306.

Burr, J. A., McCall, P. L., and Powell-Griner, E. (1994). "Catholic Religion and Suicide: The Mediating Effect of Divorce." *Social Science Quarterly*, *75*(2), 300–318.

Comstock, G. W., and Partridge, K. B. (1972). "Church Attendance and Health." *Journal of Chronic Disease*, *25*, 665–672.

Domino, G., and Miller, K. (1992). "Religiosity and Attitudes Toward Suicide." *Omega*, *25*(4), 271–282.

Durkheim, E. (1972). *Suicide*. Glencoe, IL: The Free Press.

Early, K. E. (1992). *Religion and Suicide in the African-American Community.* Westport, CT: Greenwood Press.

Ellison, C. G., Burr, J. A., and McCall, P. L. (1997). "Religious Homogeneity and Metropolitan Suicide Rates." *Social Forces, 76*(1), 273–299.

Ellison, C. W., and Smith, J. (1991). "Toward an Integrative Measure of Health and Well-Being." *Journal of Psychology and Theology, 19*(1), 35–48.

Faberow, N. L., and Schneidman, E. S. (1961). *The Cry for Help.* New York: McGraw-Hill.

Fairchild, R. W. (1980). *Finding Hope Again: A Pastor's Guide to Counseling Depressed Persons.* New York: Harper and Row.

Feltey, K., and Poloma, M. (1991). "From Sex Differences to Gender Role Beliefs." *Sex Roles, 25,* 181–183.

Freedman, D. N. (1992). *The Anchor Bible Dictionary.* Vol. 6. New York: Doubleday.

Freud, S. (1957). *Mourning as Melancholy.* London: Hogarth Press.

Greening, L., and Dollinger, S. J. (1993). "Rural Adolescents' Perceived Personal Risks for Suicide." *Journal of Youth and Adolescence, 22*(2), 211–217.

Grollman, E. A. (1988). *Suicide: Prevention, Intervention, Postvention.* Boston: Beacon Press.

Horney, K. (1950). *Neurosis and Self Growth.* New York: W. W. Norton.

Jamison, K. R. (1995). *An Unquiet Mind: A Memoir of Moods and Madness.* New York: Knopf.

Joubert, C. E. (1994). "Religious Nonaffiliation in Relation to Suicide, Murder, Rape, and Illegitimacy." *Psychological Reports, 75,* 10.

Jung, C. (1964). *Manhood Between Symbols.* New York: Dell.

Kok, L. (1988). "Race, Religion, and Female Suicide Attempters in Singapore." *Social Psychiatry and Psychiatric Epidemiology, 23,* 236–239.

Martin, W. T. (1984). "Religiosity and United States Suicide Rates, 1972–1978." *Journal of Clinical Psychology, 40*(5), 1166–1169.

Menninger, K. (1938). *Man Against Himself.* New York: Harcourt, Brace and Company.

Minear, J. D., and Brush, L. R. (1980–1981). "The Correlations of Attitudes Toward Suicide with Death Anxiety, Religiosity, and Personal Closeness to Suicide." *Omega, 11*(4), 317–324.

National Center for Health Services. (1991). *Health, United States, 1990.* Public Health Service, Hyattsville, MD.

Shagle, S. C., and Barber, B. K. (1995). "A Social-Ecological Analysis of Adolescent Suicidal Ideation." *American Journal of Orthopsychiatry, 65*(1), 114–123.

Siegrist, M. (1996). "Church Attendance, Denomination, and Suicide Ideology." *The Journal of Social Psychology, 136*(5), 559–566.

Sorri, H., Henriksson, M., and Lonnqvist, J. (1996). "Religiosity and Suicide: Findings from a Nationwide Psychological Autopsy Study." *Crisis, 17*(3), 123–127.

Stack, S. (1980). "Religion and Suicide: A Reanalysis." *Social Psychiatry, 15,* 65–70.

Stack, S. (1981). "Suicide and Religion: A Comparative Analysis." *Sociological Focus, 14,* 207–220.

Stack, S. (1983a). "The Effect of Religious Commitment on Suicide: A Cross-National Analysis." *Journal of Health and Social Behavior, 24,* 362–374.

Stack, S. (1983b). "The Effect of the Decline on Institutionalized Religion on Suicide, 1954–1978." *Journal for the Scientific Study of Religion, 22*(3), 239–252.

Stack, S. (1991). "The Effect of Religiosity on Suicide in Sweden: A Time Series Analysis." *Journal for the Scientific Study of Religion, 30*(4), 462–468.

Stack, S., and Wasserman, I. (1992). "The Effect of Religion on Suicide Ideology: An Analysis of the Networks Perspective." *Journal for the Scientific Study of Religion, 31*(4), 457–465.

Stack, S., and Wasserman, I. (1995). "The Effect of Marriage, Family, and Religious Ties on African-American Suicide Ideology." *Journal of Marriage and the Family, 57,* 215–222.

Stack, S., Wasserman, I., and Kposowa, A. (1994). "The Effects of Religion and Feminism on Suicide Ideology: An Analysis of National Survey Data." *Journal for the Scientific Study of Religion, 33*(2), 110–121.

Zhang, J., and Jin, S. (1996). "Determinants of Suicide Ideation: A Comparison of Chinese and American College Students." *Adolescence, 31*(122), 451–467.

Bibliography

Breault, Kevin D. "Suicide in America: A Test of Durkheim's Theory of Religious and Family Integration, 1933–1980." *American Journal of Sociology* 92 (1986): 628–656.

Hoelter, J. "Religiosity, Fear of Death and Suicide Acceptability." *Suicide and Life-Threatening Behavior* 9 (1979): 163–172.

Kranitz, L., et al. "Religious Beliefs and Suicidal Patients." *Psychological Reports* 22 (1968): 936–940.

Lester, David. "Religion and Personal Violence (Homicide and Suicide) in the USA." *Psychological Reports* 62, no. 2 (1988): 618.

Stark, R., D. P. Doyle, and J. L. Rushing. "Beyond Durkheim: Religion and Suicide." *Journal for the Scientific Study of Religion* 22 (1983): 120–131.
Funded by a grant from the National Institute for Juvenile Justice and Delinquency Prevention, Law Enforcement Assistance Administration, U.S. Department of Justice.

Templer, D. I., and D. M. Veleber. "Suicide Rate and Religion Within the U.S." *Psychological Reports* 47, no. 3, Part 1 (1980): 898.

8

Alcohol Use and Abuse

ALCOHOL HAS BEEN present since the beginning of time and has always been associated with various social occasions such as the celebration of births, marriages, funerals, and various religious ceremonies. While alcohol has seemingly valid and legitimate uses, it is obvious that the excesses of alcohol use have contributed to various intractable social, economic, personal, and family problems. The social consequences of alcohol abuse have led inevitably to the condemnation of alcohol by various religions as well as regulation by governments.

In the United States, the Women's Christian Temperance Union led the fight against alcohol, which ultimately led to alcohol prohibition being enacted into law in 1920. While this legislation represented a victory of sorts, the prohibition of alcohol was repealed thirteen years later and was considered to be a failure as a method of control.

The often chronicled negative effects or consequences of alcohol use and abuse include psychological, social, spiritual, family, and economic costs. One measurement of the economic consequences of alcohol use and abuse is the so-called "cost of illness" studies, which attempt to quantify what it costs society to deal with problems related to alcohol. A study by Rice and colleagues (1990) estimated that in 1988 the cost of alcohol abuse in the United States was nearly 86 billion dollars.

The Office of Applied Studies within the Substance Abuse and Mental Health Services Administration conducts a National Household Survey annually. Findings from the 1994 survey, which included personal and self-administered interviews with 22,181 respondents, indicate that 66.9 percent used alcohol within the past year.

The preponderance of research has consistently indicated that being religious makes it less likely that a person will use or abuse alcohol either as an adolescent, college student, or adult. For example, Jessor and Jessor (1975) found that greater religiosity increased the likelihood of abstinence among high school students. Middleton and Putney (1962) found that there was less alcohol use among Protestant college students who were believers than among students who were agnostics. Burkett and White (1974) found an inverse relationship between church attendance and the use of alcohol. Mullen, Blaxter, and Dyer (1986) conducted a review of the research linking religious adherence to alcohol use and found that the literature clearly indicates that religious involvement and religiosity may be associated with lower alcohol use. According to Khavari and Harmon (1982), religious adults consumed less alcohol than adults who did not consider themselves to be religious. And Midanik and Clark (1985) analyzed a national sample and concluded that religious persons are less likely to have drinking problems.

Nusbaumer (1981) undertook a longitudinal study to measure how religion and religiosity has influenced alcohol use over a fifteen-year period. He compared data from the National Opinion Research Center (NORC) obtained in 1963 with a second set of data collected in 1978. He determined that some Protestant denominations were more abstinence- oriented than others, with Baptist and Methodist denominations clearly considered abstinence-oriented denominations, while Catholic, Lutheran, Presbyterian, and Episcopalian were nonabstinence-oriented denominations. Analyzing the two sets of data, he found a decline in the impact of religious affiliation on the use of alcohol from 1963 to 1978, with Baptists and Methodists experiencing a rather dramatic 7 percent decline in the number of abstainers over that period of time.

Cochran, Beeghley, and Bock (1988) studied the relationship between religiosity and alcohol use and perceived misuse. They focused on adults rather than adolescents and distinguished among specific Protestant denominations. Using data from the General Social Surveys (GSS) from 1972 to 1984, they obtained a sample size of 7,581 people, all of whom were eighteen years of age or older. Their analysis found that religiosity is inversely related to alcohol use, but does not seem to be related to the perceived misuse of alcohol. They found that the patterns of use and perceived misuse are indeed consistent with the expectations and social teachings of the various denominations, some preaching a moral message proscribing the consumption of alcohol altogether while others tolerate the use of alcohol in moderation. They found that persons with no religious affiliation were likely to use alcohol at a rate of 88 percent, Catholics 86 percent, Episcopalians 86 percent, Lutherans 85 percent, Presbyterians 82 percent, Methodists 71 percent, and finally Baptists at the lowest rate of 56 percent.

Hawks and Bahr (1992) suggested that religious affiliation inhibits and delays the first use of alcohol and also influences the frequency of alcohol use later. Their findings confirm that church and synagogue attendance has been consistently, inversely related to alcohol and other substance use.

Schlegel and Sanborn (1979) sought to clarify the relationship between religious affiliation and drinking among adolescents. In a 1974 study, they examined 750 students in the ninth through twelfth grades who were randomly selected from two southern Ontario high schools, one rural and the other urban. They found that among high school students who attended church, those who were fundamentalist Protestants were less likely to drink than are those who were liberal Protestants or Roman Catholics. They also found that students who did not attend church at all were more likely than churchgoers to be heavy drinkers.

Hadaway, Elifson, and Petersen (1984) conducted a comprehensive study of six hundred students drawn from twenty-three thousand students enrolled in twenty-one public high schools located in the metropolitan Atlanta, Georgia, area. They found that religion had a significant effect on reducing alcohol and drug use. They also found that church attendance is inversely related to the use of alcohol, marijuana, and other drugs. They concluded that higher levels of religiosity are associated with lower levels of drug and alcohol use.

Lorch and Hughes (1985) conducted a fascinating study of 13,878 junior high and high school students from the Colorado Springs metropolitan area in May 1983. They found that church membership is a deterrent to both alcohol and drug use. They also found that students who were affiliated with fundamentalist denominations had the lowest percentage of substance use. However, it was the importance of religion to the individual that was found to have the most impact on deterrence. This is consistent with the notion that if religion is important to the person, beliefs along with religious values are more likely to be internalized and hence serve as a deterrent to illegal alcohol use or abuse.

In an attempt to better understand the complexity of religion as a variable they developed six religious dimensions: 1) religious membership, 2) degree of fundamentalism or liberalism of the religious group, 3) church attendance, 4) the importance of religion to each student, 5) a combination of church attendance and the importance of religion, and 6) a combination of fundamentalism or liberalism of religious groups and the importance of religion to the subject. They found that the best predictor of youth avoidance of substance abuse was the importance of religion to each student. Church membership was ranked second.

Perkins (1985) studied a population of 1,514 college students at an undergraduate liberal arts college in New York State. His sample included 40 percent Protestants, 33 percent Roman Catholics, 17 percent Jews, 7 percent with no religious background, and 4 percent of some other religion. Perkins found that the consumption of alcohol is related to the specific religious background of the student. Catholic students had the greatest consumption of alcohol followed by Protestants, students with no religious background, and Jews respectively. His findings demonstrated that the drinking behaviors of Catholic, Protestant, and Jewish college students was the same as that found by Snyder (1958) thirty years earlier. Perkins also was able to conclude that alcohol use and drug use steadily increases as the importance of one's faith decreases and that increasingly liberal attitudes toward alcohol and drug use are associated with a decrease in religious commitment. Finally, his findings confirmed earlier studies that demonstrate that Jews appear to drink far less than Catholics, with Protestants falling somewhere in between these two groups. Unfortunately, the restraint observed with regard to alcohol use among Jews does not carry over into other forms of substance use. Perkins found that Jewish students reported the highest levels of drug use among all of the groups represented. He concluded that "a relatively strong faith commitment to a Judeo-Christian tradition remains as a significant moderating influence on alcohol/other drug use" (p. 15).

The Seventh-day Adventist Church is considered a conservative Protestant denomination in the United States. Dudley, Mutch, and Cruise (1987) sought to identify those factors that might produce drug and alcohol use by young people who were members of that denomination. From a sample of 801 Seventh Day Adventists between the ages of twelve and twenty-four drawn from 71 churches in North America, Dudley, Mutch, and Cruise concluded that a self-reported "commitment to Christ" was the strongest predictor of abstinence from alcohol, tobacco, and all drugs combined. The desire to be in control of one's life as well as a concern for one's health were also listed as significant factors of nearly equal strength. Regular church attendance was most highly related to abstinence in alcohol and all drug categories.

Amoateng and Bahr (1986), using a national sample of over seventeen thousand high school seniors taken from the Annual Survey of High School Seniors conducted by the Survey Research Center at the University of Michigan in 1982, found that level of religiosity was positively associated with alcohol and marijuana use among all religious denominations. This was in contrast to their findings that the level of parental education and the employment status of the mother were not related to the use of alcohol or marijuana. They also found that adolescents who lived with both parents were less likely than adolescents in single-parent homes to use marijuana. Among all the variables studied, religiosity had the most consistent relationship with drug use, with those who were more religious being less likely to use either alcohol or marijuana. As had been reported earlier, Amoateng and Bahr also found that Catholics had the highest frequency of alcohol use and also consumed the most alcohol. Those without any religious affiliation were the most likely to use marijuana. Amoateng and Bahr concluded that high school students who were high in religiosity were less likely to use alcohol and marijuana than adolescents who were not involved in religious activities.

Binge drinking and other forms of problem drinking in American society have become increasingly difficult societal issues, particularly among American college and university students. Perkins (1987) undertook a study in which he found that the religious orientation of the parent of a college or university student is an important influence on the student's drinking behavior. Specifically, he found that Gentiles were at a greater risk for developing drinking problems than Jews, as were students who were not strongly attached to any particular religious orientation. Not surprisingly, students who were the offspring of an alcohol abuser were also at greater risk. Perkins sought to analyze the intergenerational transmission of alcohol problems and found that the religiosity of parents is related to at-risk categories as well. He concluded that the religious commitment of parents and their degree of religiosity determine the religiosity and commitment of their children "which, in turn, influence the student's drinking" (p. 340).

Hardesty and Kirby (1995) also found that if the family is religious, there is less likelihood of using or abusing illegal substances. The authors took a sample of 475 students attending a nontraditional high school. They reasoned that this group would be of particular interest because many of the students attending such alternative schools already display risk factors associated with drug and alcohol use and abuse. Such students typically have a low commitment to school and learning, and often have extensive illicit drug abuse histories and families that are dysfunctional. The authors found that after controlling for other family social climate variables, a significant variance of peer use of alcohol, marijuana, and other illegal substances could be attributed to family religiousness. The authors speculated that the reduced likelihood of using or abusing illegal substances could be attributed to the opportunity to bond with positive community groups such as church or youth groups, which had the effect of lessening the opportunity to develop relationships with other adolescents who use or abuse illegal substances. Second, they reasoned that families that are active in their religious practices would be less conflicted and more cohesive as a family unit. And finally, they calculated that parents who practice religion may be better role models for their children with respect to the nonuse of illegal drugs. "If families raise their children within a religious orientation, this could influence peer group formation and ultimately have an impact on illicit drug use behavior" (p. 422).

A study by Larson and Wilson (1980) examined the religious life of alcoholics. Noting that the success of Alcoholics Anonymous has been attributed to the spiritual dimension of its twelve-step program, Larson and Wilson set out to investigate a sample of eighty-one male alcoholics using structured interviews. They obtained data on (a) the denominational preferences of the subjects and their parents, (b) the beliefs of the subjects and their parents, and (c) the pattern of church attendance of the subjects and their parents. They found that alcoholics were less involved in religious practices, had less exposure to religious teachings, had fewer religious experiences, and withdrew from religion more frequently during adolescence than did a group of normal subjects. They concluded that "the early-life religious experiences of an alcoholic are most conflictual and lead to religious confusion rather than commitment" (p. 723).

Koenig and colleagues (1994) examined the relationship between alcoholism and various religious activities. They found that persons who frequently attended church, engaged in prayer and Bible reading, or considered themselves "born again" had significantly lower rates of alcoholism.

Booth and Martin (1998) summarized the findings dealing with religiosity and substance use and abuse by concluding that "despite inconsistent assessment measures with poor psychometrics, and the traditional putative view of 'religiousness' by psychology, the literature has consistently revealed an inverse relationship between religiousness and substance use, abuse, and recovery" (p. 175).

References

Amoateng, A. Y., and Bahr, S. J. (1986). "Religion, Family, and Adolescent Drug Use." *Sociological Perspectives*, 29(1), 53–76.

Booth, J., and Martin, J. E. (1998). "Spiritual and Religious Factors in Substance Use, Dependence, and Recovery." In H. G. Koenig (Ed.), *Handbook of Religion and Mental Health* (pp.175–200). San Diego: Academic Press.

Burkett, S. R., and White, M. (1974). "Hellfire and Delinquency: Another Look." *Journal for the Scientific Study of Religion*, 13(4), 455–462.

Cochran, J. K., Beeghley, L., and Bock, E. W. (1988). "Religiosity and Alcohol Behavior: An Exploration of Reference Group Therapy." *Sociological Forum*, 3(2), 256–276.

Dudley, R. L., Mutch, P. B., and Cruise, R. J. (1987). "Religious Factors and Drug Usage Among Seventh-Day Adventist Youth in North America." *Journal for the Scientific Study of Religion*, 26(2), 218–233.

Hadaway, C. K., Elifson, K. W., and Petersen, D. M. (1984). "Religious Involvement and Drug Use Among Urban Adolescents." *Journal for the Scientific Study of Religion*, 23(2), 109–128.

Hardesty, P. H., and Kirby, K. M. (1995). "Relation Between Family Religiousness and Drug Use Within Adolescent Peer Groups." *Journal of Social Behavior and Personality*, 10, 421–430.

Hawks, R. D., and Bahr, S. H. (1992). "Religion and Drug Use." *Journal of Drug Education*, 22, 1–8.

Jessor, R., and Jessor, S. L. (1975). "Adolescent Development and the Onset of Drinking: A Longitudinal Study." *Journal of the Study of Alcohol*, 36, 27–51.

Khavari, K. A., and Harmon, T. M. (1982). "The Relationship Between the Degree of Professed Religious Beliefs and the Use of Drugs." *International Journal of Addictions*, 17, 847–857.

Koenig, H. G., George, L. K., Meador, K. G., Blazer, D. G., and Ford, S. M. (1994). "Religious Practices and Alcoholism in a Southern Adult Population." *Hospital and Community Psychiatry*, 54(3), 225–231.

Larson, D. B., and Wilson, W. P. (1980). "Religious Life of Alcoholics." *Southern Medical Journal*, 73(6), 723–727.

Lorch, B. R., and Hughes, R. H. (1985). "Religion and Youth Substance Use." *Journal of Religion and Health* 24(3), 197–208.

Midanik, L. T., and Clark, W. D. (1985). "Drinking Problems in the United States: Description and Trends (1984–1990)." *Journal of Studies on Alcohol*, 56, 395–402.

Middleton, R., and Putney, S. (1962). "Religion, Normative Standards, and Behavior." *Sociometry*, 25, 141–152.

Mullen, K., Blaxter, M., and Dyer, S. (1986). "Religion and Attitudes Toward Alcohol Use in the Western Isles." *Drug and Alcohol Dependence*, 18, 51–72.

Nusbaumer, M. R. (1981). "Religious Affiliation and Abstinence: A Fifteen-Year Change." *Journal of Studies on Alcohol*, 42(1), 127–131.

Perkins, H. W. (1985). "Religious Traditions, Parents, and Peers as Determinants of Alcohol and Drug Use Among College Students." *Review of Religious Research*, 27(1), 15–31.

Perkins, H. W. (1987). "Parental Religion and Alcohol Use Problems as Intergenerational Predictors of Problem Drinking Among College Youth." *Journal for the Scientific Study of Religion*, 26(3), 340–357.

Rice, D. P., Kellman, S., Miller, L. S., and Dunmeyer, S. (1990). *The Economic Cost of Alcohol and Drug Abuse and Mental Illness*. San Francisco: Institute for Health and Aging.

Schlegel, R. P., and Sanborn, M. D. (1979). "Religious Affiliation and Adolescent Drinking." *Journal of Studies on Alcohol*, 40(7), 693–703.

Snyder, C. R. (1958). *Alcohol and the Jews: A Cultural Study of Drinking and Sobriety*. Glencoe, IL: The Free Press.

Bibliography

Adlaf, E. M., and R. G. Smart. "Drug Use and Religious Affiliation, Feelings, and Behavior." *British Journal of Addiction* 80, no. 2 (1985): 163–171.
A study conducted by researchers from the Addiction Research Foundation. The relationship between drug and alcohol use and religious affiliation, intensity of religious feelings, and frequency of church attendance was examined in a sample of 2,066 adolescents. King notes that "while religious affiliation was not significantly related to drug and alcohol use, church attendance had a stronger negative association with drug use than did religious beliefs; however, the effect of religious beliefs had greater impact among females than among males. Overall, the impact of both variables increased as the drug under consideration moved toward the upper end of the licit-illicit continuum"(King, 107).

Alcoholics Anonymous. *Alcoholics Anonymous*, 3rd ed. New York: Alcoholics Anonymous, 1976.

Bachman, J. G., L. D. Johnston, and P. M. O'Malley. "Smoking, Drinking, and Drug Use Among American High School Students: Correlates and Trends, 1975–1979." *American Journal of Public Health* 71 (1981): 59–69.

Bock, E. W., J. K. Cochran, and L. Beeghley. "Moral Messages: The Relative Influence of Denomination on the Religiosity-Alcohol Relationship." *The Sociological Quarterly* 28, no. 1 (1987): 89–103.
This study reports that "while religiosity or religious beliefs were not associated with misuse of alcohol, after controlling for standard sociodemographic variables, the impact of religiosity on alcohol use appeared greatest among denominations that took a strong stand against its consumption. This was mainly because religious beliefs constituted a significant reference group for church members"(King, 108).

Briggman, L. P., and W. M. McQueen. "The Success of Alcoholics Anonymous: Locus of Control and God's General Revelation." *Journal of Psychology and Theology* 15 (1987): 124–131.

Brizer, D. A. "Religiosity and Drug Abuse Among Psychiatric Inpatients." *American Journal of Drug and Alcohol Abuse* 19 (1993): 337–345.

Burkett, S. R. "Religion, Parental Influence, and Adolescent Alcohol and Marijuana Use." *Journal of Drug Issues* 7 (1977): 263–273.

Cancellaro, L. A., D. B. Larson, and W. P. Wilson, "Religious Life of Narcotic Addicts." *Southern Medical Journal* 75 (1982): 1166–1168.

Christo, G., and C. Graney, "Drug Users' Spiritual Beliefs, Locus of Control and the Disease Concept in Relation to Narcotics Anonymous Attendance and Six-Month Outcomes." *Drug and Alcohol Dependence* 38 (1995): 51–56.

Coombs, R. H., D. K. Wellisch, and F. I. Fawzy. "Drinking Patterns and Problems Among Female Children and Adolescents: A Comparison of Abstainers, Past Users, and Current Users." *American Journal of Drug and Alcohol Abuse* 11 (1985): 315–348.
Supported by a grant from the California Department of Alcohol and Drug Programs.

Dearden, M. H., and T. F. Jekel. "Pilot Program in High School Drug Education Utilizing Nondirective Techniques and Sensitivity Training." *Journal of School Health* 41 (1971): 118–124.

Desmond, D. P., and J. F. Maddux. "Religious Programs and Careers of Chronic Heroin Users." *American Journal of Drug and Alcohol Abuse* 8, no. 1 (1981): 71–84.
Supported by a research grant from the National Institute on Drug Abuse.

Ellis, A., and E. Schoenfeld. "Divine Intervention and the Treatment of Chemical Dependency." *Journal of Substance Abuse* 2 (1990): 459–468.

Engs, Ruth C., David J. Hanson, Louis Gliksman, and Cynthia Smythe. "Influence of Religion and Culture on Drinking Behaviors: A Test of Hypotheses Between Canada and the USA." *British Journal of Addiction* 85 (1990): 1475–1482.

Gorsuch, R. L. "Religious Aspects of Substance Abuse and Recovery." *Journal of Social Issues* 51 (1995): 65–83.

Gorsuch, Richard L., and M. C. Butler. "Initial Drug Abuse: A Review of Predisposing Factors." *Psychological Bulletin* 83 (1976): 120–137.

Gruner, Leroy. "Heroin, Hashish, and Hallelujah: The Search for Meaning." *Review of Religious Research* 26, no. 2 (December 1984): 176–186.

Isralowitz, Richard E., and Teck-Hong Ong. "Religious Values and Beliefs and Place of Residence as Predictors of Alcohol Use Among Chinese College Students in Singapore." *International Journal of the Addictions* 25, no. 5 (1990): 515–529.

Keller, J. E. "Spirituality in Treatment and Recovery." In *Alcohol Use and Misuse by Young Adults*, edited by G. S. Howard and P. E. Nathan, 109–132. Notre Dame, IN: University of Notre Dame Press, 1994.

King, Donald G. "Religion and Health Relationships." *Journal of Religion and Health* 29, no. 2 (1990): 101–112.

Kohn, George F. "Toward a Model for Spirituality and Alcoholism." *Journal of Religion and Health* 23, no. 3 (1989): 250–259.
Kohn discusses the apparent relationship of the balance between brain hemispheres and alcohol abuse. "Excessive use of alcohol 'anesthetizes' the object-based, language-oriented functions of the left hemisphere, associated with an 'action mode of consciousness.' This allows greater engagement of the right-hemisphere 'receptive mode,' which is also associated with religious experience." Kohn argues that a "model of spirituality based on achieving a balance between hemisphere functions and modes of consciousness could provide a non-chemical alternative to excessive use of alcohol."

Krause, Neal. "Stress, Religiosity, and Abstinence from Alcohol." *Psychology and Aging* 6, no. 1 (1991): 134–144.
Some funding for the collection of data provided by the National Institute on Aging.

MacDonald, C. B., and J. B. Luckett. "Religious Affiliation and Psychiatric Diagnoses." *Journal for the Scientific Study of Religion* 22 (1983): 15–37.

Maddox, G. L. "Drinking Prior to College." In *The Domesticated Drug: Drinking Among Collegians*, edited by G. L. Maddox, 107–120. New Haven, CT: College and University Press, 1970.

Matthews, Dale A., and David B. Larson. *A Bibliography of Research by Scientists on Spiritual Subjects*. Philadelphia: John Templeton Foundation, 1991.

McIntosh, William Alex, Starla D. Fitch, J. Branton Wilson, and Kenneth L. Nyberg. "The Effect of Mainstream Religious Social Controls on Adolescent Drug Use in Rural Areas." *Review of Religious Research* 23, no. 1 (September 1981): 54–75.

Monteiro, M. G., and M. A. Schuckit. "Alcohol, Drug, and Mental Health Problems Among Jewish and Christian Men at a University." *American Journal of Drug and Alcohol Abuse* 15, no. 4 (1989): 403–412.

Muffler, J., J. Langrod, and D. Larson. "There Is a Balm in Gilead: Religion and Substance Abuse Treatment." In *Substance Abuse: A Comprehensive Textbook*, 2nd ed., edited by J. H. Lowinson, P. Ruiz, R. B. Millman, and J. G. Langrod, 584–595. Baltimore: Williams and Wilkins, 1995.

Parfrey, P. S. "The Effect of Religious Factors on Intoxicant Use." *Scandinavian Journal of Social Medicine* 3 (1976): 135–140.

Singer, Merrill. "Spiritual Healing and Family Therapy: Common Approaches to the Treatment of Alcoholism." *Family Therapy* 11, no. 2 (1984): 155–162.

Vander Veldt, A. J., and R. J. McAllister. "Psychiatric Illness in Hospitalized Clergy: Alcoholism." *Quarterly Journal for the Study of Alcohol* 23 (1962): 124–130.

Walters, O. S. "The Religious Background of 50 Alcoholics." *Quarterly Journal of Studies on Alcohol* 18 (1957): 405–416.

Zimberg, S. "Sociopsychiatric Perspectives on Jewish Alcohol Abuse: Implications for the Prevention of Alcoholism." *American Journal for Drug and Alcohol Abuse* 4 (1977): 571–579.

PART THREE

The Relationship of Realized Religion to Future Research

9

The Need for Religious Values in Empirical Research

IN 1967, BERGER (1967) expressed grave doubts about the ability of disciplines such as sociology or psychology to provide viable empirical results for the study of religion. He insisted, for example, that religious assumptions cannot be imported into empirical studies without undermining their epistemological status.

> In other words, the ultimate epistemological status of these reports of religious men will have to be rigorously bracketed. "Other worlds" are not empirically available for the purposes of scientific analysis. . . . Put differently, whatever else the constellations of the sacred may be "ultimately," empirically they are products of human activity and human signification—that is, they are human projections (pp. 88–89).

Berger was open to interaction between the empirical sciences and normative disciplines such as theology, but discounted the possibility of an "empirical theology" (p. 179).

Is Berger correct? If empirical science continues to observe that certain types of specifically religious behaviors and attitudes, *frequently shaped by a definite religious content*, yield verifiable benefits or harm, can we not posit at least a strong correlation that is empirically based? Must theology only proceed in "step-by-step correlation with what can be said about man empirically"? Or is it not equally possible that theological constructs might well serve in aiding researchers in the construction of their empirical experiments? Is not Berger's insistence that the sacred is divorced from the possibility of empirical demonstration in itself an untested metaphysical assertion? Causality between God/the supernatural/the spiritual and the natural world cannot be proven decisively, but strong correlations between definite theological concepts, religious behavior, and human well-being are plausible hypotheses, unless one has previously decided on metaphysical grounds that such correlations are an empirical/epistemological impossibility.

Hood (1989), for example, explained how theology might aid researchers in understanding how people form their images of God. Research in this field has been dominated by the assumption that images of God are "primarily if not totally rooted in family experiences." Hood believed that while the correlations between family experience and images of God can be demonstrated, images of God cannot be "totally conditioned" by familial context.

> It may be more reasonable to say that one's life experiences eventually culminate in views that are "awakened" and lead to images of reality and truth no longer conditioned totally by one's particular experiences (p. 338).

Instead, what if one hypothesizes "that images of God exist in the light of the possibility of there being a God—the awareness of which some persons come to appreciate as a viable, indeed realistic, possibility" (p. 338)? Might such a construction actually lead to a more mature understanding of God and of our family background? According to Hood, the answer is yes. One can both accept the imperfection of human fathers, and draw nearer to a mature comprehension of perfect fatherhood as understood and explicated in "the great theological traditions" (p. 339).

> Once this is properly awakened one no longer projects an image of a deficient father, idealized and perfected onto a God who is "as if" a perfect biological father. Instead, perfection is now attributed to the appropriate "ontological object" and one realizes that it is God the Father, not merely my biological father who is perfect (p. 339).

Hood's example appears to explain how images of God in "mature religious developments" can help researchers to understand the

role theological constructs play in molding and developing "images
of persons, and not simply how images of persons, particularly parents, are projected onto an assumed nonexistent God" (p. 339). The
disheartening reality, however, is that researchers frequently ig-
nore the theological resources available to them for the construction
of their theoretical models and empirical experiments. Naturalistic
presuppositions and biases too frequently blind them to the potential use of theology for shaping new experimental paradigms. When
researchers do employ theological concepts such as guilt or sin in
their experiments, their formulations tend to be ill-informed and
naïve.

The influence of metaphysical presuppositions and values on
empirical research is analyzed well in two significant articles produced in the past decade. Watson, Morris, and Hood(1987) focused
on the ideological conflict present in many empirical studies of religiosity and self-functioning in their article, "Antireligious Humanistic Values, Guilt, and Self Esteem." They noted that heated
debate continues within the scientific community concerning the
relationship between "self-functioning and orthodox religious
commitment." Psychologists such as Ellis and Maslow have asserted
that orthodox religious commitment is incompatible with healthy
rational and emotional development. Writers from the orthodox religious camp have responded by critiquing the "encroachment" of
alien psychological ideas into orthodox life.

According to Watson, Morris, and Hood, the debate would be advanced if empirical evidence could be clearly adduced pointing to
the veracity of one or the other side of the issue. Unfortunately, the
waters remain muddy precisely because "research has been largely
unsuccessful in demonstrating reliable relationships between religiosity and self functioning" (p. 535). Part of the difficulty lies in the
ambiguous multidimensional complexity of religiousness in its
influence on other spheres of human existence. The empirical literature on the relationship between religion and mental health "contains numerous conflicting results," according to Bergin (1991),
with the outcome that "persons with differing biases can select the
evidence they prefer" (p. 399).

The combination of natural complexity with theoretical or metaphysical bias inevitably leads to skewed results. Watson and colleagues (1987) argued that the nature of the measures used to gauge the functioning of the self are themselves "biased against the orthodox and that religious self esteem cannot be fully appreciated from a secular perspective" (p. 536). That is to say, the personality scales employed by researchers to determine healthy self-functioning are prejudiced against theistic value systems.

> Orthodox subjects may appear as maladjusted, not because of a poor self image, but rather because personality scale items conflict with religious beliefs about the self. Similarly, expression of self-deprecatory statements relating to sin may arise from an intellectual assent to dogma rather than from a self-punitive emotional state (p. 537).

The distinction made by Hood between a theologically mature understanding of sin and an unhealthy emotional state, though, is precisely the nuancing absent from many studies. A greater willingness on the part of social scientists to move beyond theological caricatures and naiveté could well lead to new theories, models, and empirical insights. This is not a call to acceptance of theological doctrines, but rather to the serious investigation of their possible contribution to scientific progress. If this possibility has been gainsaid from the outset, research must inevitably remain locked within a pre-empirical naturalistic framework.

Watson, Morris, and Hood have demonstrated that when prejudicial values and language are statistically controlled, "overwhelmingly positive" relationships are yielded between self-functioning and forms of religiousness related to an intrinsic orientation, where "religious faith is lived as an end in itself, functioning as a foundation for one's life choices, and giving meaning to life's experiences" (Genia and Shaw, 1991, p. 274). While this outcome is in itself significant, perhaps even more important is the cogent reminder that all empirical studies are encompassed by an "ideological parameter," a presuppositional boundary that affects both what researchers observe empirically and the interpretation they give to the data itself.

Bergin (1980) has published extensively on the role of values in psychotherapy and on the relation of religion to mental health. He has noted that a major article he published in 1980 on psychotherapy and religious values elicited over one thousand comments and requests for reprints, a reaction indicating a widespread interest in the relationship between religious values and empirical research.

In his 1991 article, "Values and Religious Issues in Psychotherapy and Mental Health," Bergin contended that religious values can make three major contributions to our understanding of mental health and mental healing. First, religious values provide a conception of human nature, "the view that there is a spiritual reality and that spiritual experiences make a difference in behavior." He argued that this hypothesis can be subjected to empirical tests, "just as the invisible processes of biology and physics have been subjected to tests. An example of this would be to correlate verbal reports of religious experience with mental health criterion variables" (p. 398).

> The self-reports gathered in such studies do not provide conclusive evidence, but they do provide a basis for inferring phenomena that are unlikely to be inferred by other theories. The process is not different in principle from that which guided the discovery of genes of biology or atomic particles in physics (p. 398).

Second, according to Bergin, religious values provide a moral frame of reference for psychotherapy and mental health. He rightly observed that "professional and personal ethics that guide change are always grounded in ontology, or a way of looking at human nature" (p. 398).

Some of the questions readers must ask as they evaluate the entries in this bibliography are: What are the researchers' criteria for mental health? How is spiritual maturity defined? What values determine normal behavior and how are they measured? Are the value structure and religious presuppositions of the researcher openly recognized and acknowledged? According to Bergin, almost all professional psychologists and psychiatrists do ground their work in "value judgments about the mental health implications of various behaviors and attitudes." At the same time, he called for the constraining influence of "clinical experience and empirical data wherever possible, to avoid turning the clinical setting into a values free-for-all" (p. 398). The same can be said for research in general. Values cannot be avoided, and indeed shouldn't be. On the other hand, empirical observation must function as an important bridle on undisciplined speculation and unwarranted bias.

Third, Bergin advocated the use of "spiritual techniques" in the therapeutic process. As an example of a spiritual technique he proposed "the transitional figure" method, in which "the client is taught to become a transitional person in the history of the family by adopting a redemptive role" (p. 398). In this method clients are encouraged to see themselves "at the crossroads of their family history" and to "realize that forgiveness rather than retribution is more likely to engender health than is dwelling on having been the victim of pathologizing events" (pp. 398–399). Here we have the combination of an experimental hypothesis incorporating a spiritual value, and the opportunity to test the hypothesis empirically. Indeed, Bergin related that a "number of cases have improved substantially as a result of reconciliation experiences facilitated by adoption of the transitional figure role" (p. 399).

Propst (1980b) has also produced research indicating the viability in psychotherapy of spiritual techniques rooted within the Christian tradition. Propst (1980b) reported, for example, that the use of religious imagery in the treatment of mild depression in religious individuals "showed significantly more treatment gains" than self-monitoring or nonreligious imagery treatments. Propst commented that this success might well be related to the "religious nature of the participants" and reinforced the importance of taking "the assumptive world of the client" into account in psychotherapy.

In an earlier article Bergin (1983) argued that before empirical evidence for the positive or negative effect of religion on mental health is evaluated, scientists need to recognize that the issues involved are not only empirical in nature. Rather, they relate "also to the frame of reference of human sciences and scientists" (p. 170). Bergin maintained that this broader framework was apparent in at

least three different ways. First, the theoretical axioms and paradigms formed by scientists were influenced by values and ideology,
which themselves had "subjective as well as empirical bases." The
central assumptions of modern psychology, for example, were "naturalistic and humanistic rather than theistic and spiritual." These
"intuitively chosen positions" were often veiled by "professional
language," which gave the impression that they were derived from
empirical fact. The continuing result is that much research is dominated by a "non-religious bias" fostered by professional usage.
"These orienting constructs often exclude spiritual phenomena or
cast them in negative terms" (p. 171).

It is interesting and enlightening to observe that scientists with
a naturalistic perspective frequently object to the introduction of
the spiritual/religious domain into the psychotherapeutic relationship and the empirical study of mental healing for fear that un-
proven doctrines or ideas will jeopardize scientific integrity. Bergin
(1988a), however, reminded us that

> the critics forget that their critiques can be just as aptly applied to
> any of the dominant approaches, such as psychoanalysis, behav-
> ior modification, and the humanistic and cognitive approaches.
> Isn't it abundantly clear that advocates of these "doctrines" have
> strong beliefs, tend to over generalize, believe their approach is
> better, inculcate clients with predetermined views of what is
> healthy, and believe that their models have universal applicabil-
> ity? Is it not indefensible for critics to attack the spiritual ap-
> proach on the basis of criteria they are not willing to apply to their
> own orientations (p. 57)?

Second, this "conceptual bias" is linked to a marked insensitivity
within the scientific community and particularly within the mental
health care professions to the significant role religion plays in the
"subcultures" of our society. Bergin (1983) noted that within the
scientific community the level of professional interest in religion
was markedly less than that of the broader population, and that this
disparity caused the scientific community to "underestimate the
significance of religion in people's lives; when they do perceive it as

significant, they too often consider it a negative force" (p. 171). While a 1981 Gallup survey on religion in America indicated that 93 percent of the respondents stated a religious preference and 55 percent ranked religion as *very important* in their lives, religion still remained "an orphan in academia" (p. 171).

Third, these "conceptual and attitudinal biases" have been incorporated into much of the empirical work done on mental and physical well-being, "so religious factors either are excluded from measurement and manipulation or are included in such a way as to prejudice the results" (p. 171). As we note in our discussion of various listings in this bibliography, measures of mental health are too often slanted against the religious individual. For example, Bergin observed that measures of authoritarianism, ethnocentrism, dogmatism, ego strength, and irrational thinking frequently scored proreligious responses negatively. He commented that on Barron's Ego Strength Scale (1953), five out of a possible seven proreligious responses were counted against a person's ego strength.

Here one can clearly see that measurement of mental health is affected by mental health criteria that are often "subjective values." The result is that many empirical demonstrations of religion as a source of mental illness or malfunction are "tautologies," or circular arguments in empirical clothing. Bergin has not discounted previous empirical inquiry, but has warned that many studies may be "limited by scientific designs that have defined religious phenomena in such a way as to axiomatically preempt the possibility of healthy religion" (p. 172).

Is it genuinely possible to investigate empirically the relationship between mental and physical health and realized religion? Bergin (1988b) answered yes, and again argued that the procedure in investigating the "structures and processes" in such relationships "is not different in principle from inferences made about invisible and indescribable 'genes' in the history of biology, or subatomic particles in the history of physics" (pp. 23–24). These concepts proved to be "enormously useful . . . as indirect evidence" before the technology was developed that could directly observe these phenomena. In the same way, Bergin hypothesized plausibly that "these scientific developments may have more similarity to the quest for the spiritual than the historical estrangement between science and religion suggests" (p. 24).

Bergin argued that this kind of empirical investigation is not a regression back into magic, dogma, or unscientific thinking. Instead, he believed that a scientific approach might be better related to the spiritual than the "supernatural." Perhaps, Bergin speculated, spiritual reality "may be different from ordinary matter, but it still seems to be natural in that it proceeds according to the laws or principles." If this is so, even scientists with no religious commitment should be able to execute effectively this type of empirical research, as long as they maintain an awareness of their own presuppositions.

Bergin (1988b) announced that his own studies of people who report spiritual experiences indicate that these spiritual experiences are linked to mental healing. Indeed, these self-reports might "provide a basis for making inferences about possibly powerful aspects of human nature that are unlikely to be inferred by means of other theories" (p. 23). Marks (1978), for example, wrote after observing dramatic behavioral changes correlated with significant religious experiences:

> When it works, faith healing has a power for surpassing existing psychotherapy technology. *The order of magnitude of this difference is like that between nuclear and more conventional explosives* (our emphasis). But we have not yet harnessed nuclear power satisfactorily, and our understanding of faith and religious processes is far more primitive than knowledge of subatomic particles. Given a prepared mind, however, some paths into this labyrinth might be laid down. The important point is for hard-nosed experimenters to be alive to these possibilities, while retaining their methodological rigor (p. 530).

It is the work of scientists such as Bergin and Hood, research linking together the spiritual and the empirical, that forms the body of this bibliography. The best researchers demonstrate an adequate awareness of their own metaphysical presuppositions and biases, formulate a hypothesis to be explored empirically, and document the results.

Readers should also note that Bergin's analysis should itself be subjected to empirical scrutiny. Houts and Graham (1986), for example, conducted research generally supportive of Bergin's call for greater sensitivity on the part of psychotherapists to the influence of religious values in psychotherapy. They questioned, however, whether their findings supported Bergin's concern "that secular clinicians may routinely perceive religious individuals as more disturbed." Instead, strength of religious conviction appeared to be a more important factor in whether an individual's religious life was classified as healthy or pathological. "Both religious and nonreligious clinicians perceived the moderately religious client as having a more pessimistic prognosis and greater psychopathology than the very religious client . . ." (p. 270). Houts and Graham suggested this judgment might be consistent "with the cultural legacy of viewing religious belief as a crutch." Religious individuals who appeared to be lukewarm in their convictions might be more prone to be viewed as "disingenuous and disturbed." They hypothesized that religious doubt might "in fact be correlated with more objective measures of therapeutic prognosis and psychopathology," a surprising thought in light of Batson's conception of doubt as a sign of religious maturity.

It seems to us that it is no longer necessary to view the empirical study of religiosity and its effects on health and well-being as an impossible task; difficult, yes, but certainly not impossible. The psychological versus theological explanations for human motivation and behavior are not inherently mutually exclusive or necessarily in opposition to each other.

The current state of research increasingly embraces the validity of studying religion (including belief, practice, commitment, and knowledge) from a multidimensional research perspective. It should be remembered that all science involves value-laden issues. It appears that some, if not many, social scientists have adopted an anti-religious bias because they themselves are not believers. These values and biases need to be acknowledged and considered explicitly if progress is to continue. In the end, we agree with Albert Einstein that "science without religion is lame, religion without science is blind" (1940).

References

Barron, F. (1953). "An Ego Strength Scale Which Predicts Response to Psychotherapy." *Journal of Consulting Psychology, 17,* 327–333.

Batson, C. D. (1975). "Attribution as a Mediator of Bias in Helping." *Journal of Personality and Social Psychology, 32,* 455–466.

Berger, P. (1967). *The Sacred Canopy: Elements of a Sociological Theory of Religion.* Garden City, NY: Doubleday.

Bergin, A. E. (1980). "Psychotherapy and Religious Values." *Journal of Consulting and Clinical Psychology, 48*(1), 95–105.

Bergin, A. E. (1983). "Religiosity and Mental Health: A Critical Reevaluation and Meta-Analysis." *Professional Psychology, 14,* 170–184.

Bergin, A. E. (1988a). "The Spiritual Perspective Is Ecumenical and Eclectic (Rejoinder)." *Counseling and Values, 33,* 57–59.

Bergin, A. E. (1988b). "Three Contributions of a Spiritual Perspective to Counseling, Psychotherapy, and Behavior Change." *Counseling and Values, 33,* 21–31.

Bergin, A. E. (1991). "Values and Religious Issues in Psychotherapy and Mental Health." *American Psychologist, 46*(4), 394–403.

Bergin, A. E., Masters, K. S., and Richards, P. S. (1988). "Religiousness and Mental Health Reconsidered: A Study of an Intrinsically Religious Sample." *Journal of Counseling Psychology, 34,* 197–204.

Einstein, A. (1940). *Science, Philosophy, and Religion.* New York: Conference on Science, Philosophy, and Religion and Their Relation to the Democratic Way of Life.

Genia, V., and Shaw, D. G. (1991). "Religion, Intrinsic-Extrinsic Orientation, and Depression." *Review of Religious Research, 32*(3), 274–283.

Hood, R. W., Jr. (1989). "The Relevance of Theologies for Religious Experiencing." *Journal of Psychology and Theology, 17*(4), 336–342.

Houts, A. C., and Graham, K. (1986). "Can Religion Make You Crazy? Impact of Client and Therapist Religious Values on Clinical Judgments." *Journal of Consulting and Clinical Psychology, 54*(2), 267–271.

Marks, I. M. (1978). "Behavioral Psychotherapy of Adult Neurosis." In S. L. Garfield and A. E. Bergin (Eds.), *Handbook of Psychotherapy and Behavior* (p. 530). New York: Garfield.

Propst, L. R. (1980a). "A Comparison of the Cognitive Restructuring Psychotherapy Paradigm and Several Spiritual Approaches to Mental Health." *Journal of
Psychology and Theology*, 8(2), 107–114.

Propst, L. R. (1980b). "The Comparative Efficacy of Religious and Nonreligious
Imagery for the Treatment of Mild Depression in Religious Individuals." *Cognitive Therapy and Research*, 4(2), 167–178.

Watson, P. J., Morris, R. J., and Hood, R. W., Jr. (1987). "Antireligious Humanistic Values, Guilt, and Self Esteem." *Journal for the Scientific Study of Religion*,
26(4), 535–546.

10

The Christian Faith as a Model
of Realized Religion to Health Research

THE OVERARCHING MESSAGE of the majority of studies presented and analyzed in this survey of religion and health affirms the positive effect of religious belief and practice on significant health issues. The work of Larson, for instance, has demonstrated that religious people experience higher levels of well-being in a number of areas. For example, men who attended church had lower blood pressure levels than those who did not attend church and cared little about religion. Even after other factors such as weight, smoking, habits, and age were controlled, church attendance still was linked to lower blood pressure levels.

Not only lower blood pressure levels have been correlated with religious belief. Fully 80 percent of the psychiatric research on religion and health shows that religious belief is highly beneficial. Church attendance, prayer, and the social support network available in religious communities are significant positive factors in helping patients. According to Larson, people "with the potential for mental health problems improve or will be protected if they are religiously committed" (Hall, 1992, p. 20). Stress, Larson believed, is reduced by religious commitment before it develops into mental health problems. Even people who have only attended church for a short period of time seem to improve in their mental health status.

The prophylactic benefit of religious belief is quite striking. In a review published by Larson, nineteen out of twenty studies demonstrated the positive benefit of religious commitment in preventing alcoholism. Sixteen out of sixteen studies indicated lower suicide rates for religious people. Religious belief is also correlated with lowered rates of mental disorder, drug use, and premarital sex.

Religious faith that is consistently practiced also is associated with higher levels of life satisfaction. Larson reported that religious people who live out their faith "are more likely to say they are enjoying life, that they like their work, their marriage, their family. Religiously committed people on the whole enjoy living" (p. 20). Even people suffering stress from physical or mental illness "are more apt to report they are enjoying life than people not religiously committed" (p. 20). Research on the parents of children suffering from cancer, for example, indicates a positive role for religion in effective coping.

Are specific ways of being religious helpful or harmful? According to Larson, the answer is both. On the one hand, "an honest commitment to God," moderate flexibility, openness to change, and a willingness to acknowledge the need for assistance from others raise levels of health. On the other hand, a conservative theology that is not purposefully lived out can be harmful. It is "extremely unhealthy to have conservative religious beliefs and not be going to church," wrote Larson. In addition, it is "unhealthy to have strong religious convictions but not have those convictions actually producing concrete changes" (p. 22).

What theological sense can we make out of this extremely interesting and enlightening data? Is it even fair to raise the question of theology? Does the content of one's faith, what one specifically believes or disbelieves about God and God's actions in the world, make a difference in levels of mental or physical health? Is a Moslem or Buddhist as likely to be healthy as a practicing Christian? Is it the practice itself that produces health, or can a particular belief-system—with unique and specific ideas about God and religious practice—be an important factor in religion and health? That is to say, does theology make a difference? Even more specifically, how might Christian belief—as encompassed in the Scripture, tradition, and practice of the church—respond to the research of Larson and other researchers represented in this volume? Indeed, would a Christian perspective consider mental and physical health as viable criteria for determining the truth or efficacy of religious faith?

In a recent interview with Larson, we addressed a number of these questions. For instance, is a liberal or conservative Christian theology associated with increased or decreased levels of mental or physical health? Larson's response was that "[w]e have not done enough research to say." The principles for wise living entailed and advocated in the wisdom literature of the Old Testament did seem to be validated. As Larson put it, "It makes a difference if you come to the house of God and experience God's love within that context. You will generally have a longer and happier life" (p. 21). In addition, the Christian insistence on living out one's faith, the crucial connection between faith and practice, does seem to make a difference in levels of health. A "healthy devotional life, giving to the poor, and the serving or volunteering ministry of all believers appears to be highly beneficial" (p. 22).

And yet might not the same be said for the Jewish believer who regularly attends synagogue and follows the Torah, the Moslem firmly committed to living out the religious life commanded by Mohammed in the Koran, or the Hindu faithfully worshipping the plethora of Hindu gods? The ethical practices of all four religious traditions—Christianity, Judaism, Islam, and Hinduism—might be quite similar and their theological underpinnings drastically different. All four believers might have elevated levels of mental and physical health and yet possess incommensurable cognitive religious belief structures undergirding their behavior.

Larson's own religious background, experience, and reflection on his religious formation is a case in point. We asked Larson about the frequently voiced critique that religion is simply a crutch for people who can't make it in life. He responded, somewhat surprisingly, by affirming that religion is a crutch for many people and that this is not necessarily a bad thing. He himself had grown up on welfare in a single-parent family. "I certainly need the 'crutch' that knowing Christ provides. Indeed, Jesus taught that he came to help those in need." Larson explained that this is perhaps why minority groups are "much more religious than whites, and women more than men" (p. 21), less-educated people more religious than well-educated, and the aged more religious than the young.

His theological conclusion? "Findings like these fit with what Christ is saying in Luke 4. These are the people he has come to assist. . . . This indicates to me that God is very willing to be an enabler of those who admit they need such a crutch. He says, 'I have come to the broken, to those who are in chains, to those who need healing, to those who are in bondage.' Do they need a crutch? Yes. Do I? Yes" (p. 21).

Do other religious traditions offer the same theological grid for interpreting Larson's empirical data? How would the experience of the poor be interpreted in the Buddhist or Hindu traditions? Would the willingness to accept a crutch from God fit either tradition? Or the tradition of Islam? Clearly further research is needed on the relationship between theological content, practice, and levels of physical and mental health.

How might one explore the issue of religion and health from a strictly Christian perspective? That is to say, how might a Christian theological perspective interpret the empirical research on religion and health that has already been produced? And how might a Christian world-view, with its accompanying theological underpinning, point toward new areas of research that have yet to be explored?

What, for example, of the issue of physical healing? Jesus' ministry is sprinkled with remarkable examples of miraculous healings. The shortest and most concise story of Jesus' ministry, the Gospel of Mark, is replete with examples of Jesus' concern for the sick and his ministry to them. From the very beginning of Jesus' ministry, healings take place on what seems to be a regular basis.

Shortly after Jesus inaugurated his public ministry he healed the mother-in-law of Simon Peter of a fever by taking her by the hand and lifting her up (Mk. 1 : 29−31). This single instance of healing is repeated on a more broad scale. Mark tells us that "the whole city gathered around the door" and that "he cured many who were sick with various diseases" (Mk. 1 : 33−34). On one of Jesus' first teaching tours through Galilee he healed a man suffering from leprosy

(Mk. 1:40–45) and connected this healing with his proclamation of the arrival of God's reign in human history. Some days later Jesus healed a paralytic in Capernaum and associated his healing with the forgiveness of the paralytic's sins (Mk. 2:1–12). Those who witnessed the miracle "were all amazed and glorified God, saying, 'We have never seen anything like this'" (Mk. 2:12).

As we move through the Gospel of Mark the healings continue in what Mark emphasized are illustrations of a broader pattern. Jesus seemed to consider healing as a normal, specific, significant aspect of his ministry. Indeed, Mark commented that "wherever he went, into villages or cities or farms, they laid the sick in the marketplaces, and begged him that they might touch even the fringe of his cloak; and all who touched it were healed" (Mk. 6:56).

Mark was insistent that Jesus was also concerned about the mental well-being of the people he encountered, and he recorded a number of dramatic exorcisms in which people were restored to mental health after Jesus drove out the demonic presence tormenting them. Of course, the idea of demonic possession is highly controversial, and few of the empirical studies mentioned in this volume explore the subject. Jesus himself, however, consistently affirmed the reality of angels and demons, following the Pharisaic party in its affirmation of this wider reality, and unhesitatingly confronted the demonic when he discerned its manifestations in the life of Israel.

It should be noted, however, that Jesus did not invariably couple demonic oppression or possession to instances of mental or physical disease. Luke, a physician by profession, was careful to distinguish between Jesus the healer and Jesus the exorcist. "As the sun was setting," Luke related, "all those who had any who were sick with various kinds of diseases brought them to him; and he laid his hands on each of them and cured them. Demons also came out of many, shouting, 'You are the Son of God!' But he rebuked them and would not allow them to speak, because they knew he was the Messiah" (Lk. 4:40–41).

We misunderstand the significance of Jesus' healing ministry if we separate Jesus' healing acts, whether on the physically or mentally sick, from his wider role as Israel's promised Messiah. As we have just seen, Luke interpreted Jesus' healing acts as messianic pointers, acted parables announcing the arrival of God's anointed in Israel's midst. Indeed, Matthew, Mark, Luke, and John speak with one voice in their insistence that Jesus' healing miracles cannot be adequately understood apart from his broader proclamation that in him God's reign is breaking into history.

Jesus' miracles cannot stand on their own. If we attempt to view them as simply miraculous works, Jesus becomes one of many wonder-workers present in Israel in the first century. In fact, the distinguishing mark of Jesus' healing ministry is its inseparable connection to a wider purpose. In him, Jesus unapologetically proclaimed, God's kingdom has arrived. If so, the evidence of its arrival in his person was Jesus' ability to perform works that manifested the character of God's kingdom. The question to ask, then, regarding a specific miracle is, What's the message in the miracle? Is it specifically significant, for example, that Jesus purposely healed people who were blind, a type of healing that is never recorded as taking place earlier in Israel's history?

This question can be answered only by taking a closer look at Jewish eschatological expectations during the time of Jesus' life and ministry. The word "eschatological" is closely related to the Greek word *eschatos*, the common Greek word for "last." Viewed theologically, the "eschaton" is "the last" or "end time," the time when God's plans and purposes for history come to their fruition and culmination. "Eschatology" is the branch of systematic theology that focuses on the "last things," with a particular emphasis on biblical prophecy. "Jewish eschatological expectations," therefore, are extremely important if we are to understand Jesus' ministry and why he did the things he did. In short, what did his Jewish audience expect would take place when the Messiah, God's anointed, entered human history? What actions would manifest his arrival and the time of the end?

While Jewish messianic and eschatological expectations were quite varied in Jesus' day, we can identify certain widely held viewpoints. When the Messiah came, many Jews believed, this "present evil age" would draw to a close and the "age to come" would begin. History was clearly demarcated between these two ages. The first, this present evil age, was characterized by sickness, sin, the demonic, the oppression of Israel by its enemies, and the continuing triumph of evil people over those attempting to follow faithfully Yahweh, the God of Israel revealed to Moses on Mount Sinai. The age to come, introduced by the arrival of God's anointed, the Messiah, would be characterized by health, peace, freedom from foreign oppression, the breaking of demonic power, and the flowering of justice throughout the land. Most importantly, with the arrival of the Messiah this present evil age would draw to a close and the age to come would begin.

Hence, when Jesus began his public ministry and announced that the kingdom of God was now drawing near (Mk. 1:14–15), he ignited a host of Messianic expectations. For example, he needed to heal the sick if he was the promised Messiah. To fail to do so would severely undercut his claim to be Yahweh's promised anointed. Conversely, if Jesus worked healing miracles, these parables in action would announce that God was drawing human history to its conclusion. This present evil age was ending. The age to come was beginning. And Jesus' works backed up his message.

Or at least at first glance they seem to do so. Isaiah, for instance, had predicted that when the Messiah came to Israel certain perspectives and attitudes would characterize his arrival: good news preached to the oppressed, liberty proclaimed to the captives, and release granted to the prisoners. The presence of God's anointed would announce the year of the Lord's favor (Isa. 61:1–2). In fact, Jesus' first sermon, recorded in the Gospel of Luke, points to this prophecy of Isaiah as fulfilled in him. "He has sent me to proclaim release to the captives and recovery of sight to the blind, to let the oppressed go free, to proclaim the year of the Lord's favor" (Luke 4:18–19).

And yet, surprisingly and abruptly, Jesus stopped in midsentence in his reading of Isaiah's prophecy. Isaiah had written "to proclaim the year of the Lord's favor, *and the day of vengeance of our God*" (italics added). Jesus read up through "to proclaim the year of the LORD's favor" and stopped. He then announced to his audience that "Today this scripture has been fulfilled in your hearing" (Luke 4:21). Why didn't Jesus read the entire passage? What is the significance of his sudden pause?

Jesus purposely separated or divided a drama that almost all of his Jewish listeners believed would be one scene. In other words, a one act play now became two acts, with profound implications that continue to ripple out through human history. To generalize, the Jewish expectation was that when the Messiah came fallen history would draw to a close. The "eschaton" or "end" of this present evil age, inaugurated and completed by the coming of the Messiah, would naturally entail the dissolution of its fundamental characteristics: sin, evil, and disease. All these would end in the final judgment upon human history introduced by the Messiah. In Isaiah's words, "the day of vengeance of our God" would come with the arrival of the Messiah.

Jesus crucially modified the prevalent Jewish expectations for both the "eschaton" and the Messiah himself. As for the eschaton and the fundamental relationship between the ages, Jesus shocked his listeners by teaching that the end of the ages had arrived, the kingdom of God was breaking into history with the arrival of his person and acts, and yet this present evil age was to continue, at least for a time. Unexpectedly and paradoxically, Jesus posited an overlap between the ages that no other Jewish teacher had foreseen or taught.

The implications of Jesus' teaching regarding the relationship between the ages must be deeply explored for a number of reasons, including the issue of religion and health. For example, if this present evil age with its accompanying characteristics is still present with us it should be no surprise to the Christian that sin, mental and physical disease, struggle, pain, and death remain inescapable contours of the human landscape. Indeed, a Christian perspective would insist that a major component of mental health is the ability to acknowledge the difficulties inherent in human life and the call from God to live a wise and loving life in the midst of these difficulties.

The presence of this present evil age is only half the story, though, at least as Jesus presented it. For Jesus simultaneously taught that the age to come had in him penetrated into the midst of this present evil age. His healing miracles and exorcisms demonstrated this very reality. With this interpenetration, then, Christ taught and the church has consistently expected that the reality and life of the age to come will occasionally manifest itself—sometimes dramatically— in the midst of the disease and death characteristic of a fallen world. Again, we will have to explore the implications of this invasion and the mingling of two worlds in our reflections on religion and health.

Before we do so, however, we have to ask a further question. Why this overlap between the ages? What was the purpose of Jesus' entrance into human history? And what of his ministry, death, and resurrection? Why would he come and then leave? What did he come to accomplish? And what is he still doing in this present in-between time between his first and second comings?

To answer these questions we need to return to a crucial juncture in Jesus' ministry. It was at Caesarea Philippi, in the north of Israel, that Jesus drew his public ministry to a close and began to teach his disciples privately about the purpose of his coming and what awaited them as his disciples. Jesus was evidently concerned that the disciples themselves didn't understand the rhyme and reason of his coming. They, too, were expecting history to soon draw to a close and the kingdom of God to become fully manifest. After all, they had seen Jesus performing wondrous works for close to three years, works that pointed to divine power and wisdom resident in him and manifested for the specific purpose of teaching Israel that the kingdom of God was at hand. Surely the story would soon reach its conclusion, the disciples thought. Soon God would reveal the undisguised glory of the anointed one to Israel, and the Messiah, along with his faithful disciples, would be welcomed and honored in glory.

Take, for example, the apostle Peter. At Caesarea Philippi Jesus asked his disciples, "Who do people say that the Son of Man is?" In answer, the gathered disciples fired off a number of responses reflecting common Jewish expectations. "And they said, 'Some say John the Baptist, but others Elijah, and still others Jeremiah or one

of the prophets.'" Jesus, however, wanted to know what the disciples
themselves thought. Peter, the leader of the group, responded, "You
are the Messiah, the Son of the living God." We must remember that
when Peter said this, his statement was enfolded in the messianic
expectations we have been discussing. That is, for Peter to identify
Jesus as the Messiah was also to say that he expected history to soon
change dramatically. The glory of the age to come was at hand. The
present evil age was ending. Suffering, pain, disease, evil, and death
would soon be no more. What Jesus had already taught and acted out
had convinced Peter that the last time was at hand. What could be
better? What better time to be alive and invited to follow him?
(Matt. 16:13–16)

Note that Peter's identification of Jesus as the Messiah was
affirmed by Jesus himself. In fact, Jesus exclaimed that Peter's
words were inspired by God. "Blessed are you, Simon son of Jonah!
For flesh and blood has not revealed this to you, but my Father in
heaven" (Matt. 16:17). Peter was right. Jesus was the promised
anointed one. God had revealed this to Peter. And then come the
shocking, unexpected words. "From that time on, Jesus began to
show his disciples that he must go to Jerusalem and undergo great
suffering at the hands of the high priests and scribes, and be killed,
and on the third day be raised" (Matt. 16:21).

The anointed, promised one of God rejected, killed, and then
resurrected? While this aspect of the Christian story is familiar to
the Christian community, it was terribly shocking news to Jesus'
disciples and made little sense to them historically, theologically, or
emotionally. When the Messiah came he was to reign in glory. When
the Messiah came he was to judge the oppressors of Israel. When the
Messiah came he was to inaugurate the age to come. When the Messiah came he was to end the present evil age. When the Messiah
came evil, sin, pain, and sickness were to be eradicated. How, then,
could the Messiah himself be devoured by the evil and death of this
present evil age?

No, Peter thought, Jesus must be wrong. And so he rebuked him.
"And Peter took him aside and began to rebuke him, saying, 'God
forbid it, Lord! This must never happen to you'" (Matt. 16:22). Je-

sus' response to Peter was immediate and pointed. "Get behind me, Satan! You are a stumbling block to me; for you are setting your mind not on divine things but on human things" (Matt. 16:23). Jesus shockingly identified Peter's words with the very demonic realm he had come to conquer. His coming then, could accomplish its deepest purposes only through an unforeseen and inexplicable route, death on a Roman cross.

We must not overlook the troubling theological meaning such a death would have communicated to the disciples. Moses' words in the Torah taught that "anyone hung on a tree is under God's curse." For example, Mosaic legislation demanded that a murderer's body be publicly hung from a tree as a sign that God's curse rested upon the murderer. His execution represented God's judgment (Dt. 21:23). And now not only was Jesus predicting that Gentiles would put him to death, but in a manner teaching that God's curse rested upon him. How could this be? How could the cursed of God be the blessed of God, God's promised Messiah?

As Mark continued his narrative of the last few weeks of Jesus' life, he presented the disciples—people who will later be described as the foundation stones of the church—as confused, depressed, and terribly bewildered. They didn't understand why Jesus was predicting future suffering for himself and for them. They didn't comprehend why Israel's religious leaders, the very people who should welcome the Messiah upon his arrival, would reject him and turn him over to the Roman authorities on a charge of attempting to lead an insurrection against Caesar.

At least three times in the final weeks of Jesus' life he predicted his betrayal, suffering, death, and resurrection. The familiarity of most people with this story anesthetizes them to the shock, horror, and confusion the disciples felt when they heard Jesus' predictions for the first time. Mark commented that after the second time Jesus made the prediction of future suffering the disciples "did not understand what he was saying and were afraid to ask him" (Mark 9:32). As Jesus resolutely continued to make his way toward his painful destiny in Jerusalem his followers "were amazed, and those who followed were afraid" (Mark 10:32).

We should note that Jesus' prediction of a resurrection after three days seemed to offer scant comfort to his closest disciples. Although Old Testament teaching will in retrospect help his followers to understand the necessity of his suffering, their comprehension of the Old Testament had not prepared them for the idea of a resurrected Messiah. Again, the key question was to raise its head repeatedly: How could the cursed of God be the blessed of God? A crucified Messiah clearly appeared to be a contradiction in terms.

Those who followed Jesus during his earthly ministry were not the only ones who would struggle with the idea of a crucified, resurrected Messiah. As events played themselves out as Jesus had predicted, there were many who once opposed Jesus' message and ministry who subsequently responded in faith. The Peter who had been filled with doubt and fear, indeed, had denied Jesus three times at the point of his greatest need, was found in the Temple area forty days later preaching the message that Jesus had been raised from the dead. Thousands in Peter's audience—almost entirely Jewish—responded to his message and believed in the resurrected Jesus as Israel's promised Messiah.

Some, though, continued to reject this possibility, and none more so than Saul, later to be known to his readers as Paul. For Saul the Pharisee the message of the early Jewish Christian community by definition had to be false. Why? The cursed of God could not be the blessed of God. For Saul, the manner of Jesus' death—crucifixion on a Roman cross—demonstrated that Yahweh, the God of Israel, had rejected Jesus. Even the early Christian community, Saul's theological opponents, seemed to agree that in some way God had separated himself from Jesus at the time of his death. It was publicly known, for example, that close to the time of Jesus' death Jesus had cried out, "My God, My God, why have you forsaken me?" (Matt. 27: 46).

If Jesus was cursed of God, Saul reasoned, he could not possibly be the blessed of God, God's anointed, the Messiah. Saul concluded that the early Christian accounts of the resurrection must be fabrications and its theological underpinnings blasphemy. In his zeal for the faith of Israel he began to persecute ferociously the fledgling Christian community. The basis of his accusation against them was that they were lying about God—committing blasphemy—a capital offense.

Luke, the author of a two-volume account of Jesus and the early Christian community, related that Saul asked Caiaphas, the Jewish high-priest who had resided over Jesus' trial, for letters authorizing him to arrest members of the Christian community in Damascus. Luke wrote that as Saul approached Damascus "suddenly a light from heaven flashed around him" and a voice addressed Saul, asking "Saul, Saul, why do you persecute me?" (Acts 9:4). Saul asked in return, "Who are you, Lord? The reply came, 'I am Jesus, whom you are persecuting. But get up and enter the city, and you will be told what you are to do'" (Acts 9:5–6).

The emotional, spiritual, and theological revolution produced by this appearance of Jesus in Saul's life cannot be overestimated. Not only did Saul (now referred to as Paul) find himself with innocent blood on his hands, but he was forced to admit that something that had made no theological sense to him was actually the work of God. Somehow, Paul had to admit, the cursed of God was the blessed of God. The next seventeen years of Paul's life would be spent in trying to make theological sense out of a life, death, and resurrection that at first glance made no sense at all.

Paul's answer to the riddle of Jesus' life and death is found in the first theological tract he ever composed, a short letter he penned to churches he had founded in the Roman province of Galatia. The question Paul had mulled over for years had revolved around the issue of cursing and blessing. On the one hand, Jesus' death on the cross surely indicated that God had in some way deserted him; he was the cursed of God. And yet Jesus' subsequent resurrection, attested irrefutably by his appearance to Paul on the road to Damascus, declared that Jesus was indeed the blessed of God, God's promised Messiah. Paul's theological task was to resolve theologically these two seemingly contradictory propositions.

Paul did so in the third chapter of his Galatian letter. There, in what only can be described as a theological tour de force, Paul argued that cursing and blessing, at least in Jesus' case, can be resolved. How so? Paul's argument runs as follows.

All those who "rely on the works of the law are under a curse"

(Gal. 3:10). That is to say, if sinful human beings attempt to use obedience to the law of God as the basis of obtaining a righteous relationship with God, they will end up cursed, that is, separated from God. Why? Paul provided two reasons. First, the law was never given to Israel as a means of obtaining a relationship with God. Israel's relationship with God had already been established on the principle of faith, the pattern of the great patriarch Abraham's response to the promises of God.

Second, and more significant for Paul's argument in Galatians 3, fallen human beings cannot use obedience to the law as the basis for establishing their relationship with God because if the law is used in this manner, that is, as a means of salvation in and of itself, perfect obedience is required. Even one act of disobedience to the law is sufficient to separate a person from God, a separation Paul described as being under a curse. As Paul put it, "Cursed is everyone who does not observe and obey all the things written in the book of the law" (Gal. 3:10). Paul argued that if we attempt to use the law in a manner that the law was never designed to fulfill or facilitate—obtaining salvation on the basis of human obedience—separation from God can be the only unfortunate result.

Indeed, Paul argued that salvation is obtained on the basis of a different principle, that of faith. After all, Abraham had believed or trusted that the promises God had made to him would be fulfilled and on the basis of that faith had been declared to be in a righteous relationship with God. Those who believe or follow the pattern of Abraham's faith, Paul contended, receive a righteous relationship with God—on the basis of the principle of faith.

The question for Paul then became, Faith in what? or Faith in whom? Or to rephrase the question, If all human beings exist in a state of separation from God because of their sinful condition and the acts that flow from that condition, how can this condition be overcome? They themselves cannot overcome it because they represent the problem itself. It is they who are separated or cursed. They lack the power, condition, or qualification to overcome their own cursed situation. To employ David Larson's phrase, human beings do "need a crutch." There is, as Larson's research indicates, a human need to look beyond itself for strength, healing, and restoration, but Paul insisted that left to ourselves we remain in a state of alienation, from God, from others, from ourselves. It was at this juncture that Paul turned to Jesus and offered his life's story as the solution to what seemed to be an intractable problem.

How has Paul resolved his fundamental theological dilemma? "Christ," Paul contended, "redeemed us from the curse of the law by becoming a curse for us—for it is written, 'Cursed is everyone who hangs on a tree' . . ." (Gal. 3 : 13). In a dramatic theological about face Paul had taken his fundamental objection to the early Christian community—its assertion that the cursed of God is indeed the blessed of God—and made this assertion the foundation of his own understanding of spiritual reality. In doing so, he answered the question Jesus' closest disciples could not comprehend in the days before the crucifixion and resurrection.

Exactly what is entailed in Paul's assertion that Christ has become a curse for humanity so that humanity might be blessed in him on the basis of faith? And what might be the implications of Jesus' and Paul's teaching for future research on the relationship between religious faith and health?

Both Jesus and his apostle Paul were convinced that sin and evil had deeply affected, indeed infected, all of human life and experience. Things at present are not what they should be. Something has gone wrong. Jesus' own phrase for this grave time was the common Jewish one, "this present evil age." Paul contributed to Jesus' teaching by showing how deeply evil has affected human nature, indeed crippling it so severely that God must act directly in Christ to rescue humanity from its dire situation. Neither Paul nor Jesus downplayed the seriousness of the human dilemma. That human life continues to be characterized by physical and mental illness, addictive behaviors, moral blindness and depravity, and death itself would be no surprise to them. Both were realists. And yet their realism refused to succumb to pessimism, cynicism, or skepticism. Indeed, it was a realism marked by a deep hope of restoration and healing, both for this present life and for the future. How so? How can realism and hope be combined without succumbing to naiveté on the one hand or disillusionment on the other?

We can begin to resolve this question by looking back on Jesus' teaching on the kingdom of God from a post-resurrection perspective. Recall that the disciples were terrified and confused by Jesus' prediction that he must suffer, die, and be raised from the dead (Matt. 16: 21–28). Such dire predictions undercut their Messianic expectation that when God's anointed one arrived God's kingdom would be manifested in glory and power. Jesus' teaching and deeds had clearly manifested the presence of the kingdom, but the prediction of suffering and death seemed to belie his claim that God's reign was uniquely invading history through him.

As events unfurled, Jesus' predictions proved true. He was rejected by the religious authorities of Israel, handed over to a Roman procurator for trial on a trumped-up charge, and finally executed on a Roman cross. The one who so clearly had manifested God's blessings to Israel died under God's curse. Cursing, though, was not the final word. Jesus had predicted that after three days he would be raised from the dead, a sign that the curse of sin and death had been overcome in him. And on the third day, according to all four Gospels, Jesus rose from the dead.

The resurrection fomented the same theological struggle and ferment in the disciples as it would later actuate in the apostle Paul. Somehow, in light of the resurrection, Jesus was simultaneously the cursed of God and the promised Messiah. The resurrection demonstrated irrefutably that in Christ the age to come had indeed arrived. The great surprise was this: although the age to come had arrived, this present evil age continued with its pain, disease, evil, and death. In Christ the end of history seemed to have arrived and yet history continued on its normal, ferocious, skewed path. Augustus still ruled the Roman empire. Pilate continued to crucify rebellious Jews. People continued to suffer from disease. Death remained the final word for all.

How could the dynamic between this present evil age and the age to come be explained? And how might this dynamic inform research on religion and health conducted within a Christian theological framework?

Gordon Fee, professor of New Testament at Regent College in Vancouver, British Columbia, described and analyzed the new theological dynamic introduced by Christ. Fee (1993) first insisted that "the basic theological framework of the entire New Testament is eschatological," the position presented in this chapter. As Fee put it, the Jews of Jesus' day "thought they lived at the very brink of time, when God would step into history and bring an end to this age and usher in the age to come" (p. 131). The new age introduced by the Messiah "would be a time of righteousness (e.g., Isa. 11:4−5). Sin and sickness would be done away with (e.g., Zech. 13:1; Isa. 53:5). Even the material creation would feel the joyful effects of this new age (e.g., Isa. 11:6−9)" (p. 132).

After the resurrection of Jesus the disciples were forced to grapple with a remarkable new reality. Jesus' ministry had been validated by God and yet history was continuing on its course. Initially this made little sense for them. As they asked in the Book of Acts, would this not now be a good time for Jesus to "restore the kingdom to Israel?" that is, to draw this present evil age to a close and fully introduce the life of the age to come?

Jesus' response was no. Instead, Jesus returned to the Father and sent the Holy Spirit to fill his body, the church, which in turn would have the responsibility to manifest the life of the age to come in this present evil age until Jesus returned to earth. This gap between the first and second coming of the Messiah and the interim ministry of the church was entirely unexpected.

Peter's theological ruminations on this surprising and unforeseen turn of events began to show themselves in his evangelistic sermons in the Book of Acts. Take, for example, his sermon in Acts 3. Here Peter explained his realization, in Fee's words, that "Jesus had not come to usher in the 'final' end, but the 'beginning' of the end, as it were." Yes, "the blessings and benefits of the future had already come. In a sense, therefore, the end had already come. But in another sense the end had not yet fully come. Thus it was *already*, but *not yet*" (pp. 132−133).

Hence, as Fee explained matters, the Christian community, Christ's body on earth, the church, is a people that presently lives between the times—that is, between the *beginning* of the end and the *consummation* of the end.

Already they knew God's free and full forgiveness, but they had
not yet been perfected (Phil. 3:7–14). *Already* victory over death
was theirs (1 Cor. 3:22), *yet* they would still die (Phil. 3:20–22).
Already they lived in the Spirit, *yet* they still lived in the world
where Satan could attack (e.g., Eph. 6:10–17). *Already* they had
been justified and faced no condemnation (Rom. 8:1), *yet* there
was still to be a future judgment (2 Cor. 5:10). They were God's
future people; they had been conditioned by the future. They
knew its benefits, lived in light of its values, but they, as we, still
had to live out these benefits and values in the present world
(p. 132–133).

It is this tension between the present and the future, between this
present evil age and the age to come, between the *already* and the *not
yet*, that characterizes human history at the present moment and will
do so until God's acts in Christ are consummated at the second coming of God's anointed one, the Messiah. For those who choose to live
by the principle of faith that Paul had advocated in his Galatian epis-
tle, life in this *present in-between time* will always be characterized by
the fundamental tension of life between the ages. That is, the unexpected overlap of this present evil age and the age to come will determine what we can expect of life at the present moment.

From a Christian perspective of life between the ages we can develop a number of implications for the relationship between religion and health and future empirical research on this topic. What
might the paradigm of life between the ages offer for understanding
the relationship between religion and health? What further questions might it raise?

First, there is a clear sense of incompleteness to this present in-
between time. In Christ, a human being can experience the life of
the age to come in this present evil age, but that experience by
definition must be limited, incomplete, a taste of things to come,
but always short of complete fulfillment and fruition. Why? We still
live between the ages. The consummation of the ages, an event that
comes only when Christ comes a second time, is yet to be. Hence,
we can taste of the future in Christ, but at present that is all we re-

ceive. We presently may receive an appetizer, but the main course awaits the consummation.

If this is the present reality, if we can indeed sample the hors d'oeuvres of the kingdom, then faith in Christ is likely to have a positive effect on our mental and physical health. After all, when Jesus began to minister publicly, purposefully manifesting the reality of God's reign in the midst of this present evil age, he often did so by healing people. Some people received healing from physical diseases such as paralysis and leprosy. Others received healing from internal hemorrhaging and blindness. Some were raised from the dead.

Christ's healing power, always to be thought of in connection with the invasion of the reign of God, also manifested itself in the healing of the human mind and spirit. Through the forgiveness Jesus offered, people received deliverance from guilt, ingrained, harmful habits, and the oppression of evil. Simultaneously, however, life as usual seemed to go on for many. Not all were healed. All would need to be forgiven again and again. Habits didn't change overnight. Every believer would sooner or later face the reality of death. Why?

Here we see clearly the "already but not yet" dynamic of life between the ages. In this in-between time between Christ's first and second comings those who follow him are a mixture of old and new, good and bad, health and disease. And this is the very thing we should expect. This dynamic, then, should prevent us from being either overly optimistic or pessimistic when it comes to the relationship between Christian faith and health issues. For example, the dynamic of life between the ages—when the age to come and this present evil age overlap—should occasionally manifest positive health outcomes. The kingdom of God has invaded this present evil age. However, this present evil age still exists, and whatever expectations we have for health issues must be shaped by the broader perspective and purposes of the kingdom in the midst of a fallen world.

That is to say, Jesus himself never made the direct pursuit of health—mental or physical—a fundamental priority for those he called to follow him. There might well be positive health outcomes in the life of discipleship, but Jesus seemed to feel that health outcomes would be corollary to a deeper, fundamental purpose for his followers, that of witnessing faithfully to the person and work of Christ in a world contaminated by deep evil.

Perhaps C. S. Lewis's (1970) principle of first and second things may prove helpful here. Lewis advocated a hierarchy of values grounded in reality or being itself. Because of the nature of things— for Lewis because God had created things with a given structure and value—certain things were "first things" and others were "second things." There were small goods and great goods. A small good might be derived from pursuing a great good, but the reverse could never be true. Take the example of pleasure. In a hedonistic society a second thing—the pursuit of pleasure—is treated as a first thing, a fundamental rather than derived value. The assured result, in Lewis's thinking, is that such a society will always be dissatisfied, unhappy, unfulfilled, ultimately disillusioned. Why?

Second things such as pleasure can only be obtained by pursuing first things. When pursued directly, they escape us ultimately. Work, a first thing, leads to pleasure, a second thing. One has only to re- member the deep pleasure of accomplishing a difficult task or learning a demanding skill to realize the truth of the principle. In Lewis's words, "You can't get second things by putting them first; you can get second things only by putting first things first. From which it would follow that the question, What things are first? is of concern not only to philosophers but to everyone" (p. 280).

How might this principle relate to the question of religion and health and the dynamic of the kingdom? Jesus considered faith and loyalty to him and the values of his kingdom a first thing. In addi- tion, he warned of the possibility of placing second things before first things, with the result that one would lose the very thing one was seeking. "For those who want to save their life will lose it, and those who lose their life for my sake, and for the sake of the gospel, will save it. For what will it profit them to gain the whole world and forfeit their life?" (Mark 8:35–36)

In Jesus' kingdom, loss becomes gain, death to self becomes life, and confession, repentance, and forgiveness lead to reconciliation; taking the lowest place is actually the place of greatest honor, for self-denial leads to self-fulfillment. It is indeed an upside-down kingdom. But only, perhaps, from the perspective of those who have made the mistake of placing second things first, or of denying the possibility of ever distinguishing between second and first things. The result is we lose the very thing we were hoping to gain. Or as Lewis puts it, "Every preference of a small good to a great, or a partial good to a total good, involves the loss of the small or partial good for which the sacrifice was made" (p. 280).

From a Christian perspective, then, sacrifice, pain, challenge, hardship, service, forgiveness, even martyrdom itself might have long-term positive health outcomes and perhaps even short-term ones. The pursuit of first things in the light of the invasion of the kingdom might well have positive side effects. If these positive side effects are pursued directly as first things, however, they are apt not to be found or experienced.

Here, we would argue, is one of the weaknesses of present empirical research on the relationship between religion and health. If one advocates the pursuit of religious truth and commitment *because of* the health benefits correlated with religious faith, religion has become a means to an end. A second thing has become a first thing. Jesus never advocated or promoted such a reversal.

Instead, Jesus promised that a life of faith between the times will periodically seem unbearably difficult. It will demand all we have. "Take up your cross," he told his early disciples, "and follow me." I demand all that you are and have. I can promise you only sacrifice, toil, hardship, and a martyr's death. And yet it is on this path, one seemingly strewn with thorns, that Jesus promises his disciples that they will find what they have always desired. And occasionally, because the life of the age to come has invaded this present evil age in Jesus, there will be bursts of great power and glory. The surprising, unforeseen paradox is that this glory will most often manifest itself in the midst of suffering and weakness. That is, the robust faith of a dying cancer patient might teach us more about the glory of life between the ages than her miraculous healing, though the dynamic of the kingdom would allow for just such a healing. An in-between time is full of surprises.

How might the paradigm of life between the ages inform present research into religion and health? For one thing, such a paradigm demonstrates both the fruitfulness and difficulties entailed in moving away from a generic discussion of religion and health to an analysis of a specific faith tradition. And yet such a move can be made by religious researchers without specifically advocating the inherent truthfulness of the faith tradition in question. In short, it is possible to study the empirical results of specific religious ideas about God, without necessitating the truth of those religious concepts themselves.

The time is ripe for such a transition in research on religion and health. How, for example, does one's understanding of God affect health outcomes? Is it possible to have a dysfunctional understanding of God? Does a Hindu view of the divine lead to different health outcomes than an Islamic view? Research can be conducted on these questions without advocating the truthfulness of either Islam or Hinduism. And yet researchers in a pluralistic age seem to have avoided this level of specificity for fear of what they might discover, that is, perhaps specific religious concepts are psychologically or physically harmful. We will only discover so if we have the courage and skill to raise the level of specificity in the research conducted.

We should also acknowledge the limits of research on religion and health. What if Hindu theology correlated with high levels of life satisfaction and Islamic theology with low levels? What conclusions should we reach? If we make life satisfaction a first thing, a fundamental value to be pursued directly, then Hinduism in our theoretical example would likely become the religion of choice. But nothing has been decided or proven about the question of truth. Islam might be correlated with low levels of life satisfaction and yet still represent the truth about God. One will have to decide the issue of truthfulness on different grounds.

Having acknowledged the limitations of empirical research on religion and health, a number of further possibilities for research present themselves: Is a religion's understanding of salvation related to health issues? Does an emphasis on God's grace produce positive health outcomes? What of those who seek salvation through obedience to a divinely revealed set of laws or precepts? Are specific conceptions of life after death correlated with health benefits? And what of ethics? There are similarities in the ethical teachings of the great religious traditions, but also differences. Do the differences make a difference? Do the similarities nourish health? What of styles of worship? Does worship make a difference? We have listed a number of studies concerning prayer that are correlated with positive health outcomes. Does it make a difference, though, to specifically pray in the name of Allah, Christ, or one of the Hindu deities? Does research indicate that specific types of spirituality and spiritual disciplines are correlated with health issues? For example, is Buddhist meditation more closely correlated with mental health than Christian meditation?

We encourage greater specificity in research on religion and health. A Christian paradigm of life between the ages illustrates the possibilities a specific faith tradition offers for understanding the relationship between religion and health. Further empirical research based on this specific theological paradigm might well prove fruitful and lead us beyond the limitations of generic research. After all, there are few if any generic religions that humans practice or promote.

References

Fee, G. (1993). *How to Read the Bible for All It's Worth*. Grand Rapids, MI: Zondervan.

Hall, C. A. (1992, November 23). "Holy Health." *Christianity Today*, 19–22.

Larson, D. B. (1993). *The Faith Factor: Vol. 2. An Annotated Bibliography of Systemic Reviews and Clinical Research on Spiritual Subjects*. Washington, DC: National Institute for Healthcare Research.

Lewis, C. S. (1970). "First and Second Things." In W. Hooper (Ed.), *God in the Dock*. Grand Rapids, MI: Eerdman.